The Long Road
Dave Lodge

The Long Road
Dave Lodge

Pixel tweaks
PUBLICATIONS

Published in 2016
© Copyright Dave Lodge

ISBN: 978-0-9934679-4-3

Second Reprint

Cover and Book interior Design by Russell Holden
www.pixeltweakspublications.com

Pixel tweaks
PUBLICATIONS

All rights reserved without limiting the rights under copyright reserved above, no parts of this publication may be reproduced, stored in or introduced into a retrieval system, or transmitted in any form, or by any means (electronic, mechanical, photocopying, recording or otherwise) without the prior written permission of both the copyright owner and the publisher of this book, Dave Lodge

All the images in the book have been sourced by Dave Lodge, the self-publisher of this book. They are from his own personal collection or he has obtained permission from the copyright owners for their usage. Any queries regarding this can be directed to Dave Lodge at davelodgebooks@gmail.com

Acknowledgements

I'm grateful to my Aunt, Susan Cupitt for bringing literature in to my life and in so doing helped to give me an education. Reubin 'Hurricane' Carter and his book *The 16th Round*, this is the true story of a man's fight against injustice. Also my wife Margaret... she knows why.

The photographs in this book have come from a variety of sources and every effort has been made to credit the people who took them. However as some of them date back more than sixty years it has not been possible to find all of the photographers. I can however thank: A.Newton, Alice music, John Alford, The Acton Gazette, John Leng, The Leek Post & Tmes, Ricky Valance, Vicky Michelle, Mike Berry, Harry Prytherch, Billy Ruffley, Tommy Bruce, Dave Berry, John Leyton, Wee Willie Harris, Bob Harrison, Heinz, Chas McDevitt, Brian Pool, Tony Crane, Billy Kinsley, Bob Rosenthall,Vince Eager, Lee Curtis, Karl Terry, Karl Denver Jean Fergusson, Doug Mackenzie, Pete Bardsley, Dennis Brown, Les Brotherstone, Dave Sampson, Perry Smith, Brian Jones, Nicki Edwards, Brendan Dodd, Daily Express, Kathy Kirby, Frank and Dee, Tony Hilton, Chris Healy for the Billy Fury photos and also Peter Leonard. In every single case their contribution has I feel enhanced this book.

People who helped make sure that the book finally made it to completion include, Jeff Burn, Peter Leonard, Dave and Ann Robins, Johnny Mans, who also provided the picture of Norman Wisdom with his knighthood, Margaret Lodge, Tony Crane, Brian Poole,Chris Black and Mac Poole. Last but by no means least Russell Holden, my publisher at Pixel Tweaks Publications who helped me to see that his formatting for the layout and the cover was superior to mine, he has done a fantastic job.

My thanks to them all, if you enjoy this book it is as much due to them and all my friends in the book as it is to my humble attempt to write it.
Now carry your brothers and sisters ever forward and when you fall to ground, they will carry you. For together we are but seconds from greatness. Unknown.

Dedication

I dedicate this book with my grateful thanks to a man who was a gentleman in every sense of the word. This man had a code of honour, ethics and total reliability that is rarely equalled and never surpassed by anyone I have ever met in any walk of life. A man who in my opinion was the finest all round entertainer to come out of the sixties Rock 'n' Roll era. A great and talented man, a kind and generous man, a man who treated everyone he met with thoughtful and respectful consideration. This man who I was privileged to know and who honoured me by regarding me as his brother, he was quite simply the one the only, the incomparable Mr Tommy Bruce.

My thanks as always also go to my lovely wife Margaret for the love, patience and support she gives in all things. Without her I would never have achieved anything.

Contents

The Beginning of it all .. 1
Rugby 16
Sport 37
Speedway 42
Ken Eyre 44
The Quadrathon 57
Tommy Bruce 71
Clem Cattinni 78
Jess Conrad 83
Vince Hill 89
Vince Eager 92
Danny Williams 96
Billie Davis 106
Danny Rivers 112
Chas McDevitt 118
Heinz 120
Wee Willie Harris 125
Norman Wisdom 128
Billy Fury 133
Craig Douglas 135
Lynn Alice 139
Karl Denver 142
Carl Wayne 146
Mac Poole 148
Dave Sampson 152
Lee Curtis 157
Ricky Valance 161
Ronnie Carroll 166
Pete Oakman 168
Don Lang 170
Brian Poole 173
Len (Chip) Hawkes ... 178
Terry Dene 181
Freddie Garrity 184
Jet Harris 187
Jean Vincent 190
Jean Fergusson 195
Mike Berry 199
Eden Kane 204
Julie Felix 208

Tony Dangerfield 210
Kathy Kirby 212
Helen Shapiro 215
John Leyton 219
Tony Crane 227
Graham Fenton 232
Tom O'Connor 235
Philip Madoc 237
Vicki Michelle 240
Alan Crowe 244
Screamin' Lord Sutch .. 248
Leapy Lee 251
Tony Christie 253
Paul Melba 257
Ruby Murray 261
Anita Harris 264
Bob Monkhouse 268
Maggie Stredder 271
Joe Dolan 274
Mike Pender 277
Emile Ford 280
John Allison 283
Dave Berry 286
PJ Proby 289
Bill Maynard 293
Faron 296
Karl Terry 300
Geoff Nugent 303
Harry Prytherch 306
John McCane 309
Colin Paul 311
Big Jim White 314
Chris Black 317
Bob Harrison 324

Other people who have been there along the road .. 326

This is the story of my journey through life, through my childhood in the forties and fifties to the present day, incredibly in another century. It is a journey that has taken me from the world of sport to the world of entertainment and made many great friendships along the way. The story is also my attempt to show the teamwork I feel is required to make life more enjoyable.

The contents of this book are, like my sporting career and everything else in my life, based on the ethics of loyalty, friendship and team work. Teamwork helped to re-forge my friend Tommy Bruce's career by allying his incredible talent and my organisational skills. In turn that association helped make many of the friendships described in the following chapters.

It should also be pointed out that what is said about my friends in the pages that follow are reflections and memories from conversations and experiences that we shared and not on any research undertaken by others who may have written biographies about these people. My opinions of each and every person mentioned in this book are influenced only by time spent in their company.

This is perhaps a strange account of how someone who truly loved taking part in sport because of the 'rush' that physical exercise brings when endorphins is released into the brain. Someone who had no aspirations to be involved in show business let alone share in the pleasure it can bring to others. Before going on to the beginning of the journey I would just say that as an athlete I always competed as an amateur and as such had to support myself and fund my sporting activities by working in various jobs.

CHAPTER ONE

THE BEGINNING OF IT ALL

I was born a very sickly child with little hope of survival, because I was suffering from a condition known as Pyloric Stenosis.

This condition simply explained as a blockage of the intestines. These days this condition is dealt with by micro surgery but in the forties there was not a lot known in out lying areas about a possible way of rectifying the condition.

First known photo of Dave

A surgeon in Manchester decided to have a try at an experimental operation known I believe as 'Ramsted's Procedure' which he hoped would correct the problem. The plan was that as we, human being, have miles of intestine he would attempt to unblock the affected part, or even cut it out He carried out the operation on six babies four of whom died but a little girl, whose name I have never known and I survived, proving that he was right and because of him and a few other courageous surgeons thousands of babies were saved. Because he did not know what he would find he opened me up from groin to collarbone and almost seventy years later I still have a scar that has now shrunk in size to about eight or nine inches in length. Because of this condition my mother who did not expect me to live, took me to (and left me with) her mother and father. My grandmother told me years later that my mother used the words, "You can look after him, you won't have him long because he is to sickly to be reared". I thank her for that without any ill feeling because for the next eleven years, indeed it was almost twelve I had the most idyllic childhood and loving upbringing any child could have wished for.

My Grandparent ran The Horse and Jockey Hotel in Renwick, Cumbria (or Cumberland as we all knew it then). My Grandma raised me (so she told me) on a diet of whiskey and milk!

The milk, for the first twelve months of my life, would have bread broken into it to make a dish she called 'pobs' (nearly seventy years later I still find this dish delicious on a cold winter's night) and then supplemented my food intake with good fresh vegetables and meat from then on ... I don't think there was much whiskey in that early concoction, just enough to stop me crying all the time.

Feeding the hens

Just how effective this diet was is shown by the photo of me rolling a beer barrel outside The Horse and Jockey at what is clearly a very early age. My Grandma and Granda, as I called him, gave me at lot of love and I thrived under their care. My Aunty Effie, the youngest of their two daughters, took more and more responsibility for my upbringing as Grandma's health was failing and if I hadn't been told I would have thought Aunty Effie was my mother. Indeed until I was ten or eleven years old she was the only one I had.

Although my father loved me it was impossible for him to work and look after a small boy so it became accepted that Aunty Effie and her husband my Uncle Peter were in loco-parentis.

My first friend was a boy called Kenneth Cairns who lived just along the hill from me, I also used to trail around after an older boy called Frank Moses who also lived on the hill beside our home but I don't

Grandma & Grandad

Grandma in the orchard

think he was very grateful for my company. That said in later life we have been getting on very well and Margaret and I have the pleasure of getting to know his wife Nancy. Sadly since starting this book Frank passed away and we mourn the loss of a good friend.

When I was older Kenneth and I would come down off the hill and play with Dennis Armstrong and Brian Smith and two older children Norman Blackburn and his sister Jean, whose parents ran the village shop. I was also blessed to enjoy the companionship of Tommy Wells and his wife Robina, it seemed that everyone had time for a small boy in this wonderful place.

Dave gets his beer ration!

Life continued in this way until I was about seven when the Raine Family moved from a farm at Springhead to Raven Wood estate this included the squire's house at the top of the village. I met and became friendly with the whole family but with two of the boys William and Robert in particular. William was slightly older and Robert was about eighteen months younger than me but it was Robert and I who through our mutual love of horses really became fast friends a friendship that has lasted more than fifty years to date. It was though William who was kind enough to let me have use of his pony, a fell pony called Jimmy.

Grandad outside the Horse & Jockey

Robert was affectionately known to the villagers as Bronco Laine the television cowboy, because of his exceptional equestrian prowess. Robert and I spent many happy hours riding in the fields behind his home at Raven Wood.

Dave & his Granda

Really at that time I suppose we were a foursome as we were never seen without the two ponies Princess and Jimmy.

Incidentally, the first girl I ever really liked was Robert's sister Carol. Carol was a very pretty girl, indeed she still is and before I met my wife Margaret, I often wondered if Carol and I might have gone out together when we got older. During those happy days I was not aware of the disappointments that life had in store for me and that in a few short years by the age of twelve I would have to leave the wonderful hamlet of Renwick and live in Manchester, with my father and his second wife Fran.

Robert on Princess and Dave on Jimmy

Fran was a truly wonderful woman and I regard her as my mother to this day. I never really felt I belonged in Manchester and despite the best efforts of my father and new mum I was unable to fit in.

I did not know then that I would spend the best part of next fifty years trying to get back to live in Renwick, finally making it in 2008. The delay in returning was caused by the fact that I, like millions of other people, have always been constrained in my choice of dwelling by the need for employment so had to always live where the work was. In spite of this I did return three or four times every year, to spend time with Aunty Effie and Uncle Peter.

I am pleased to say that when I was in my teens Uncle Peter and I became great friends; this friendship was forged by a mutual love of the books by western writers Louis Lamour and George G Gilman to name but two, we remained friends until his untimely death when I was in my thirties.

It was only a couple of years later when Aunty Effie who I loved dearly passed away that I thought my visits would cease to have a purpose.

In that thought I was wrong because when I went to have one last look round in Renwick, I bumped into my childhood friend, Robert Raine, and in the ensuing conversation he his wife Linda asked Margaret and I to visit and stay with them.

After that first visit we returned on a regular basis and Robert encouraged my wish to return to live in Renwick. Having said how much I regret having had to leave the village it was clearly my fate to move away from Renwick. Had I not done so I would never have met my lovely wife Margaret and my two good friends Peter Leonard and the late Tommy Bruce

Granda

Returning to my early life in Manchester – at the start of what I thought was my usual six weeks summer holiday from school, my father took me aside for a little chat. He said to me, "Look David, you know things have been a bit tight financially for the family for some time now and your younger sister Christine will need to go to school for another five years so I really need you to go out to work, I hope you understand". He went on to say "I have got you a job and you start on Monday."

I started work as a milk boy at the age of fourteen my introduction to working life! I thought this was a funny start, as after doing most of my growing up in Cumberland, as we then knew it (and as I still think of it) I was extremely naïve about the world at large and I thought that when I left school I would be working on a farm. However that would not be the case (in fact that ambition would never be fulfilled).

It may have surprised him to know that I was absolutely delighted by this news. The

Auntie Effie and Dave

5

School photo

reason being that I hated school with a passion having spent my time being bullied by the pupils and the teachers alike, this had gone on from the very beginning of my school life.

Such was my fear of the schools I attended after I left Renwick, and of all the people in those schools that on one occasion so that I wouldn't have to go attend my lessons, I deliberately broke a milk bottle and slashed my hand with the jagged pieces of glass. It now seems, looking back that my fears were totally irrational but at the time they were very real and my fears consumed every waking moment of my life. I would haven given anything not to have experienced the misery of my school-days.

For example just three of the so-called best days of my life, resulted in the science teacher Mr H burning my hand with a Bunsen burner to, as he put it, 'help to concentrate my mind'. Then on another occasion because I was unable to solve what he thought was a very simple problem on the blackboard I incurred the wrath of Mr R the maths teacher.

This man seized me by my tie and commenced swinging me so that my head hit the blackboard repeatedly while at the same time he cried out for the benefit of the class, "Oh for the wings of a dove that I might fly far away from Lodge and his stupidity!"

The result being that when I fell from his grasp I was unable to breath, there was great panic as scissors were sent for so that the tie could be cut from my neck, leaving me with abrasions and cuts to my neck. My father always a gentleman sent a letter of complaint to the school in which he said, that while he understood the need for discipline, this man had overstepped the mark. Going on to say that the result of his actions was the most flagrant piece of hooliganism he had ever been unfortunate enough to witness the results of.

However the third of these incidents was to my mind was by far the worst. I would never have chosen metalwork or woodwork as a subject because I didn't then and don't now like machinery that moves fast and seem to me to have life of their own. I must have lost control of things like drills and circular saws more times than anyone and consider myself lucky that in the worst accident I had only severed one finger which I was fortunate to have sewn back on. I don't know why but I find myself drawn in by fast moving machinery becoming mesmerised by it and that proves dangerous for me and those around me. However as I had to choose one or the other I chose woodwork unfortunately for me so did all the other boys in my class. That meant that there were too many pupils who wanted to do woodwork and none who wanted to do metalwork. So several of us were 'volunteered' to be in the metalwork class, this was a disaster as I possessed no aptitude at all for this.

My pathetic efforts in making things like toasting forks and pokers were the source of constant humiliation by the teacher Mr R and my classmates as added to my ineptitude with previously mentioned subjects I was the ideal target for being dubbed the schools resident village idiot.

Although my mother, for this what she became, Fran always gave my efforts pride of place in the hearth and indeed regularly used my lopsided toasting fork to make toast in front of the fire. I am sure that my poor showing in this and almost every other subject must have been a disappointment to her. If so she never let me see any sign of her disappointment and always supported me in my endeavours.

However the experiences of my school-days were teaching me then, as I still believe now that nothing is ever so bad that it won't get worse and that no good deed goes unpunished. Add to that my is belief that a good liar will always be believed before someone like me who tells the truth, this is something that I have found to be true up to the present day. You can perhaps see in the following paragraphs how miserable my school-days really were.

However returning to Mr R who was a very powerfully built man who would frequently push or cuff any boys he felt deserved it. On this particular day he was pushing and shouting at a boy for some act of stupidity and I foolishly decided to speak. At the time I was holding with aid of a pair of tongs, a piece of metal in the acid tub to harden it and I made the mistake of speaking. "I don't think that's fair" I said, Mr. R turned and cuffed me on the side of my head and to my horror I dropped the metal and the tongs into the acid. He roared with rage and grabbing my arm said I would pick the tongs out the acid with my hand.

I am sure now that he only meant to frighten me, in this he succeeded, but would not have put my hand in the acid. On the day my fear and horror at the prospect was such that although I was only small in those days my fear made me fight like a demon. I was kicking and struggling and hitting him with my free hand and some how I caused him to fall back against the workbench. I found both hands free and continued to flail at him while sobbing and crying with fear.

The next thing I knew I was lying on the floor with blood pouring from my head, I looked up and saw Mr R standing over me with a hammer in his hand and thought my end had come.

He just told me to get up and walked away. For once the class wasn't laughing at me, everyone just stood in stunned silence. Then Mr R spoke, "Right class the lesson is nearly over so put the tools you have been using away and you Lodge can think yourself lucky you are not being sent to the headmaster for the cane".

I stood there blinded by the blood running into my eyes in total disbelief and shaking with relief, that I hadn't suffered incredible pain and mutilation. At that point the bell went to end the lesson and we all left the classroom.

It was lunchtime so those on first lunch went to the dining hall the rest went to the playground, I went home.

When I arrived home, Fran my mother was greatly distressed by my appearance my blazer and shirt were soaked in blood, which was still running down my face. At first she tried to staunch the bleeding but to no avail.

I told her what had happened and while I pressed a towel to the cut she phoned the school and asked to speak to Mr R, when he came to the phone she said who she was and asked if he had any problem with her son that morning. "No" he replied "no problem at all". "Really" she said "and where is he now?", "In the playground" came the response.

At point she told him where I actually was, and that she was taking me to hospital to have my head stitched adding the words "I will come to the school and deal with you later". She put the phone down.

Later that day with my head stitched and bandaged Mum and I arrived at the school. As she was small in stature and wearing a calliper on her leg due to polio as a child Mr R clearly thought he could browbeat her. Towering over her he blustered and shouted about how I deserved everything I got, he even went so far as to push my mother and told her to get out of the school. That's when she hit him with a left hook that Henry Cooper would have been proud of. She caught him flush on the jaw and he went to the floor, after that there was no more shouting and he didn't get up until another teacher helped him. After that I was even more isolated at school than I had been before but at least no one bullied me.

The School Headmaster was called Mr S who was a nice, but I now feel ineffectual, man because he exerted little control over his staff or the pupils and probably feeling he should support his member of staff did make an attempt to give me detention for leaving the school grounds without permission but mum soon put him right on that score, verbally on that occasion pointing out that if he had controlled Mr R the situation would not have occurred.

I never saw her hit anyone else so I think it was the realisation of what I must have been going through with this teacher that put her maternal instincts into overdrive. I do know that she loved me and I adored her until the day she died of a heart attack at the age of fifty-two. She was a wonderful lady and if I have any good qualities they were instilled by her love and care in conjunction with that of my Grandma and Auntie Effie, I will miss the three of them till the day I die.

Looking back at these incidents after nearly sixty years, I have to say that such brutish men did much to shape the way I have viewed life and it seems strange to me when I read in the papers about teachers being sacked because they have shouted at some unfortunate child.

In fairness I have to say that it is also the case that some teachers have been subjected to extreme mental and physical cruelty by their pupils.

In the time I was educated just after the war it was accepted that you would be disciplined by your teachers and that your parents would accept that situation.

Unfortunately I truly believe that some of these men who had suffered the horrors of war were so badly damaged mentally that they were unsuited for the teaching profession. I have recently written a study of Post Traumatic Stress Disorder and it is clear to me now that many of the symptoms of this condition were displayed by these men. They functioned on a daily basis and the average child may have benefited from their knowledge, but when they encountered someone like me who was dimwitted and not quite up to their required standard, their responses to the ineptitude I displayed were out of proportion.

In spite of that there was the occasional teacher along the way who tried very hard to help me, Mr Gibbons, Miss Birtenshaw, Mr Bowers and Miss Greaves and earlier Miss Dronsfield and Miss Allen come to mind, as being among those who did their best for me.

However my fear of the other teachers made it quite impossible for me to function or obtain any education in the school environment. The events of my school-days are seared on my memory. For those who doubt that I can remember so clearly after all this time I can only say the lessons taught by these acts of violence and the fear they instilled are the only things I learnt at school.

My father in regular visits to my Grandmas taught me to read, write and do my times tables by the time I was five years old and that education set me up for life. I never took an exam at school that I was able to pass and did not have any qualifications or even a leaving certificate. Yet thanks to my father's efforts and a love of reading I have achieved things, academically that I believed were beyond me not the least of these achievements have been Tommy Bruce's biography and this book. I have also obtained qualifications in English Literature, Maths and other subjects. My dad also taught me the value of teamwork and aided by my mum and the other people involved with my upbringing that love and loyalty are the greatest gifts in life. Because of this I have made good friends and my life has been and continues to be filled with wonderful things. I am pleased to be able to give the people in this book the opportunity to know and to share with everyone how much I loved and respected them.

Although I am sad that some have not lived for me to really let them know how important they have been to me and my life.

Mum and Dad

Returning to my conversation with my dad it was because of the actions of the aforementioned teachers and others like them I recall that I was totally unfazed by my father's revelation that I should start work.

Indeed I was delighted and replied, "Okay, am I going to work on a farm then?" "Not exactly" replied my father, before going in to a long rambling explanation. "You know that cows are kept on a farm don't you?" "Yes" I replied, "And you know that milk comes from cows don't you?" "Yes" I again replied a little confused by now; "Well you are going to be delivering milk." Dad paused for a moment and then said, "So you see it will be almost like working on a farm won't it? Because when you deliver the milk you will think of the cows won't you?"

Ever the obedient son I replied, "Yes dad." We often laughed in later years about because neither one had been fooling the other. He was embarrassed because he had to send me out to work. I knew I had to go to work and I was happy it would be sooner rather than later, because of my miserable school life. So while he was speaking I had been thinking, very disrespectfully In my opinion now, why he is saying this load of rubbish,

I will just have to do what I'm told. Just as we all did then, we accepted without question that we had to obey our parents even if sometimes what they said seemed unfair.

This is something, which seems to have changed for worse because it seems no one can be told anything now.

After eighteen months or so in that job, I moved on to work in a factory that made fire-lighters for a company called *Hallworths* I actually left there after about two years, to go to work in *Ainsley's Wire Factory* they made wire ties for the building trade, for an extra thirty shillings a week.

I did that for six months and then was asked to go back to the fire lighter factory as they said they had realised my value and I would receive an increase several shillings more than Ainsley's were paying me.

After doing six to eight months back in that job I found out what I have found to be a hard truth in life, *you should never go back*. This was an unhappy period in my working life and I was also learning that work related friendships could not for the most part be relied upon. I left again and went into the building trade working as a general labourer and a hod carrier, I loved this job because I felt it helped me to be fit for the reason I got up every day, to play rugby.

This way of earning a living ended when I broke my leg in a motorcycle accident. After my leg came out of its plaster cast I thought it best to go back inside and work in a warehouse till the strength in my leg returned.

I took a job as a packer, and found to my surprise that I enjoyed it. I had to write dockets and advice notes the idea of which terrified me as I had always thought that as I left school at such a young age, with no qualifications that I was incapable of doing anything that required clerical skills.

Thankfully my new employers thought differently and over the next thirty-two years I was promoted five times finishing up as the group distribution manager. The company was *John T Clarke and Son* and my wonderful employers not only supplied me with employment opportunities but also supported my sporting activities.

They did this to the point of sponsorship by way of purchasing my athletic kit and funding hotels for me to stay in on away trips. In return I took upon myself to visit clients when I was abroad and always came back from my trips with product orders by way of thanks. The other way the company was repaid was by seeing their Dormy product logo displayed in national and local newspapers.

Also on a couple of occasions we made the national television screens. I can honestly say that in a fifty-two year working career to date, I haven't given up yet, Mr Arthur Brooks, Mr Brian Sykes, Mrs Anita Henshall and it may surprise him to know, latterly Mr Alan Hayes the Financial Director, were the best employers I ever had. In Alan Hayes case there was some acrimony over my pension, this was pointless because I later lost the pension due to a take over by an Austrian company who I regard as to insignificant to advertise in these pages. Alan Hayes was a man who I liked and respected because he succeeded and advanced in his job through hard work and diligence, I hope wherever he is now he is happy and content in his life.

That these fine people were eventually replaced after a couple of take overs by a bunch of proven liars, crooks and complete charlatans. These people would be aided by one B who may believe he was acting in the best interests of the company. Be that as it may his actions cost me my job my pension and any possible redundancy. This only makes my memory of working for those special people all the more pleasurable. It is worthy of mention that I took the firm to an Industrial Tribunal and gained an apology, a reference and some financial compensation.

I have to mention two men who were not in the category of the charlatans previously mentioned, former Managing Director Malcolm Macintyre a courageous and honourable man and Robert Dixon, who was Managing Director at the time of the final take over who was horrified at the treatment I received. Indeed Robert said to me, "David I am so sorry, I know you have been stitched up, you do not deserve to lose your job in this way, sadly there is nothing I can do as I have already been replaced myself".

As I used to be a member of the board of directors of The Heritage Foundation Ltd and also Managing Director of The CIPP Ltd I am better equipped to understand Robert Dixon's position than I was at the time.

I liked and admired both these men who had risen though the ranks to achieve high office in business.

I also made two exceptional friends during that time who belied my normal rule of working relationships not being reliable as lasting friendships.

The two men were, the late Harold Winstanley and Fred Liston. Harold was my mentor during the first seventeen years of my time with John T Clarke and Son as I made the transition from being a packer into management I learnt a tremendous amount from him, both in my working surroundings and in my life, sadly Harold is no longer alive but still in my thoughts

Fred Liston who I taught as much as I could of what Harold had taught me during the fifteen years before our employment together was ended by the last take over. I will always remember them both, two very different men but each with the right approach to life and both great exponents of team work.

During the course of my progress through life and jobs I met and fell in love my beautiful wife Margaret, I was sixteen when I met her and although the early years of our relationship were marred by other people's interference. Margaret was then and is now absolutely stunning to look at as you will see from the photographs in this book, and more importantly had, indeed still has a wonderful personality.

Stockport Express Newspaper's Personality Girl of Stockport

This was proved when Margaret was voted *The Stockport Express* Newspaper's Personality Girl of Stockport in the early sixties. Luckily for me Margaret felt the same way about me as I did about her and over the years our relationship has become almost telepathic, such is our understanding of each other. People will try to tell you that there is no such thing as love at first sight; I can say that they are completely wrong. I loved Margaret the first time I saw her and fifty-one years later our love is undiminished, indeed it has grown.

Margaret on our wedding day with her parents Florrie & Fred

For me Margaret has been my reason for being. Everything I have tried to do and anything I may have achieved has been for and because of her.

She has been at my side in good times and bad and when in the bad times my resolve weakens and I am filled despair her strength carries me through until she is able to restore mine. Margaret quite simply is an incredible woman I thank God every day for bringing her into my life.

CHAPTER TWO

RUGBY
THE LOVE OF MY SPORTING LIFE

I had been playing rugby since the age of thirteen and I have to say that, it was for me a difficult sport to be a part of. Looking back I think my first mistake was playing for a club, Toc H RFC, that my father had graced with some distinction in his own playing days. The older members were for the most part former players. Like my father many of these ex-players were now officers of the club and had a perception of me as a younger version of my father.

Dave (bottom row left) age 15 in the TOC H Colts Team

Dave (bottom row, third from right) age 16 in the TOC H Colts Team

They couldn't have been more mistaken, my father was a likeable and gregarious man who thrived in the off-field camaraderie of the club. I on the other hand was a surly angst ridden youth who grew into a young man driven by demons to succeed. This desire to succeed came in spite of having my having my own misguided perception that all the senior members of the club wished to prevent me achieving my goals.

A couple of good things came out of my struggles to become a valued member of the team, indeed the club, the most important one being my friendship with Peter Leonard. I met Peter at the age of fourteen and did not like him at first but more than fifty years later he has proved to be a constant influence for good in my life.

The other important thing was actually being good enough to play for the first team. In fact in the opinion of many players and ex players who I admired from both in and outside our club was that but for a previously mentioned broken leg I may well have achieved a higher level than I subsequently did.

Be that as it may my inner demons spent twenty years or so driving me in and out of retirement from the game. This ensured that I received little pleasure from playing the game I loved until finally I came to the decision that would change my life.

At first it seemed just in a sporting sense but as time unfolded it became clear that my life could not have taken the direction it did had I not stopped playing rugby. Because of the time I dedicated to training and preparation I would not have been free to move into the world of show business and by so doing share Tommy Bruce's career and more importantly his friendship.

The end of my playing career came about in strange circumstances, indeed that season I was coming to believe that due to continued good form I might even challenge for county honours. I had been having a particularly good season having overcome the presence of a very talented and gifted player one Mike Harrison who possessed qualities that I did not.

Although I felt that I in turn had abilities that compensated for this. Mike played the same position as I did, wing forward and he was a fast moving player who had a speed of thought that matched his physical ability. On top this due to the fact that unlike me Mike was and is a likeable and friendly man he always had the much-deserved respect of his peers.

This respect allied with his playing skill and leadership qualities meant that he was appointed first team captain for a couple of years. This appointment had the effect of restricting my opportunities to compete for his place on a level playing field as it were; in fact there were several of us fighting for that elusive place in the back row.

However after hearing that he was standing down from the captaincy, I spent the off season honing my fitness and playing skills I succeeded in not just displacing Mike but holding on to the position on merit. Such were Mike's abilities and skills that I felt justifiably proud of this and determined to make it as difficult as possible for the selection committee to let him back in to the team, or indeed allow any of my other rivals to steal the march on me. My efforts were rewarded and I settled into the team and as I said set my sights on higher things, not through arrogance but due to the belief that as Mike was so gifted I would have to push myself further and harder to keep him at bay.

Phil Baliss' TOC H 'A team' (Dave is far left on bottom row)

Little did I know that there were moves afoot to force me out of the team without the need for competition from Mike or any other member of the playing staff... People like the former captain Ted Turner and some of his cronies on the selection committee decided that by fair means or foul I would be pushed out of the team.

Really as I look back I realise, it was largely the fault of my abrasive personality that I had offended these people and so they had a blinkered view of my abilities. However things came to head when it came to be that we had cup match to play and I found to my dismay that my place was given to an up and coming young player from the youth team. A really pleasant and physically gifted young lad called Tony Betts who while I was sure would be a real threat in a couple of seasons or so was not expected by most people to be ready to replace either Mike or I for some time.

I was selected to be one of the substitutes; this was disastrous in those days because it meant you would only get on if someone was to badly hurt to continue. However ever loyal to my fellows I turned up for the game. Five minutes before kick off Tony Betts had not turned up, right said the captain, who just happened to be my life long friend Peter Leonard, get changed Dave you are playing. Just as we were leaving the dressing room Tony arrived although he plainly was not fit to play the decision was taken by Peter to send him on and take me out of the team.

The effect on me was catastrophic in terms of me realising that I would never be able to continue to play in a competitive way for the club again. I was completely and utterly devastated; all my years of training and trying to improve my skills and temperament were gone for naught. I knew in that moment my days as a competitive Toc H rugby player were over, this was one setback to many. I slouched along the touchline for some of the game in complete despair. I watched as young Tony took little or no part in the game, in fact at one point his boot having come off, he spent about ten minutes behind the try line trying to unfasten a knot in his lace so he could put the boot back on.

We were losing heavily and viewing the game from the touchline I was unable to be part of trying to reverse the situation. Then the final blow was delivered, my father ever the fair man was puzzled by my situation, asked his long time friend Derek Brown who was also the chairman of selectors, "Derek, if you had two players one of whom was plainly fit and the other not, which one would you sensibly put on the field?" Derek Brown didn't even pause for reflection. "If one of the players was David Lodge he said I would put the other one on even if the other player only had one leg."

I reeled away from the touchline I couldn't have been more hurt if I had been struck in the face. I left the ground ignoring my father's pleas to return.

As I said previously I knew my playing days were over and I would not play a competitive match again. The following morning I phoned my captain, Peter Leonard and told him of my decision to retire, he expressed regret, and tried to dissuade me, but it was plain that my mind would not be changed.

I explained to Peter I had spent the best part of twenty years knowing that I would always be one vote short on the selection committee because my father would not vote for me as he felt it would be seen as nepotism. Now I knew I would not have the chairman's vote either I was not prepared to continue the unequal struggle. On top of that I had endured what I and others considered to be unfair discrimination from a man who was a boyhood hero of mine, Ted Turner.

Ted Turner was about six or seven years older than me and he had the build of a Greek god and immense natural talent. There is no doubt in my mind that had he chosen to make the step up to play at a higher level he would have achieved international status. The downside in all this was the fact that from the very beginning he treated me as being beneath contempt and that was when he noticed me at all.

If he had just genuinely believed that I was not a good enough player that would have been fine. I could have lived with that and tried by my performance on the field to change his opinion. But his seemingly deliberate actions to humiliate me and on some occasions actually do me physical harm led other players of the day to comment that he possibly feared me as a player. A suggestion I find unlikely given his physical size and his undoubted talent. I think more likely for reasons unknown to me he, simply doesn't like me.

There were occasions that he actually caused me physical harm the worst of these occasions being during a loose maul during a training session one Monday night. One of my great strengths as player was the ability to maul well and by doing so win and retain the ball for the team.

Prior to my time Ted had been the best exponent of this and it was clear to others that instead of appreciating my efforts for the team he actually resented my success. Ian Gatie a fine player and at that time scrum half for the first team said to me after one match that he could not believe the things that Ted Turner had done during the match to belittle me.

It seemed that Ted had gone out of his way make it appear that it was him not me winning the ball added to that was the verbal abuse that he gave me in the process. During the game Ian was in the best position to see what was occurring in the loose mauls and I do not doubt he was right in his assessment of the situation. But I was so used to what happened it had ceased to register with me so I just smiled and said I am used to it.

Dave (bottom row 2nd right) with John Scott demonstrating that rugby really is a game played with odd-shaped balls.

What I do know is that many of Ted's cronies treated me with the same contempt that he did in an obvious effort to curry favour with him. However I return to the training incident, Ted decided to demonstrate the technique of how to strip the ball from an opponent in a loose maul. Naturally I was to be his opponent, at first he tried to simply use what appeared to him to his superior strength and weight, when this didn't work he became agitated and irritated and went on to do something that I have not forgiven him for to this day. He grabbed the middle two fingers of my left and right hands and jerked them back so hard that he dislocated all four fingers at the knuckle. That was bad enough but then with his leering smile he added insult to injury as he loudly proclaimed; "He's not as strong as he thinks he is he?"

I missed a few games during that season because of those injuries to my hands and such was the weakness of those joints afterwards that I played for two seasons with the two middle fingers of each hand taped together. How sad that two people who both plainly wanted Toc H to be successful were unable to agree and play the game in the right way. When I saw Ted a club dinner a few years ago I thought it was time after nearly thirty years to bury the hatchet. So I approached him and engaged him in conversation.

During the conversation I spoke of the past saying that if I ever offended him I was sorry because whatever I had done was done in my efforts to a better player, his reply was that he didn't remember anything and never noticed me anyway. As I walked away I thought that his answer probably justified my feelings toward him.

As Ted Turner was first team captain for several years getting myself selected for the team proved nigh on impossible. I say this even though I had the support of wonderful people like the second team captain Graham Allington, who apologised to me on a weekly, basis expressing complete disbelief that the selection committee continued to ignore what he perceived as my outstanding play. During my time under Graham's Captaincy, I only went up to the first team for the away games, home games were denied me it seems by Ted Turner for his own reasons.

Even when I made the first team on a regular basis one season (1972/1973) Ted Turner chose to humiliate me on the day of the team photographs by asking me in front of the other players in the dressing room why I was getting changed into my kit. The other players stopped getting changed and looked at me as I stutteringly replied, "for the photograph". Ted laughed and said "you're not going on any photograph with my team and me". I started to get dressed again and ignoring any further words from him got ready to go home.

Someone whose name I can't remember said to Ted as I was leaving the building, you do know we are playing away today and by the time anyone who can take Dave's place arrives here we will already be at the away ground for the kick off. Ted relented at that point and followed me out saying; you silly young bugger can't you take a joke? Although I knew he hadn't been joking I swallowed my pride and came back. I did so because even as a young man of twenty or so I thought that I might never get another chance to record the fact that I had played at the clubs highest level.

Indeed there were occasions over the next few seasons when I could and should have been on the team photographs, but I allowed bitterness against Ted Turner not to mention my own poor judgement to cloud my thinking and did not turn up for the photographs. Thus I proved not for the first or last time my ability to be the instrument of my own disaster.

My feeling about Ted Turner have never prevented me from knowing the truth about him as a player. That truth is that Ted was the best lock forward I ever played with or against. More than that he was in my opinion better than anyone I have ever seen play the game in that position. Better than Willie John McBride, Martin Johnson, Paul O'Connell or any other player in the position that I can think of. He had huge physical strength, good technical ability, and the determination to dominate the forward battle. Sadly I never felt inspired by him as a captain in the same way I did by Jeff Burn, Jeff had a way of driving you forward by the power of his incredible mental strength. If I felt I was letting him down with my playing efforts I would always be driven to try harder and go the extra mile.

However it now gives me great pleasure, as I look at the team photos on my wall that many years after that first photo which I had to endure so much humiliation to achieve. I am also in the first team photo (1981/1982) which only has me, the incomparable Mike Harrison and the indescribably talented and determined Jeff Burn, left from the team photograph ten years previously that I so nearly wasn't part of.

Jeff Burn was the clubs outstanding player in the hooker's position, a man who should to my mind have attained representative honours. In fact there was only one player who really challenged Jeff Burn in my time, one Johnny Penk.

Johnny could strike for the ball in the scrum so quickly it defied belief, sadly he did not have Jeff's dedication to the game or his fitness ethic and so did not achieve all he might have as a player. Having said that Johnny

Dave (bottom row left) with the incomparable Mike Harrison behind. Captain Ted Turner (with the ball) and the outstanding and talented Jeff Burn sitting on his right.

was a highly entertaining character and I liked him very much. I have to say that players like Mike Harrison, Jeff Burn and Peter Leonard, who for a period of least five seasons was regarded as the best scrum-half in junior rugby, would display greater longevity both on the first team and with the club in general than I did. But given my fiery temperament and an over active sense of injustice, I feel that I achieved far more than anyone could have expected.

On the subject of Peter Leonard he always worked really hard to improve his game, he could kick tactically with either foot and had a prodigious spin pass off either hand. He also took time to teach me more about my own playing position than I could ever have learnt on my own. In life and in sport Peter Leonard I regard Peter as the most brilliant and capable man I have ever known. It is therefore no surprise that he has become my longest and indeed most trusted friend.

Another of the highlights of my time at Toc H was when in the 1972/1973 season I was awarded my club colours. This is honour which still fills me with pride today' because although I played briefly for other clubs Manchester and Burnage, that great stalwart of Toc H Wilf Lord brought me back from these brief excursions, even threatening to report Burnage for poaching Toc H players. I like to think he would have just let me go if he hadn't felt that I had some playing ability and was of value to the club. I think he knew that my heart was then and is still today more than forty years later firmly fixed with Toc H.

Also to my great delight, I was privileged at this time to be the first recipient of The Harry Bettany Cup as the most outstanding and improved player of the season. These are not my words, nor are they vanity because these are the words said to me at the presentation.

Dave was always proud to wear his club colours

Harry Bettany had been a friend and playing contemporary of my father. I can say that there can never have been a prouder recipient of this cup as having had the privilege of knowing Harry I knew the character he exemplified and so was honoured that people thought I was worthy of being the first holder of the cup.

Harry Bettany cup

I think, without being to big headed that I can claim to have been the most improved recipient of the cup. None of the other recipients ever started from such a lowly position. Nor were any of the others as inept at the outset of their playing careers as I was.

My reason for believing this is that at the time I received the cup the club was fielding five teams and I started the season on the fifth team ending it on the first. Because of these reasons I still feel great pride and pleasure at being awarded that cup. That I was in a position to be considered for this honour was largely due I think to the auspices of people like the gentle and kind man Len Cuniffe who had played in the hooker's position in earlier years, was the Club President that year. Also the man who gave me my first chance on the colt's team and helped me learn to play the game a man who was gifted player from my fathers era, Harry Foster.

I cannot leave Len Cunciffe's contribution to my success as a player without mentioning another incident which caused me distress. It was in my opinion a great honour to be selected for the President's 15 for the annual game against the colts and I was privileged to be selected by more than one President, having also been selected to play for the Colts team in earlier years. Len Cuniffe picked me for his team, the first President to do so. My heart was bursting with pride as I changed to my kit and readied myself for the game. Chris Mayer one time captain of the A team had been selected had been chosen to captain the team.

He approached me and said I think there has been mistake you are to young to play in this team; I will have to leave you out. I dressed again and stood disconsolately on the touch line watching the game. Len Cuniffe approached and said hello David, why aren't you playing, are you injured? I gave the explanation that Chris Mayer had given me, Len looked at me with what I thought was disbelief and replied there is no age restriction, my cheeks were burning with shame, I felt I had let him down by allowing myself to be talked out of my place on the team. I spoke to Chris Mayer after the game and he just shrugged his shoulders and said he had got it wrong, no big deal. He was wrong it was then and still is now a massive deal to me, I still feel that through my naivety I let Len Cuniffe down.

That was not the only time Chris Mayer would upset me, it was a strong part of my game as previously mentioned that I could stay on my feet in the tackle and retain the ball in the ensuing maul, Chris was often heard to say he could make me release the ball if he was playing against me.

In a pre-season training game one year we were picked on opposite sides and at one point I was stopped just short of the try line, the maul drove me forward and I would probably have scored, but Chris as good as his word reached down as the maul drove forward and squeezed my testicles causing me to drop the ball. I was incensed and tried unsuccessfully to land a punch on him as he ran backwards laughing and saying told you I could do it. Other players restrained me and I eventually calmed down, but I spent the rest of my time with the club unable to have any respect or liking for Chris. That said Chris was a decent player well liked by the other players and a good servant to the club. Looking back I think my response was out of proportion to the incident and did not help to change my perception that people didn't like me and that I had to succeed in spite of them, this delayed my appreciation of teamwork.

These men and some others like them recognised the supreme effort I had made to improve both my fitness and skill levels. When I decided to write this book I researched the subsequent recipients and found that as I suspected none of them had been as inept as myself and so had not had start from the bottom as it were. For my part I am glad I did because I had the benefit of playing in the company of players who, although in the twilight of their playing careers taught invaluable lessons not just in playing skills but also in the value of team work and discipline.

However due to Ted Turner's attitude to me and my own burning desire to succeed, my admiration for him turned to something bordering on hate.

To the point where as the years passed I actually much to his surprise and my lasting shame, struck him. The incident happened one day as I felt he was carrying out his ritual humiliation of me. Thereafter he was of the opinion that not only was I beneath contempt, as he had always thought but also that I was a complete nutter.

This in itself caused me further problems as it seemed that when he was no longer captain but retained his place in the team his influence persisted and I repeatedly had to prove my worth to successive captains.

When he retired from playing-and became an observer for the selection committee my match performances were always reported by him as being poor. I now see that it was my own weakness not his strength that hindered me as a player. I simply allowed him to cloud my judgement and in so doing gave him power over me.

I know I am not perfect either as a player of any sport or as a man. This was even more the case back then. Because in my youth I was possessed of a quick temper which robbed me of the ability to think clearly in moments of stress. As I matured I learned to control my temper on the field of play and in daily life and found I enjoyed everything more. Unfortunately I still continued to harbour grudges off the field because of perceived slights. That said I only ever argued with the referee once and that was when I was about seventeen years old and occurred after the game.

As often happened in those days we were being refereed by a man who was a former player for the club we were playing against. Although we had led the game and were in a seemingly unbeatable position he played at least ten minutes over time. During that ten minutes he penalized each member of our team in turn. All these penalties were awarded in front of our posts the last one being given against me. In my mind his actions were unfair and caused us to lose.

As usual my response to what I perceived as an injustice was to give him a tirade of abuse in the course of which I told him I would drown him if he got into the communal bath. It was situation that shames me to this day, but I did learn something from it.

I learned that if you want to play sport there have to be officials and because they are human they will all make mistakes and some of them will be better than others. Because of that realisation I regard the referee and the touch judges in the same light, as the goalposts and the ball and I never blame those things for reversal of fortunes. I have learned to carry that belief forward in all aspects of my life. Because in life you are responsible for your own actions, it is no good blaming other people when things go wrong, however much you might wish to.

There was one other occasion when I let myself and more importantly the team and the club down. That was on the only occasion I was sent off. We were losing a match and as a team we had been repeatedly warned for being off side during the game and the referee was loosing patience with us. We had a scrum in the opponents half and got a good push going forward, unfortunately I stumbled and in an effort to regain my balance broke from the scrum.

Now I know that as a wing forward as my position was called in those days I, like all other exponents of that position lived on the edge of being offside at all times but on this occasion I was so far off balance that far from gaining unfair advantage I put myself at a disadvantage. The referee blew his whistle and sent me off. I walked silently to the touchline keeping my previously avowed rule of never speaking to referees.

When I got there Harold Casper, another sadly no longer with us, a lovely man who had been a good player in his own time with the club, not to mention a man who had distinguished himself by his service during the war, spoke to me and asked why I had come off, and enquired if I was hurt?

To my eternal shame I berated him about his incompetence, reminding him that he was the official observer and a member of the selection committee and he really ought to have seen that I had been sent off. I went on to say that I was finished with playing rugby, as I was tired of being made to feel miserable by a group of people, the selection committee, who in my opinion were a complete shower of shit. I went on to say that he should tell them of my opinion of them, as they were long over due being told just how incompetent they were.

Because at the time I was combining playing rugby with riding speedway and as I walked away I mistakenly thought I could devote more time to that activity. I had bought a 500 Jawa and was attending the Belle Vue Training School every week. I felt I was making progress .and hoped I would make the grade and make it into the team. I was wrong in so many ways.

As I was possessed of at least some decency I was ashamed of my outburst against Harold Casper and the selection committee and I felt that I could not leave things as they were. I thought that before I left the club I should apologise to him.

Fortunately I was helped in this when I received a phone call from Bill Haynes who told me that I had to appear before the Lancashire Disciplinary Committee due to my sending off. Bill also said that he would take me there and speak up for me at the hearing. He insisted we go down to the rugby club. This gave me the opportunity to apologise to Harold Casper. He being a true gentleman kindly accepted my apology.

Needless to say people like Ted Turner commented that I would be banned till the end of the season at least, if not for life. All nonsense of course but this just served to wind me up and I angrily retorted that I was riding speedway now and couldn't care less. Nothing could have been further from the truth as I still wanted to play at the highest level in the club and prove my worth to them.

On the day of the hearing Bill kept me calm and spoke strongly in my defence as a result of that due to the fact that it was my first offence I was given a one-match ban which was suspended for a season. So that meant that provided I was never up before the Lancashire disciplinary committee again I wouldn't miss any games and the matter was closed. Bill then wisely counselled that I loved the game too much to retire going on to say that he also knew I was man enough to apologise for my verbal attack on the selection committee.

He was right I'm pleased to say on both counts. I played on for several more seasons and never fell foul of the referee's authority again.

I will always be grateful to Bill for that, in my opinion he was a great and wise man, a man who was inspiration to many young players. He certainly extended my playing career and any pleasure I found in it.

However returning to my actual retirement from the game of rugby. After I had phoned my captain Peter Leonard and told him of my intention to retire because of my belief that I was a man without true friends or honour in my own club. He could not change my mind although he tried,because I was adamant in my intention to retire from the game. This meant that I was some what bewildered to be told later that when Peter put his team for the coming weekend up for consideration there was great surprise that my name was not included.

When the selection committee members were told that my reasons for making myself unavailable included the attitude of Derek Brown and Ted Turner they were aghast. My assertions delivered via Peter that I was neither wanted nor respected either on the 1st team or in the club were greeted with disbelief as it turned out there were people who held me in high regard and were unaware of my perception of the situation.

If I had been aware that there were more people than I ever dreamed in the club who actually thought I was an asset and could play the game quite well, would I have continued to play? Who knows? What I do know is that I received many overtures to return sometimes from surprising sources. These overtures were coming from people who both surprised and pleased me with their support as they were people who had my respect for how they had played themselves and for their tireless work for the club.

In fairness as I look back I realise that Derek Brown loved the club as much as I did and he simply didn't think I was the right kind of person to be part of the club He never looked at how I well I might have been playing or that I might be maturing into a better person. He simply thought I wasn't his idea of a gentleman and that I was incapable of change and so he wanted to be rid of me. Unfortunately I gave him his wish if I had more maturity and been the man that my father was I would have stayed and worked hard to prove him wrong

However I knew that I would not recapture the love and enthusiasm I had felt for playing the game. It wasn't that I couldn't have played on lower teams; I could, indeed had and enjoyed it. But I couldn't then and still haven't to this day more than thirty years after I stopped playing recovered from the feeling of utter worthlessness that Derek Brown's words filled me with.

With hindsight had I known that, Tony Betts, who was married with children would tragically die in a car crash in his twenties, I would not have begrudged him the place that day and maybe reacted differently to the situation and behaved in a better way. Even so I think it would only have been a matter of time until my temperament caused me to over react to some other perceived slight. It was I think time for me to move on from that aspect of my life..

However it fair to say that Toc H RFC had in that period of twenty years had a selection in the wing forward position of some of the most talented players in the north if not the whole of England. That I chose to put my self up for selection against players of the calibre of the legendary Derek Lear, George Cumbes, Mike Dutch, Peter Lewellyn, David Walker, Dave Fender, George Andrews Barry Foster, John Beardmore, the Potts twins Fred and Roly and of course the incomparable Mike Harrison who were all outstanding athletes and that I was still able to achieved first team status at all, makes me very proud.

I should also say that with my blinkered view of events I didn't realise that other people who played the same position like George Andrews, Dave Fender and several others were suffering, probably more harshly than me at the strange selection policy that seemed to be in place at that time. George a fine player definitely coped better with the situation than I did, showing greater maturity, proof of this is that he is still playing for the club today.

When I look back now I think more of the people who it was a pleasure to know in the club than of the upset that was created by my desire to be accepted for myself and who I was. People like Wilf Lord, Rudi Speed, Bill Haynes, Harry Foster, Harold Casper and Len Cuniffe and of course my father Ted Lodge, who although they as part of a gentler age struggled to understand my frustration and despair as I strove to achieve what I felt was my playing destiny, always supported me even though they wouldn't have appreciated my hot headed responses to perceived slights.

I did return and play for a brief period as I missed many of my fellow players, but it was a short lived return as I once again allowed myself to take exception to meaningless remarks from a meaningless man. Even though it give me great pleasure to recall that on the day in question a man who I still hold in high regard, Jeff Burn told people that losing some one like me from the club was a disaster. In spite of his support I still left. I did come back to the clubhouse the following Saturday to officially resign and give my account of events. At that point Tommy Dunn a far better clubman than I could ever hope to be offered his opinion. Because he feared my well-known temper would result in physical violence he decided to speak. Tommy said, 'We don't want your kind of person in this club', even in my annoyed frame of mind I realised he was probably right, because I knew I would never be able to take a rational view of anything that I felt was to my detriment in that environment.

Tommy Dunn probably without realising it did me a great favour, as he helped me make the only decision possible and that was to walk away before I damaged any hope I had of anyone having good memories of me at the club.

Many years later long after I had stopped even thinking of playing, as I was in my fifties Peter Leonard phoned asked me to come and play for the fourth team as he was short of players. The call came just before the team took the field a man short. It was half-time when I arrived and one of the Toc H players was being taken off to hospital. So they were still a man short even with me there.

Toc H had lost the first half heavily and in my overweight state, due to being on the road with Tommy Bruce and having to many helpings of pie and mash, it did not look as though I would be much help. However what I lacked in pace I made up for with my reading of the game and positional sense. I also found I could still tackle like a train. We won the second half and but lost the game and I was very kindly praised by teammates and opponents alike.

But the thing that meant the most to me was Rudi Speed and Bill Haynes who were spectators came and spoke to me. These two men fine players in their day stalwarts of the club whose playing days overlapped mine were now seventy plus said how pleased they were to see me. In conversation I pointed out that my club colours awarded years before that I wore on my jersey with such pride were lost. Bill looked at me with a smile and replied, David you never needed them because we all knew the clubs colours were tattooed on your heart.

At that moment I knew that I had misjudged many people and that if I had stayed with the club they would not have allowed me to be pushed aside on the whims of a couple of people and that I could have played on.

What really amazed me was that I had some how managed not to leave behind me the impression of the unpleasant young man that I thought I was.

People like Rudy, Bill and many others had realised that the pride I felt in playing for the club and my desire to contribute to its well being caused me to be consumed by frustration and rage against things that I felt prevented me making my full contribution to the cub. Also whilst raging against perceived injustice I had wished to be liked and admired by the many excellent people in the club, not realising that I had achieved this in spite of myself.

There are many people who I admired, men like Brian Head Rapson a former first team captain who retired from playing due to serious injury. Then took up refereeing at high level. Derek Squirrel who was kicking goals from inside his own half long before the advent of the light white ball. The incredibly talented Billy Thompson a fly half who with a drop of his shoulder could beat two men before his feet had even moved. He played for the county of Berkshire and for the Combined Services against France, during his National service and there is no doubt in my mind that with just a little more luck and training he would have played for England. Harold Payne a lovely man who in spite of suffering great pain from a knee injury, I believe suffered during the war, served both club and country with great distinction.

Keith Jackson a good friend and a scrum half with sublime skills who as captain of the colts team in conjunction with the team manager Harry Foster gave me my first real chance to play rugby on a regular basis. Peter Leonard, who in his day was rated one of the finest players around, helped me hone my skills as a wing forward.

Peter Bradley a cracking bloke who achieved much with the support of his lovely wife Mary. Peter played some of his best rugby in France before being badly injured. In spite of that injury he came back to Toc H when he recovered and served the club with great distinction both as a player and as an officer of the club.

Jack Rawson an athletic lock forward, Richard Brawn a talented fly half, these men and others like them are all remembered by me for their contributions to the club and for making it a pleasure to play in their company.

Jeff Burn who played on till he was all but sixty and then broke his neck playing as captain for the fourth team. This man apart from being the best hooker of his generation proved what courage and determination are all about to fight back from initial paralysis to walk again. Jeff is a truly remarkable man whose modesty will probably not allow him to appreciate my saying that he was real inspiration to all the players of my generation, both as a player and a man. He and his wife Ann have taken ever opportunity to demonstrate their friendship to Margaret and I in some of the most difficult times.

All of these men are worthy of more mention than I have given them here. Others who I have not mentioned at all played their part in my journey from being a boy to the man I hope I have become today. All I can say to those people who were part of the club during my time there but for a couple of previously mentioned exceptions I have been honoured and privileged to know you all . I can also say hand on heart not for the first time, that every time I pulled on my Toc H jersey I wore it with as much pride as I would have an England jersey.

Peter Leonard, who I have not said half enough about in this book either as a man or a rugby player has since told me that the Toc H players today would like to have the club emblem put above the door of the changing room so that they can reach up and touch it as they go out to play a match. This would remind them to play with pride in the club, I am sorry if they need to do that.

Dave (bottom row right) Jeff Burn sitting to his right.
Captain (holding the ball) is Peter Leonard and Mike Harrison on his right.

For my part I only had to touch my jersey and look in the faces of the great players around me to be filled with immense pride at the honour I had been given by being allowed to play for Toc H RFC.

CHAPTER THREE

SPORT

A DEFINING TIME OF MY LIFE

This story actually has two beginnings one being the beginning of the end of my love affair with playing the game of Rugby and my transition into Marathon running, Race walking, Triathlon, and most notably the Quadrathon.

Although the time frame is slightly out I feel it is an opportune moment to mention that the transition would also bring me into contact with great people like Dick and Zena Smith of the Lancashire Walking Club. This club has a great team ethic and because of that I was able to achieve some very rewarding sporting moments.

Thanks to Dick Smith's excellent coaching and the support of fantastic team mates like Ronnie and Stuart Marsden, Johnny Grocott and Bill

Dave proudly holding two of his many sporting trophies

Cowley I had the pleasure of having trophies for both the Lancashire and the Northern 10 mile championships on my mantle piece.

I also received the gold medal for the northern 10-mile race and the silver for the northern 50-kilometre championships thanks to my incredibly athletic and talented team mates. I received a badge for the 10k inside one hour time trial, three successive time standard medals for the Manchester to Blackpool 50 mile race and two third place trophies, in consecutive years for the Lancashire team in The Bradford 50k walk.

Dave on his way to silver in the Northern 50K

I also had the honour to lead the Blackpool race alongside the very competitive Yorkshire walker Paul Briggs on one occasion. Although some of the better athletes had gone off course that year, it is part of the skill of distance racing to keep going in the right direction. Ironically my team mate Ronnie Marsden missed his chance to win the race that year. He being the great sportsman that he is chased those who had gone off course and guided them back to the route and still finished the race in a great time. What a privilege to compete with men like Ronnie Marsden.

I cannot continue my memories of this wonderful club without special mention of a really talented member of our ladies team, Hazel Cross. Hazel under the guidance of Dick Smith trained with me every week and my speed and racing action improved greatly as I chased her round an industrial estate in Stretford in the shadow of the M62 motorway.

My thanks also go to Ronnie Marsden and his son Stuart who trained with me every Sunday morning around a course that include the aptly named Hareshill Road, we were often joined by the veteran Johnny Grocott and my competitive skills and stamina where honed on these outings.

Also I must mention that cakes made by Sammy Shoebottom for the after race tea. Thinking of Sammy brings fond memories of the camaraderie shared by team mates past and present. I have no doubt that these wonderful sportsmen kept me tied to an earlier and I have to say for my part better age. A time when concern for the well being of your fellow man was stronger and contrasted with the what's in it for me syndrome that is so prevalent today.

How I long for the spirit engendered by men like Dick Smith, an incredible man who in his sporting career achieved multiple cycling and race waking championships. Added to this following his management of the British team at the European Games, Dick was a guest at 10 Downing Street, of no less than three Prime ministers. Dick Smith was a man for whom the team was the important thing. He would demonstrate his belief in this when leading many a long distance walking race he would hear from supporters at the roadside that one of his team was struggling he would drop back down the order until he found his man. Then while still walking would give his team mate vocal encouragement, use his technical skill to get the man's racing action going again, bring him up through the competitors until they caught up to the next team member, give both of them another pep talk and then forge ahead once more. Many team prizes where achieved because of his actions, although Dick would certainly have won more individual prizes if he hadn't done this. Incidentally we called this action chain horsing, for obvious reason that the slower man got pulled along

Dick Smith and others who shared the same ethic as him won many medals and trophies but they are best remembered for their love and support of their fellow man. I have tried to follow their ethic in my life and in my sport. I will be very

Dave and Paul Briggs take the lead in the Manchester to Blackpool race (with Hazel Cross, of the LRWC, acting as feeder on the road just behind)

contented if at the end of my life I merit one quarter of the respect that these excellent men received.

I am proud to say that Dick Smith became my friend and sporting mentor. His technical knowledge and ability, added to any small talent I may have possessed brought me most of my sporting achievements. Also Dick Smith, along with his wife Zena, who was the first lady to be made a judge for race walking events helped Margaret and I through some difficult times in our lives. They remain forever in my memory as the epitome of what all human beings should aspire to be.

I cannot leave this part of the story without mentioning what I think is a very amusing story about the first time I competed in the Isle of Man TT race walk. This race is held over the motorcycle race course including the mountain section. I was there due to the kindness of my team mate Ronnie Marsden, Ronnie had won a free ticket over there in the previous years race and instead of using it himself gave it to me as he thought I would enjoy the experience and paid for his own ticket.

As we thought we did not have someone who could take the individual title on that occasion it was decided by Ronnie as team captain that we should race as a group and help each other so hopefully gaining a team prize.

After about an hour on the road we went past a commentary box manned by the President of the Race Walking Association, sadly I have forgotten his last name, but he had been a fine athlete in his own right and we all knew him by his first name John.

John was announcing the name of each competitor to the crowd and as we passed he said, "ladies and gentlemen here we have The Lancashire Walking Club, a fine body of men, still warming up". We could all have been disqualified there and then as our walking actions disintegrated and we all fell about laughing.

This happy memory only serves to remind me what a fantastic sport race walking is and how much fun we all had taking part in it.

I should also mention that two fine players and past first team captains of Toc H Rugby Club were spectators that day, Brian Goldsmith, who lived on the island, sadly Brian passed away while I was putting this book together, and Mike Harrison who was visiting him at that time. I have no doubt it amused them greatly to see one of their elderly former team mates struggling round the course.

I also had a brief flirtation with motor sport in the form of speedway riding and although it was most enjoyable experience I did not have the success in that sport that I was fortunate enough to enjoy in the others I took part in. In fact as it turned out, my success in other sports would be made more difficult my breaking my left leg in a motor cycle accident. That injury left my left leg at least two inches shorter than the right. I have to say in all honesty that while other people commented on how well I performed in all sports with such a limp, it was never an issue for me.

The second beginning was when in the company of my wife Margaret I met sixties singing star Tommy Bruce on a car park outside a Manchester Club in the early seventies. Starting a friendship that lasted to until his death on July 10th 2006 more than thirty five years.

Indeed as I have said many times since he is my friend and not seeing him doesn't change that, our friendship will remain as long as I'm alive and I will continue to look after business for him and his wife and family as long as I am able. After all he gave me total autonomy over all matters to do with his career although we never had a contract. I just have to continue to be worthy of his trust in me.

CHAPTER FOUR

SPEEDWAY

I was playing rugby for Toc H but I had long held the desire to try the sport of speedway. I had missed a great opportunity when a very fine rider Gordon Mc Gregor, a former Belle Vue rider, offered to take me under his wing and train me. Unfortunately at that time I just wasn't sure I was ready to stop playing rugby so didn't take Gordon up on his kind offer. I always regretted missing that chance as I feel any talent I had would have been enhanced by Gordon's training. So when a young lad came along to Toc H Rugby Club saying his name was Ken Eyre, I thought I might have a chance of a trial at Belle Vue. He was very friendly and invited me down the pits for the next meeting. The trouble was when I got to the pits and asked for Ken Eyre, a completely different person than the one I was expecting came to speak to me. Rather than being an embarrassing encounter Ken, being the man that he is, invited me into the pits and our friendship began.

I bought my first bike, a 500cc Jawa, in 1969 from Dave Hemus a really nice guy and a good rider. He had a good career, riding first for Wolverhampton and then Belle Vue and he also spent a brief period in the Exeter team. After buying the bike we became good friends. Dave would only be around for a couple more years as he emigrated to South Africa.

In my efforts to make it as a rider I received great support from Peter Leonard who acted as my mechanic and an old school friend, Phil Derbyshire, was kind enough to transport us to the tracks in his father's furniture van. After seeing me race at Crewe Speedway I was fortunate to be given a contract by the then Belle Vue team manager Dent Oliver. Dent had been a great rider in his day and he seemed to rate my abilities so I misguidedly thought that was were my sporting future lay and he signed me as a junior rider for the club. Although I feel he thought I was a half decent rider my decision to sign that contract would signal the end of my aspirations to be a rider ... because he never gave me a ride. There had been interest from Berwick Bandits and Workington Comets but I didn't give them a second thought. This was because I was naive enough to think that I had made it. I thought Dent Oliver wanted me in the Colts team, I was not alone in this belief as several other lads made the same mistake.

I regard Dent Olver as the most successful speedway manager there has ever been. He had built up the Aces and the Colts, they were League champions in their own respective divisions. I think perhaps he decided to sign riders who showed even the slightest ability so that they wouldn't be riding for opposing teams. If that was the case I don't blame him one bit. Some of the other lads with a greater desire to succeed got out of their contracts and moved to ride for other clubs, in fairness to Dent he did suggest I went to ride at Rochdale and try to break into the team there. I decided to call it a day, because I knew I would never be good enough to make the grade at Belle Vue. That said, I did enjoy the experience of finding out. For example on one occasion at Belle Vue one of the other junior riders was unable to take his allotted ride so Dent Oliver said send out that new lad, Dave Lodge. "Great" I thought, "I'll show them", I leapt on my bike and made my way to the starting gate. I pulled in the clutch and wound the throttle back ... then, as the tapes went up so did I, turning a back somersault and landing hard, catching my heel in the back wheel and wrenching my knee. During this time Peter Leonard was watching open mouthed. We hadn't eaten all day so thinking I wasn't due out on track he had gone to get us a pie. That would have been fine, except he had been adjusting the handlebars and they weren't tightened up because he wanted me to check their position.

Then in one race I was in a distant 3rd place, but last to finish because a guy called Geoff Pusey had come off. As I entered the pits bend Stan, who raked the track between races, pulled out ahead of me on his tractor. I got to know that area of the track and the fence very well.

The most spectacular of my many attempts to get to know tracks really well, came at Crewe. I was having a really good night, I usually did there because the banked track suited me. With a win and two second places earlier in the evening, my confidence was high. At that time the second half of the meeting was being run on a handicap basis with 5 riders in the race so, because of my earlier success I was coming from halfway down the straight before the starting gate. My start was electric and as I came down from the top of the first bend I was in second place, I was flying and I thought I would take the guy in front of me, Barry Booth in his blue boots on the outside. He rightly moved over to his right. "No problem" I thought, "front wheel right up alongside his back wheel close to the fence, I'll lean back and lift my front wheel over to the left side and go past him". I had never seen even the best of riders attempt this, but I had no doubt I could do it ... after somersaulting six times down the back straight I realised why nobody ever did this! In spite of that fiasco it was that evening that Dent Oliver gave Paul Callaghan and I our contracts.

I met and I am privileged to know Peter Collins a modest man who went on to be world champion. Like all great riders Peter had great courage. This was shown when he defended his world championship. He rode with courage and determination to finish third despite breaking his leg prior to the event. Peter Collins is a fantastic ambassador for his sport. He and his wife Angie were kind enough in later years to share their time and company with my wife Margaret and I. Unfortunately Peter suffered a stroke but with good medical care and the loving support of his wife he has been able to make a good recovery. Margaret and I wish them both good health in the future.

It was my honour to know many other great riders and ride against some of them. In particular Alan Wilkinson, a great and courageous rider sadly paralysed in a crash. Alan has something every man among us strives for, but only a few of us achieve, the companionship of a loving and loyal wife, Alan has Jean who epitomises those things in abundance, it is a privilege to know them both, although time and personal problems have meant that we have not seen as much of them as Margaret and I would have liked.

Others include Chris Pusey known as The Polka Dot Kid, Tommy Roper, Norman Nevitt, Cyril Maidment, Dave Hardy, Taffy Owen, Eric Broadbelt, Chris & Dave Morton, Gary Middleton, Tom Owen, Tom Leabitter, Arnie Pander, Ole Nygren, Bernie Lagrosse, Soren Sjosten, Gary Peterson, Sandor Levi and multiple world champions, Ole Olsen, Barry Briggs and Ivan Mauger to name just a few.

The fab four - Peter Collins, Ken Eyre, Eric Broadbelt & Alan Wilkinson

One man who was not a speedway rider who but who remains to this day one of the worlds greatest competitive motor cyclists. This man must be mentioned at this point in the book as I met him when I was riding in the speedway training school at Belle Vue, Mick Andrews. Mick is the holder of more championships in Scrambling, Moto Cross as it is called today and Trials riding than anyone I have ever known or heard of. Once again we are proud to say that he and his wife Jill, the lady with the sparkling eyes have shared their friendship with Margaret and I.

I have to say that the people we have been privileged to meet throughout my sporting life have enriched us in a way that money never could. I enjoyed many great evenings and afternoons watching Ken, racing to victory, aided by his father Len, who had been a great rider himself and his mechanic Dave Shipstone. Ken really did achieve fantastic wins against outstanding competition. These wins often came against more experienced riders; Ken's skill would bring the acclaim of other riders like three times world champion Ole Olsen and also brought him international honours.

At this point I think I should tell the story of how I met and became friends with Ken Eyre. I met him by default and by mistake really, but I'm very glad I did.

Ken Eyre

Ken Eyre is quite simply a thoroughly decent man who deserved far more than his chosen sport was able to return to him. That said the way he has lived his life is an example to those of us who try to live our lives in the right way. Ken's ideals of hard work, dedication, reliability, loyalty and decency make him a man who I proud to call my friend.

It came as no surprise to anyone that knew Ken in his younger days that he would succeed in some form of motorcycle sport. The reason being that as soon as he started to ride in any form of competitive motorcycling sport it was clear that he had a competitor spirit. Added that his father Len had been a rider of some distinction who was successful in trials riding and most notably speedway and Ken had clearly inherited some of his dad's love of motorcycles. As well as being a fine rider Len was also a wizard with an engine something that would later help Ken's quest for success on the speedway track. Indeed had it not been for the advent of World War Two Len would certainly have been an outstanding rider for Belle Vue. That said Ken was not the first of Len's sons to have success in the world of motorcycling. That early fame fell to Ken's brother Norman who was four years older.

Norman Eyre was one of the outstanding trials riders of his generation, winning many trophies while riding works bikes for Royal Enfield, Triumph, Bultaco and

Ken Eyre, Ace in the pack

Len Eyre

DOT factories. Although I didn't know him well Norman always treated me kindly on the occasions that I met him, I like think that he recognised that I would always be a good and loyal friend to his brother. I hope I have lived up to that.

One of the great things for me about knowing Ken Eyre is that his mum and dad, Eileen and Len always made me welcome in their home, really making me feel like friend of the whole family.

Norman Eyre

Of course returning to Ken himself he showed early on in his riding career that he had the skill to ride very well in, trials scrambling, and grass track racing before he took up speedway. Although he had done two seasons very successfully on grass he was still ready for another challenge. That challenge was speedway and his performance right from the start was a revelation. Because it seemed that no sooner had Ken turned up at Dent Oliver's training school in the winter of 1967/68 with his 500cc Jap grass engine fitted in a rolling chassis, that he was in the Belle Vue Colts team competing in the new Division Two.

I watched Ken Eyre in his first race meeting for Belle Vue Colts, and he scored a paid maximum, this was unbelievable because he was competing against riders who had been around for some years and had ridden in the top division as reserves and second strings, indeed some of his own team-mates had outing with the Belle Vue Aces. How could Ken do this? I just don't know, like all the other fans I watched in awe as he flew round the track. All I can do is tell you is that Ken Eyre was blessed with an unbelievable talent, his style and technique were clearly a gift from God although he always worked hard to improve them, added to that he had a racer's brain. But what really set Ken apart was his determination to win, his tenacity to hang in there when it looked as though the guy in front might have faster bike. Putting it as simply as I can Ken Eyre possessed instinctive and superior track-craft to that of most riders and could use it to great effect.

The other things that made a difference for Ken was his dad tuning his engines and supporting him all the way. That allied to Ken's friend Dave Shipstone acting as his mechanic on race nights meant that Ken could concentrate on doing what he did so well-winning races. Something else that Ken never forgets is the advice offered to him by that great Swedish rider called Torbjorn Harryson. The most memorable thing I think Torbjorn told Ken was to ditch the banana seat, because you tend

Belle Vue Colts circa 1969.
L to R - Bill Moulin, Ken Moss, Jim Jacoby, Alan Middleton (manager), Chris Bailey (on the bike), Steve Waplington, Eric Broadbelt and Ken Eyre

to slide up and down on it when you are riding, get a small seat. Ken took his advice and the rest as they say is history.

Because of Ken I met the other riders including Dave Hemus who I bought my own bike from and I became a regular in the pits and more importantly from a personal point of view enrolled in the Belle Vue Training School, I thought I was on my way.

With hindsight I realise I should have forgone my own excursion into the sport and used my money to sponsor Ken as there was a time in his career that with more financial support there is no doubt he would have made even bigger strides towards the success and stardom that his hard work and talent deserved.

Incidentally the other Ken Eyre never turned up at the rugby club again, which was a pity because he had already shown himself to be a talented rugby player and was a likeable lad.

Ken Eyre the speedway rider was proving himself to be a great asset to Belle Vue, top scoring on tracks up and down the country for the Colts and gaining International selection. He was having a tremendous start to his career he couldn't have ridden better.

The riders with the best points average in the division towards the end of the season were selected for the Division Two Riders Championship. Belle Vue Colts had a strong contingent of riders, including as I recall Taffy Owen, Eric Broadbelt, Chris Bailey and of course Ken Eyre. There would be no team riding though, it was every man for himself. Ken was flying and his engine was superb, thanks to his dad and Ken Eyre was far and away the best of the Colts riders that night.

Ken out in front for England

Ken could and indeed should have been the Division Two Riders Champion that night, had it not been for what was in my opinion an incorrect refereeing decision to rerun a race that had already completed three laps and started the last lap with Ken in the lead. This decision by the referee meant that Ken finished the rerun in third place, behind actual winner of the meeting Graham Plant, who couldn't believe his luck and his own team-mate Taffy Owen, who was having an awful night up to that point. This result left Ken in second place in the Championship, but Ken was far to much of a sportsman to begrudge Graham Plant being the Champion. That said it was definitely a poor refereeing decision and the referee that night should in my opinion hang his head in shame.

What none of us knew then of course was that a complete lack of understanding of the rules by the referee cost Ken Eyre the only major individual championship that he would because of injury, have the chance to compete for. Of course young Ken still had many successful years ahead and during the course of them he would achieve multiple league championship medals for both the Colts and the Aces. What a man, what a champion.

L to R Ken Eyre, Graham Plant & Graham Smith

There is no doubt that if Ken Eyre had remained in the second division he would have won that title in the future but his talent was to great for that to be allowed to happen. The reason for that was because Dent Oliver knew that Ken Eyre was the outstanding rider of his generation and his value in the Belle Vue Aces team would be immense. In this. Dent was proved right as Ken's points average elevated him from reserve to the No2 Race Jacket in the team. Ken rode in both the Colts and Aces team in 1969, becoming a full Ace in 1970.

With multiple Word Champion Ivan Mauger being Belle Vue's No.1 rider It seemed that Ken's rise to fame would continue unchecked in spite of various injuries he picked up along the way, one to his knee which he seemed to shrug off as though it was nothing and of course a hand injury that meant in order to keep riding he had the clutch lever and the throttle on the same side of the handle bar so that he could operate them with the same hand. To do this and keep winning races required unbelievable skill but Ken was a special kind of rider and more importantly is a special kind of man.

During this time Ken met and fell in love with an absolutely stunning girl called Chris, he would go on to marry her. Chris is a rare person because her physical beauty is enhanced by an even greater inner beauty that radiates from her eyes. Chris is a wonderful, kind and generous person who makes you feel that you are the person that she most wanted to speak to whenever you meet up with her. Always busy Chris works as a PA , has been chair of the Parish Council on more than one occasion and is a School Governor. I am delighted to able to tell you that Chris has been honoured for all her years of selfless work for her community with the award of a British Empire Medal, well deserved. Amazingly with

L to R Chris Pusey, Ken Eyre, Ivan Mauger, Tommy Roper, Dave Hemus, Bill Powell , Eric Broadbelt & Soren Sjosten

all her efforts Chris always has time to help other people and most of all provides 100% support for Ken and their wonderful son Torbjorn.

Torbjorn, affectionately known to us all as Toby was named Tobjorn in honour of the Swedish speedway rider Torbjorn Harryson, who is mentioned earlier as having advised Ken at the start of his career. This being a sign of how much Ken liked and more importantly admired Torbjorn Harryson as a rider.

Unfortunately misfortune was waiting round the corner for Ken Eyre as a rider at Belle Vue. In July 1972 He was challenging for the lead in a race against Swindon Robins when he hit a ridge in the track left by the grader- Ken fell heavily but the rider behind Ken, did not react quickly enough to situation and rode straight into him as he lay on the ground, fracturing Ken's shoulder blade in five places as well as other injuries. The specialists later said that Ken must have had a spine like sprung steel as the wall of his stomach had been bruised by the impact-he also punctured his stomach falling on his handlebars.

After three consecutive First Division League Championships for The Belle Vue Aces The ACU rider control decided to dismantle the "dream team" thereby reducing their strength and transferred Ivan Mauger to Exeter and Ken Eyre to Wolverhampton. The Wolves were keen to have Ken Eyre in their team. With World Champion Ole Olsen riding at number one and with two riders he already knew, Tom Ledbitter who scrambled with Ken and Aussie Gary Petersson in the team, Ken agreed to move. Sadly both Tom and Gary are no longer with us.

It seemed to Ken that this would be the right move to help his career. What Ken didn't realise and neither did anyone else at the time was that the

Ken and Chris Eyre

Leading the field at Hyde Road

damage to his back was more serious than had been thought and it wasn't lack of form or riding ability that was letting him down but the ongoing effects of the back injury which had been serious enough to cause the vertebrae to fuse in his spine.

After a solid start with this new team in 1973 the next season started with great promise Ken had been made a heat leader. In late May 1974 an unfortunate accident at Wimbledon in a World Championship qualifying event left Ken lying on the track for a while. We couldn't know it then but writing was on the wall for the end of Ken's career. He turned up for his next meeting but retired after one ride. The man who in my opinion and that of three time world champion Ole Olsen, was the greatest British rider never to be World Champion had ridden his last competitive race and I am not ashamed to say I wept at the cruelty of the hand of fate.

Ken moves to Wolves in 1973

Needless to say I was wrong to do so, because over the last forty years Ken Eyre has shown himself to be a man possessed of great courage, a man with an indomitable spirit who has the admiration and respect of all who know him. In spite of ill health Ken worked hard and in his spare time became an accomplished trials rider despite the pain this pastime must have caused him.

Ken Eyre achieved much in an all to brief career - in his first season riding for Belle Vue Colts, 1968, he scored an average of just under nine points a match, out of a possible twelve, winning his first Division Two Championship medal, the following year, 1969, with a match average of just below ten points he helped the Colts to their second Division Two Championship gaining his second medal whilst also riding 21 matches for the Aces with an average of 4.21. The same time Promoted to the Aces 1st team he won three consecutive medals for the First Division Championship, in 1970, 71 and 72, one of only two British riders to achieve this. Added to that he was part of the team that claimed the Knock-out Cup in 1972. Together with Aces team-mate Eric Broadbelt, Ken Eyre holds a world record for five consecutive League medals for the same club.

Back - L to R,
George Hunter, John Irskine, Tom Ledbitter, Dave Gifford
Front L to R Ken Eyre, Ole Olsen, Gary Petersson

In 1990 the opportunity came for Ken to let his son Toby see him ride as a guest in the Chris Morton Farewell Meeting, a one off challenge match between the former Hyde Road Aces and the then current Kirkmanshulme Lane team, it had been 16 years since Ken last rode, Ken only rode in two races but with two fine second places he showed just how good a rider/racer he really had been. Needless to say the Hyde Road Aces won.

As I stood proudly watching on the centre green with Ken's son Toby beside me I was able to tell the story of the great rider his father had been and how but for injury he would in my opinion have been world champion.

Eric Broadbelt, Ken Eyre & Steve Waplington represent England

I hope this made a fantastic day even better for Toby because Ken is far to modest a man to ever boast of his own achievements, but I believe his abilities should always be remembered. Both Ken and his wife Chris are truly examples of the best that members of the human race can ever be and they remain two of the closest friends Margaret and I have.

I would like to praise Toby for his fantastic achievements as a competitive trials rider and as a man. He wins competitions on a regular basis and recently won the Clubman Dave Rowlands Trophy for the fourth time, a

Ken and Eric Broadbelt, triple Champions

trophy that he first won ten years ago! He also regularly runs marathons especially the London, and half marathons, raising an incredible amount of money for charity. Recently Toby went a long to the Scunthorpe speedway track with his dad Ken to see if he could master the skill required for that sport. In no time at all he was tearing round the track at full chat. As the photograph of him shows he possesses all the skill necessary to have succeeded had he chosen to follow his dad into the sport.

Like Toby his wife Claire is an amazing person who supports him in all he does. To the extent that when they were married in 2005 they took part in the London Marathon while on their honeymoon Claire wearing her wedding veil and Toby in Top Hat and Tails. Claire is also

Toby Eyre after completing the London Marathon (again!)   Toby & Claire's Wedding Day

Toby Eyre at full chat at Scunthorpe and over the rough ground

an accomplished horsewoman whose skill with her horse is of a very high standard.

I am pleased to say that Toby and his wife Claire have also become our friends and they both display the same exemplary qualities of kindness and consideration that Ken and Chris have always demonstrated.

All in all the Eyre family are exceptional people who enhance the lives of all who know them.

Ken Eyre, Margaret, Dave & Chris at Claire & Toby's wedding

CHAPTER FIVE

THE QUADRATHON

Preface By Geoff Wiles.

Although I don't know Dave Lodge all that well, I would hazard a guess to say that having seen him compete in The Quadrathon, a race that I was partly responsible for putting on, I have some idea about the character of the man. As I told Dave when I spoke to him, while he was writing this book, he and the other competitors had to be in the top one percent of the population of the World just to take part. That Dave is one of a few who competed in it twice shows he had a high level of fitness and determination. Endurance athletes are special breed and Dave Lodge is an example of that breed.

Geoff Wiles British Professional Cycling Champion

This athletic endeavour would span 15 years. I joined Sale Harriers and with the help of athletes like Steve Green, Dave Farmer and Steve Edmonds I became a reasonable distance runner at club level. I also had the privilege of training with a man called Kelvin Breeze who but for health problems would most certainly have achieved international status.

Once again I would make mistakes which with hindsight probably affected my performance and level of success. I decided that being over thirty years of age I would go for quantity not quality and for twelve of those years I competed in between four and six marathons a year as well as races over other distances ranging from five to twenty miles.

An example of this was that one Easter I ran two marathons and twenty-mile race in the space of four days. The twenty-mile race was the most successful position wise as I finished fourth. But the marathons were to my mind a great success. The day after the twenty-mile race I ran a time of two hours fifty two minutes for the marathon and then followed this two days later on a very hilly marathon course in near Stoke with a time of three hours nine minutes.

Results of this type gave me the consolation I thought, of knowing that had I tried this wonderful sport of distance running ten years earlier, it was possible that I could have been very good indeed. It was only in later years when I reflected on my running career I realised that had I limited my competitive running to maybe two marathons a year I might have achieved great success.

At the age of 58, six weeks after I had competed in the Malta international Triathlon, I was hit by a fork lift truck. This accident left me disabled in the leg area and ended any sporting ambitions I may have still harboured. It also partly explains my overweight appearance in the later photographs you see in the book. The other contributing factor is the helping of double pie and mash, with green liqueur, eaten in Tommy Bruce's company.

However I have no regrets and look back with a degree of pride that I developed a level of fitness that allowed me to be competitive at an age when many people have reached for their armchair and slippers.

That fitness would also make the foundation of an even more enjoyable and successful period in my sporting life.

My father, ever the interested spectator at my sporting endeavours, noticed an article written by Sports correspondent Len Gould in *The Daily Express* in December of 1982. The article was about an event called the Quadrathon to be held in September 1983. Competitors would have to:

- Swim Two Miles In The Sea
- Race Walk For Thirty-Two Miles
- Ride A Bike For One Hundred Miles
- And Finish Off By Running A Twenty-Six Point Two Mile Marathon.

He drew the article to my attention and I sent for an entry form and then started to train for the event. My basic fitness was good from the marathon training but I had not ridden a bike or done any swimming except on holiday since my school days.

Initially I bought a second-hand racing bike and added a forty mile measured cycle ride to my daily run of fifteen miles. I waited impatiently for the Christmas holiday to be over as my local swimming baths would not be open until the end of the first week in January. When I finally got in there I was to have one of the greatest pieces of luck I could have possibly have had in my sporting career.

Dave with Dale Gartley

The two pool attendants at Levenshulme Baths where kindness itself to this middle aged man who was floundering about in the pool. Their names are Dale Gartley and Doreen Madden, both of whom are fine athletes in their own right, Doreen is a ladies running champion over distance and Dale in his athletic career is a champion fell runner Their help and advice with my swim training was invaluable. Right from the start they explained how far I would need to swim in training on a daily basis to have any chance of being ready for the race.

I thought at first that I would not be able to achieve the target which was sixty-six lengths of the pool, (the equivalent of one mile) every day Monday to Friday and on a Saturday and Sunday double that. The reason given for this extra effort on those two days was that, as I would have more energy due having to go to work on those two days. Surprisingly it was only a few weeks before I was up to

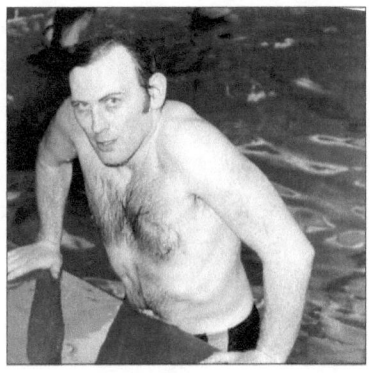

Leaving the pool after a training session

59

speed and more to the point my performances stated to improve in the other disciplines as well.

At this point Dale decided it was too easy for me and decided to create how he thought it would be swimming in a stormy sea. He did this by training the high powered hose that they used for cleaning the pool on me as I swam length after length. This was very effective and helped increase my strength and endurance. These two wonderful people also helped with my travel expenses when I went down to Brighton for the race. I still have great respect for both of them and regard them as my friends to this day.

I had the great good fortune to be sponsored by Raleigh Cycles and this sponsorship proved to be a valuable assistance to me. My training on the old bike I had was good but the new bike just seemed to fly. Athletic clothing for three of the four events was provided by the company I worked for (Dormy Ltd) on condition that I had their Logo printed on the clothing.

When I set off down to Brighton for the race I could not have been better prepared. With hindsight this was a somewhat misguided view but I was a rather naive competitor in this particular sport.

There was only one negative aspect to consider Raleigh Cycles who had provided me with a bike and cycling shorts had also promised to provide me with a cycling jersey, they were unable to fulfil that promise in time for the race. Although they subsequently did for future events.

This problem was solved with a call to Geoff Wiles the great cycling champion, who was one of the organisers; he had a cycling shop he told me not to worry as he would sell me one on the day of the race at a reduced price. As it turned out he lent me one of his own, as due to the pressure of organising the race he had not had time to go back to his shop. I still have that cycling Jersey and that I wore it in competition is the source of great pride to me.

SPORT STARTS HERE

Superman Four lunges into a cycle of torture

By Bryn Davies

THANKS A MILLION AS OLSEN THE LEGEND BOWS OUT WITH A FINAL FLOURISH

Ole Olsen

By Phillip Rising

The morning of the race *The Daily Express* having been to my home to interview me and photograph me, paid me the tribute of writing about me first on their sports page putting me above great athletes like Olympic Javelin Champion Tessa Sanderson and three times World Speedway Champion Ole Olsen. The headline read '*Superman Four Dives Into A Cycle of Torture*' I didn't deserve to be placed above these great names and the comparison was only made because like Clark Kent and I wear glasses but I was very proud I that I had my two minutes of fame.

Cutting & Photograph courtesy of Daily Express

61

I travelled down to Brighton with my friend and one of the only two men I felt a brotherly affection for, Peter Leonard. After we had booked into the hotel and registered for the race. Peter who had volunteered to be my feeder during the race and I decided to relax and enjoy the pre- race atmosphere. Unfortunately that evening I succumbed to something that has been the bane of my life, migraine! It was a shocker I was up all night being sick and neither Peter nor I got any sleep.

On the day of the race things would only get worse. In the morning Peter Leonard and I went down to the beach to view the start. We decided after consultation with the lifeguard on the beach that in spite of the flag flying warning swimmers not to go in it would be all right for me as I was obviously a strong swimmer or I would not be in the race. Peter decided he would swim a short way but soon turned back due the heavy waves and also due the fact that he possesses more common sense than I do.

I revelled in the conditions and with powerful strokes had soon swum out past the end of the pier. This was not deliberate but due to the fact that the waves were so high I could not see the pier. Unbeknown to me this was causing great consternation on the beach. Peter and the lifeguard were in a state of some agitation and the lifeguard assured Peter there was no way I could get back to shore.

Peter said are you going in after him? You've got to be joking was the reply; I can't swim in those conditions. Peter being quite concerned asked what will you do then? I will have to call the lifeboat out he said and we will be lucky if they get to him before he drowns. Unaware of all this I happened to have swum onto the crest of a wave and noticed that I was level with the end of the pier. I thought to myself you had better turn back if you do not want to finish up in France.

Peter and the lifeguard saw me turn so delayed the call for the lifeboat. Swimming with the power that my training had produced I arrived back on the on the beach only a few feet lower down from where I had gone in, only to be told of the excitement my little jaunt had caused. I was to realise later that expending that much energy on the morning of the race would have a detrimental effect on my performance, even though the race did not start until four o' clock in the afternoon.

I plunged into the sea at the start of the race with dreams of glory running through my brain. My fitness and conditioning were at their peak and I have never looked or felt better. I swam with the power of a man half my age and as I passed people swimming the crawl, I was swimming breaststroke, thought to be a slower stroke, I felt exhilarated.

As the race progressed in spite of the rough sea I was eating up the two-mile distance and felt confident of a good performance. Although I could hear the cries of swimmers in distress due to cramp and hypothermia and I found this quite unnerving.

Inflatable motor boats sped around us pulling those competitors stricken by the various ailments from the water. In this they were also aided by canoeists who allowed people to hold onto their craft to take a breather. Air sea rescue helicopters with their blades spinning, were making an horrendous noise which terrified me and spurred me on to find the shore. These helicopters had men dangling from rope ladders and they were plucking people from the sea. It seemed to me, from the cries of those in the water that people were dying all around me but I could not see because of the height of the waves. I am pleased to say that I was wrong in my thoughts, nobody died.

Ploughing through the sea 2 miles at Brighton

I prayed as I have never prayed before or since and promised God that if I could just get to land, I would not put myself in harm's way again (how quickly I forgot these promises and prayers when competing in similar events). Luckily, thanks to the bravery and skill of the men in the support services, no one died in the sea that day. But out of one hundred of the fittest people in the world only something between thirty and thirty five of them completed the swim, I was one of those who made it but it was a heavily decimated field that started the race walking section.

I was pumped up by surviving the ordeals in the sea and thought in my naivety that all I had to do was keep going and I would win the race. As I strode purposefully out at a good marching pace of five miles an hour, I thought to myself, "This for you Dave will be the hardest part of the event." I thought that if I got through the thirty-two miles of the walk in a reasonable time I would be able go on to win this race and be a world champion.

How wrong I was. The trained race walkers moved incredibly fast and soon passed me. In my efforts to chase them I put my foot in a hole in the road and hurt my ankle. Still refusing to be denied I limped on, falling further behind. The only ones I was passing were others who had dropped out of the race standing at the side of the road. My thoughts now on the hundred-mile bike ride possibly in my mind my best event.

At the end of the walk section, all competitors were given a medical examination. The doctor who examined me thought, because of the damage to my ankle that I had no hope of reaching my destination at Brands Hatch, never mind fifty laps of the track when I got there. On hearing this Geoff Wiles commented that I might as well give back the cycling jersey he had lent me, as I had no chance of continuing in the race. I very nearly did return it and retire from the race, because if ever there was a man to respect it was Geoff Wiles as he is one of the greatest cyclists this country has ever produced. In the event I rode like a man possessed and turned in a very fast time for that section of the race.

Those of you who haven't followed cycling may not be aware that Geoff Wiles has been a great champion in the sport. Geoff started as an amateur in 1960 riding for the Medway Club he won many local and national races before turning professional. On turning professional his many Palmares included winning the Professional Cycling Championship in 1976 beating riders of the calibre of Sid Barras and Phil Corley. Geoff made a courageous defence of the title in 1977 coming third.

He also won the British Professional Madison Championship. On top of this he graced two World Championships and represented Great Britain with distinction. As his riding career was coming to an end he became a coach to the British Triathlon Team. In fact I recently hard that his career as a racing cyclist is not over, because he is still winning medals in his seventies, including golds in the World Masters Championships.

At the end of the cycling section the great Geoff Wiles came to me and told me that the jersey he had lent me was the one he wore when he won the British Professional Cycling Championship. He went on to say that when I set off at the start of the ride he thought I was so far behind that if he could he would have taken the jersey back.

Dave cycling section Brands Hatch

However he said had heard the reports of my pace and progress throughout the hundred miles and that now he was so proud of me that he wished me to keep the jersey. His wife followed that up by saying that she couldn't believe her ears as he had taken the jersey with them everywhere they went since he won the title. I was more proud than words can describe to have this tangible recognition of his approval. I still have that jersey to this very day and regard it along with Geoff's words as the finest award that I received in my long sporting career.

At that point in the race you had to give a urine sample and have your blood pressure tested before being allowed to start the marathon section. In the medical tent the doctor remembered me and said he was surprised to see me and that he couldn't believe the speed of my ride given that I had literally torn the ligaments in my left ankle to shreds when I put my foot in the pot hole.

The doctor then said I had blood in my urine, I replied I am not surprised as due to making up time I had neglected to take enough fluid and sustenance on the road. His response was that since I was aware of my physical situation and was going to rectify it by drinking milk and eating food he would allow me to continue in the race. I think he knew that my race was run because only a mile or so into the marathon section my ankle gave out completely.

I came back the next year and finished the race; I think only about twenty five of the one hundred starters made it to the finish and I was far from last. It was a very strange race and I am proud to have my name in the record books along with the other finishers, Richard Crane won the first time and Steve Upton the second they were both incredible athletes. Also to have had my own competition within the race with the great Australian distance racer Joe Record and to have beaten him was a real honour.

Joe who I believe was sponsored by Hoover was an incredibly determined competitor who went on to achieve record times in many other events. As I look back now it seems wrong that I had been so fit the previous year and due to injury did not get to the end of the race. Then in the second year I was able to finish the race and an athlete of Joe's calibre could not.

That said he went on travelling the world and winning competitions for many more years. He was a great athlete and a really nice man. He is counted among the people who I am privileged to have met and raced against. The race itself was a very strange experience.

Well into the Marathon section in The Quadrathon

The reason why I found the experience very strange was that I was unable to walk properly never mind train for the event until February of the next year due to the severity of my ankle injury sustained in the previous year's event. Added to this when I eventually did start training my father who had been diagnosed with cancer just after the previous race was spending a lot of time in hospital. So I spent more time visiting him than I did training.

Then he sadly died a couple of weeks before the race and I was left with the decision as to whether or not I should compete.

I decided to take part and hope that my fitness from the previous year would carry me through to the end of the race. In effect I was right but there were a couple harrowing moments which could have brought a very different result. The worst of these being during the swim, which on this occasion was held in the marina as the sea, was so rough.

The waves were so high they were coming in over the sea wall and it was very choppy causing the boats, which were marking each end of the course to move on their moorings. On the last turn with about half a mile from the end of the swim my leg got caught in the mooring rope and each time the boat bobbed up and down I went under. I really thought I was done for but a guy leapt out of the boat in a duffel coat and wellingtons to help me, as we both went under the water I thought well that's both of us done for. He knew better and got me free.

I remembered the pre-race talk about outside assistance so, with remarkable clarity of mind I resisted the efforts to pull me in the boat and asked if I could continue without disqualification someone said I could and I swam on. Then because my leg had been rigid it started to spasm with cramp, I very soon got cramp in my other leg.

A canoeist who was paddling up and down the course checking the competitors said hold on top the canoe and I will get you to safety as you can not swim the rest of the way with just your arms. I said I could swim the remaining distance, however doubting that I could, he paddled along side me till I reached the jetty. He then wished me luck and went back to help others. During that swim I was very afraid that I would not survive, the reason I did was because I was sure my late father was in the water with me and I spoke to him saying I could not do it with out him. Fear has a strange effect on you in moments of stress but I really did feel his presence.

My troubles were far from over because when I tried to climb the ladder my legs refused to respond so I dragged my self up with my arms as I neared the top people seeing that I was struggling tried to help me. But I urged them to leave me, as I was still fearful of being disqualified.

When I got on to the jetty my good friend Peter Leonard who was feeding me during the race, asked if I could go on, I replied they will have to put a bullet in me to stop me now. Joe Lancaster the great sports journalist heard that remark and the next day the newspaper headline read *'Even A Bullet Can't Stop Iron Man Lodge'*. A stupid thing for me to say, which led to an embarrassing headline, but I really felt I had to keep going.

Dave with Peter Leonard at the end of the Quadrathon

The race walking section went well because I had been coached and trained in the discipline by that great former athlete Dick Smith, I excelled in the cycling and ran a strong marathon. The medal I received for achieving my ambition is one of my proudest possessions, second only to Geoff Wile's cycling jersey.

It is only right that I mention two great athletes who won the race in the two years I competed in it, Richard Crane and Steve Upton, they seem to be forgotten now, but they were great athletes in their day. They needed to be in order to win an event that was rightly dubbed the toughest race in the world. 2 miles swim in the sea, 32 miles race walk, 100 miles cycle ride, and to finish a 26 miles 385 yards marathon. Well done them both and to every other competitor who took part. I was proud have met you all.

A little aside to the swim saga is that a guy called Jim Ryan who is a great stunt co-ordinator who knew I had dived off this jetty to start the race asked me if I would be free to do it as a stunt man for a television drama. My reply was that I wasn't free but that if he took my advice he would be cautious about how he hit the water, as it would be like hitting concrete from that height. In the event he broke his shoulder and I have always felt guilty about that because he is brilliant at being knocked down by cars and falling without ever getting hurt. I should have gone down to Brighton done it for him.

I went on to take part in many more races including triathlons and I raced internationally abroad. My last race was the Malta International Triathlon. In this race I was lucky enough to compete against the great Maltese Champion, international Nicky Feruga. I beat him due to him having to pull out during the race. Nicky was a fantastic athlete and a really powerful man who had swum from Malta to Sicily on a previous occasion. During my long career I was lucky enough to win some of my races including the Northern and Lancashire ten mile Championships. I kept up the race walking for several seasons picking up individual awards and team prizes along the way under the auspices of my mentor and friend Dick Smith who actually managed the British team at the European Championships. He was a champion cyclist before the war and a great race walker. Dick and his wife Zena were a great support and I had my most successful period in sport under his auspices. Zena was a wonderful woman and Dick was a great man, without their support I would never have achieved as much as I did in sport.

Returning to Geoff Wiles, he has kindly agreed to write a foreword for this section of the book and in conversation he has once again given me this time verbally a great

Flying without wings!

prize. Geoff reminded me of something I had forgotten, that was I had to be in the top one percent of the population to be fit enough to compete in the event. The fact that I was able to finish the race on so little training the second year, was testament to my father's spiritual presence in the sea, added to my own mental strength and my athleticism and the support of Peter Leonard. That a great athlete such as Geoff uttered those words to me is, if I may misquote the bible 'a prize beyond rubies'. If those words from Geoff are to be the final statement on my sporting career I could not have kinder words from a finer athlete or a better man.

Just a few of the medals and trophies I picked up along the way.

Chapter Six

Tommy Bruce

I had thought that I would go on competing until old age one way or another probably taking part in Masters Events and competing for age group prizes. But to my surprise something that I had been doing in conjunction with my sport would gradually take over and ensure that I could not train as I would wish to and therefore I would have to make the break from sport. I thought I would go back at some time but the previously mention action put paid to that idea.

A chance meeting on a car park after a sixties show in the early seventies ensured that I would be fortunate enough to share a friendship and a career with a quite remarkable man Tommy Bruce.

Our time on the road together would span more than half my adult life to date, resulting in an affection and friendship for each other that is seldom seen and that I have only been fortunate enough to share with only one other man, Peter Leonard. Although in that friendship I have relied more on Peter than he on me.

Tommy outside the house with the car Barry Mason saw him cleaning... and the rest is history!

The time that Tommy and I spent together has been well documented in Tommy's biography, *Have Gravel Will Travel*. However it is fair to say that it was because of him that I have come to know most the people who make up the next chapters of this book. With that in mind this chapter is made up of a brief account of the early years in the life of the truly legendary man with the gravel voice, my mate indeed my brother in all but name Tommy Bruce. He was the most special of men who always showed warmth and consideration for others throughout his life.

Tommy was born within the sound of Bow Bells; he grew up and went to school in and around Camden Town until he was tragically orphaned in the early years of the war. Tommy and his sisters went on to grow up in a Middlesex Orphanage. Tommy left the orphanage in 1952 with the usual outfit of clothing, all the children leaving the orphanage were given two of every thing, shirts, trousers underpants and socks, but only one pair of shoes, The authorities at the orphanage found Tommy a job in engineering and placed him in a boys hostel. His introduction to the outside world was unpleasant to say the least.

Tommy having a drink

Tommy was forced to crawl under moving machinery in order to clean it, most his wages were taken by the hostel. He soon took the decision to move on. Tommy found himself a job on the delivery vans for Smiths crisps, and thanks to an uncle, who lived in London, found accommodation there. Before long Tommy changed jobs again starting work with the same uncle in Covent Garden Market.

Tommy in the National Service

National Service called when Tommy was eighteen. He joined the Royal Ordinance Core and was given the duty of working in the stores. During his National Service Tommy led an ordinary soldier's life getting into a few scrapes, mostly for returning late to camp, due to always thinking he would have one extra pint before returning to camp. While in the army Tommy served overseas in Belgium and Germany receiving an honourable discharge at the end of his time. His commanding officer said of Tommy when completing his discharge, 'you have been a good soldier Bruce, a credit to the regiment. This doesn't cover just how good Tommy's character was because I have to say after knowing him for more than thirty five years that in his whole life Tommy Bruce was never anything less than a credit to himself and everyone who knew him.

Back in Civvy Street, Tommy settled back in to work at Covent Garden. He needed somewhere to live so he quickly found himself a place to rent. That place being the downstairs rooms in a house and settled down to having the life of normal young man.

Tommy the barra' boy

Before long Tommy met the young man who was living with his girlfriend, Tommy's landlady, in the upstairs rooms. Their meeting would irrevocably change both their lives. Because that young man was Barry Mason; Barry would one day become a famous songwriter. Tommy and Barry became friendly. Before long, Barry who was already making inroads into the music business, asked Tommy to come down to a recording studio, to see a group he was managing and also singing with make a Demo disc.

Barry Mason, Harry Fowler and Tommy Bruce

After the group, The Tony Ross Trio had done their bit, there was still some time left so Barry said 'Tommy would you like to try?' Tommy refused at first, but when pressed he said that he only knew two songs,' Why' and 'Ain't Misbehavin'. Tommy didn't know what key he sang in but Tony Ross who backed him on piano worked it out, so both songs were recorded Tommy enjoyed the experience, but thought that was end of it; when in fact it was only the beginning.

Barry took the Demo to Norrie Paramour, recording manager for Colombia EMI, hoping that he would sign the group. Norrie didn't,

Tommy Bruce classic Rock and Roll pose

think there was anything different about the group but having heard the unusual quality in Tommy's, voice and liked it and decided he would give him a recording contract. Norrie then put a rock cha cha arrangement to *'Ain't Misbehavin'*. It was released it and the rest as they say is history, that first recording sold a million and went to the top of the charts. Tommy Bruce had a Gold Disc and a career that was to last for forty six years until the end of his life.

The fact that Tommy has died has made no difference to his popularity. This is because his fans recognise that he was unique and by buying his CD's and his biography keep his memory alive. The interest that continues to surround the great man in the years following his death has meant that even now his success continues.

I will always remember his funny little phrases, like '*What's 'appin' Davy*', he must have said that at some point in every day we were together. Another classic that was used to put down the occasional heckler at his shows, 'just because you are a right Nana, don't mean you're one of the bunch,' delivered in his cockney accent this would have audiences convulsed with laughter. Another one usually delivered when he lost patience with some ones stupidity, was '*Do that again an I'll eat Ya*', there was also an expression that he paraphrased, during his contribution to Charlie Drake's hit '*My Boomerang Won't Come Back*' on that occasion using the words 'Throw that fing at me and I'll step on yer 'ead'. Always a kind and gentle man Tommy had the build of a middleweight boxer and his imposing physical presence added to his gravel voiced delivery of these phrases, would very often stop people in their tracks. At which point the warmth of his laughter would be heard and everyone joined in, a truly special and lovely man.

I must take this opportunity to correct something from the start of Tommy's biography, I gave his name as Thomas Charles Bruce, this was deliberately only partially correct. His full name was Thomas Charles Joseph Bruce. His son Thom, asked me why I had done this and I explained that his dad had asked me to do this for the following reason. It was to do with the initials, TCB, Tommy wanted it be to known that he was 'Taking Care of Business' from the day of his birth, long before Elvis coined the phrase. I take this opportunity to put the record straight out my great respect for Tommy's son.

I would just like to add something which I always believed to be true, if you are fortunate enough to take care of business for an artiste, you should always remember you work for them, not the other way round. I have seen far to many problems and difficulties leading to disappointment when this truth is forgotten. As a manager you should suggest but not demand, remember were the talent lies. Of course I was lucky I managed Tommy Bruce, I had the easiest job in show business.

Thanks to Tommy Bruce I as a fan who bought the records of many of the people who follow in this narrative, have also been fortunate to work with and become friendly with them and I believe gain the respect of this remarkable generation of people.

I hope you enjoy the insights into their lives that I am about to share with you the reader. Every single one of them is remarkable human being and it is a privilege to know them all.

L to R - Pete Langford, Dave Sampson, Tommy Bruce, Dave Lodge & Tony Harte

SECTION TWO
ENTERTAINMENT

My meeting with Tommy Bruce would ensure that not only would I be involved in a life in show business but that it would become a life of hard work and pleasure. Also that the hard work and pleasure would be shared with good companions. One of those companions, Clem Cattinni would come to say, "Dave we, the entertainers of the sixties, are a family and you are part of that family." Thus Clem Cattinni encapsulates everything I will try to say in the following pages.

Five

Clem Cattinni

Preface by Clem Cattinni

Dave Lodge has been around our business for a long time and he is well liked and respected by us all. He really became known to us as Tommy Bruce's manager. It quickly became clear to us that Dave was different he actually cares what happens to us all and of course he and Tommy were like brothers. Dave was never in the game to make money and I told him once, 'Dave we the guys from the sixties are a family and you are part of that family'. I meant it then and I still mean it now. We are all glad that Dave and his lovely wife Margaret came on the scene.

Clem Cattinni and the Dave Lodge

To refer to a man who has played on more than forty No.1 hit records as an unsung hero, is strange indeed. But such is the nature of Clem Cattinni that anyone meeting him would not immediately think that this quietly spoken, courteous, modest man is one of the most respected musicians in the world.

Like many of his contemporaries Clem started his career in the late fifties at the famous 2i's Coffee bar working in a Rock and Roll group that also touring with Max Wall. He soon moved on to join one of most popular and enduring favourites of the popular music scene, Terry Dene in his group The Dene Aces.

Other luminaries of the day to benefit from Clem's distinctive drumming style include Vince Taylor and Chas McDevitt. He was an integral part of the sound created for the Larry Parnes Rock and Roll Shows backing the exciting young stars of the day, names we all remember like, Billy Fury, Marty Wilde, Joe Brown Vince Eager and Nelson Keene, to mention but a few. He left these tours to join Johnny Kidd and the Pirates and played on the legendary No.1 hit *Shakin' All Over*.

Once Clem had joined Terry Dene and The Dene Aces, he soon became a respected musician, who would be in great demand. In 1960 Clem made the move to be a founder member of a group destined to change the sound of popular music, working in Joe Meeks studio the group recorded a tune that would top charts on both sides of the Atlantic, making them the first group to have a No.1 record in America.

None of us who heard and bought Telstar will ever forget the thrill and excitement of the new sound. Staying with the Tornados until 1965 Clem achieved more recording success keeping the new sound going with tunes that captured our imagination, *Globetrotter, Ice Cream Man* and *Robot* being just a few of these.

Needles to say we will never forget Clem's contribution to Johnny Kidd an the Pirates, great hit *Shakin' All Over*. The Pirates were a great band with Clem on Drums, Brian Gregg on bass and of course Alan Caddy on Lead Guitar.

Always willing to diversify but never compromise on quality of performance Clem joined the Ivy League on leaving the Tornados playing on their numerous hits including *Tossin' and Turning*.

At the end of this period Clem made a decision that some

Clem on drums with the original Tornados

of the finest vocalists in the world have reason to be thankful for, he went in to session work playing on No.1 Hit recordings to many to list but here are a few – *Devil Woman* (Cliff Richard) *Last Waltz* (Englebert Humperdink) *Green Green Grass* (Tom Jones) *Everlasting Love* (The Love Affair) *Something's Gotten Hold of My Heart* (Gene Pitney) *Bonnie & Clyde* (Georgie Fame).

Other artists Clem has recorded with include, The Kinks, Paul McCartney, The Bee Gees, Lulu, Lou Reed, Dusty Springfield, Bay City Rollers, Sandy Shaw, Tony Christie, Classic Rock, (LSO), Clodagh Rodgers, Marvin Welch & Farrar, Paul Jones, Ike and Tina Turner, The Bachelors and delightfully for the kids, The Wombles. It is all but forgotten now that Clem even played on John Leyton's recording of *Wild Wind*, this musical relationship being rekindled when John made his return to musical performance after many years in America.

Twelve years of Clem's career were spent in the Top of the Pops orchestra, backing the likes of Stevie Wonder, Michael Jackson, Gladys Knight and Abba.

Touring also formed a large part of Clem's working life, artistes he has toured with include Cliff Richard, Roy Orbison, Englebert Humperdinck, Sandy Shaw, Dusty Springfield, The Kids from Fame, Neil Sedaka, The Drifters, Lulu, Grace Kennedy and Sonny and Cher.

Clem has appeared in many TV shows and series as part of the orchestra, providing music for Benny Hill, Lulu, Michael Barrymore, Tommy Cooper, Freddie Starr, Grace Kennedy, Keith Harris and Orville and Crackerjack the list goes on and this period of Clem's life is worth a book never mind a chapter in its own right...

Clem Cattinni has been much in demand to play on film soundtracks his credits include, *Just for Fun, The Krays, The Golden Disc, Swinging UK and Superman.*

In October 2000 Clem received the long overdue award of a Gold badge from BASCA for his services to the music industry. In my opinion he should get another award for his service to the performers he backs and the audiences he continues to give pleasure to.

Clem Cattinni epitomises everything, which is good in the entertainment industry, he is happiest at home with his wife Maria and his family or watching the Arsenal, 'the best football team in the world', As a Manchester United fan I know this because Clem told me. Clem has the love and respect of all the people I have met in the business and even more that I have not. Clem has a passion for the game of football and the Arsenal in particular, the club welcome him and the contribution he makes with his support of the youth team.

Not to long ago Clem Cattinni was part of a band that included Ray Fenwick, the legendary James Burton and Dave Sampson they performed a tribute to Ricky Nelson at the Floral Pavilion New Brighton on the Wirral. As always Clem held the beat as only he can keeping things tight for the rest of the band. I doubt that anyone but Clem was thought of for this gig as very few drummers could have brought what was required to the stage.

There are many talented drummers, but only one Clem Cattinni, a gentleman in the truest sense of the word, a good family man who is loved by all who come in contact with him.. Clem Cattinni is an unsung hero not just for his musical achievements but for the way he conducts himself he is a fine example to anyone starting in the business, my life has certainly been enriched by knowing him and I look forward to seeing and hearing him play for a long time to come.

Clem Cattinni, Dave Chrevon & Dave Sampson

From a personal point of view I feel that it is amazing that Clem grew to be what I would call a perfect English gentlemen. The fact is that Clem had a difficult time during the war because of what the government of the day termed the management of aliens. This meant that Clem's father being Italian would be viewed with suspicion, for no good reason, The policy then was for people to be put in interment camps which meant perfectly good citizens like Clem's father would be separated from their family for the duration of the war. This was especially hard for Clem's mother, who although being British born herself had to report her movements to the police, not even allowed to see Clem and other members of her family without reporting where she was going and again when she got back. In some ways it was harder for her than for Clem's father because having filled paper work to say he was friendly to the country he was able to ply his trade as a chef, for the county's benefit of course, he had freedom of movement in the environment in which he lived. Sadly these restrictions of family life meant that Clem did not get to now his father until he was 14 years old. In spite of this desperately unfair treatment of his family Clem Cattinni grew to be a man of great courage and character, a man who will never let you down and Margaret and I are very proud to call him our friend.

Recently Clem had a hip operation, which prevents him from playing the drums, as he put it. "The way I want to play". We are sorry to hear that because Clem has a very special talent which the public still want to share in. Thankfully we all have the fabulous recording he had made over the last sixty years to enjoy.

Six
Jess Conrad OBE

Preface by Jess Conrad

I first got to know the author of this book, Dave Lodge more than thirty years ago when my great mate Tommy Bruce brought him along to a gig. When Tommy said that Dave was going to be his new manager, I have to say that I did not think much of the idea, saying to Tommy, 'look Tom, Dave is just a funny little man from Manchester he won't do you any good'. Dave proved me wrong many years ago by being a loyal friend and astute manager to Tommy and always doing his best to look out for the rest of us as well. He has never hesitated to help any of the sixties guys, as was proved one year when I was in pantomime in Leeds with no chance of getting home to my wife Renee for Christmas. Dave and his wife Margaret came to see the Christmas Eve show and then took me home in his car, a round trip of four hundred miles for him. If I hadn't known before why Tommy thought so much of Dave I certainly did then.

So when I was asked recently to describe what I think of Dave Lodge I was delighted to have the opportunity. Having though about it for a moment I then replied, Dave is a thoroughly decent person, the type of guy who will always go the extra mile for you. On top of that he is as honest as the day is long. I am very proud to have him as my friend.

Jess Conrad & the Author

Sixties Icon Jess Conrad.

When I hear people say, "I don't like Jess Conrad" I always smile and reply, "Oh, so you don't know him then?" Because, for me it would be quite impossible not to like the man behind the myth. Jess on the other hand when reading this is probably saying, "Everybody loves Jess I'm the sixties icon, what are you talking about?"

With the possible exception of Screamin' Lord Sutch Jess is in my opinion the most successful image-maker of his time. He is frequently heard to say, "I'm a poseur not a singer" but he is so much more than that. Jess Conrad is one of this country's most talented entertainers, he vastly under rated because of his successful portrayal of a vain arrogant man note another of his quotes, "I don't do humble love".

Jess is also quite simply the sixties icon, because he portrays everything that I like about that period in time and has been able to sustain it. But if you take the trouble to look below the surface and you will find something very different

Jess Conrad was born in Brixton and christened Gerald James, but his name was soon changed by his schoolmates to Jesse after the notorious American outlaw Jesse James. I am sure his school friends did not realise just how remarkable Gerald James was and just how famous he would go on to become.

It has to be said that Jess Conrad just seemed destined for the show business world. As he grew up Jess matured into a tall and exceptionally good looking young man, Jess had then and still has now great strength of character this being the case he was determined to succeed in his chosen field.

At this point I should tell you I don't think he is exceptionally good looking; I know he is because he told me. In order to fulfil his ambitions Jess Conrad would spend no small amount of his money and time in the stalls at the London Palladium learning timing and stagecraft by watching the big American stars of the day like Jo Stafford and Danny Kaye.

Before long he had enrolled at a Drama School in East London determined to make his way in entertainment. Money was not easily come by so he paid his way working on his fathers flower stall in Marble Arch. Jess showed great promise in his drama class, so he decided to apply for and got his Film Artistes Association Union Card. The next step along his career path was for Jess was to join Central Casting. This he did and that enabled him to set about learning everything he could about studio technique.

Jess Conrad appeared in many films during the fifties and sixties, receiving considerable acclaim for the parts he played. These film appearances included an outstanding performance in The Boys appearing alongside Dudley Sutton and Richard Todd.

Jess also continued to practice his art to great effect touring with The Charles Danville Company. It was during his time with Charles Danville that he came to the attention of television producer Daphne Shadwell who saw him in an advertisement for The Daily Sketch Newspaper. Incidentally she would later have a helping hand in the careers of Tommy Bruce, Vince Hill and Kathy Kirby when she produced Stars and Garters.

Even Daphne Shadwell could not have realised the impact she would have on Jess's career when she cast him as Barney Day in the television play Rock-a-Bye Barney. The legendary Jack Good saw the play and thought "the boy looks like a pop star" and cast him for the brand new TV music show Oh Boy! The success of his appearances on this show led to Jess becoming a Decca recording star. The release of songs such as *Cherry Pie, Mystery Girl* and *This Pullover* added to the image of Jess Conrad as a Teen Idol.

After being voted England's 'Most Popular Male Singer' in the 1961 NME annual poll Jess Conrad played the London Palladium the very theatre were he had first nurtured his show business dream. Jess Conrad's popularity with audiences continued and he found himself working and touring with the British and American stars of the day, these stars included Gene Vincent, Eddie

First Christmas card from Jess and Renee

Cochran, Billy Fury, Tommy Bruce, Marty Wilde and Joe Brown to name just a few.

While he was continuing to make records for various labels, President, Colombia, Pye and the previously mentioned Decca the seventies would see a change in the type of work Jess Conrad was doing. More acting roles some of them in TV soaps such as Crossroads would come his way. Added to this Jess was making many appearances on celebrity quiz shows. This made Jess Conrad one of the best known entertainers in the country.

Always a hard worker Jess Conrad did not rest on his laurels he improved his status with the general public and agents alike by creating his own unique cabaret show, with this show Jess went on to tour not just the United Kingdom but the rest of Europe and South Africa.

However for Jess Conrad one of the really big breakthroughs in his career came with his cross over from the world of pop to that of stage musicals. Initially playing the Role of Jesus Christ in 'Godspell'. This was a role that Jess Conrad always says that with his initials was made for him. It is` fair to say that his performances' in the role brought him rave reviews.

Once again always eager to surprise and indeed confound the critics Jess Conrad went on to create the role of Joseph in 'Joseph And his Amazing Technicolor Dream Coat'. Jess was regularly appearing in the West End and these appearances led to him breaking box office records during the 1982 summer season. Having seen and heard his performances I have no doubt that the role of Joseph has never been played better than it was by Jess Conrad, in spite of the impressive list of names that

Jess Conrad with his magnificent looking dog who through his apprearances in a good many TV adverts was on the television more than Jess at one point.

have played the role of Joseph in the shows many subsequent successful incarnations.

Jess Conrad continues to perform in the UK and Europe in sixties revival shows and in cabaret making cameo appearances on TV. Recently, he completed a role in *The Last of the Summer Wine* in this he played the puzzled tourist looking over the wall at the geriatric Stars of the show getting up to some very strange antics. This showed the public once again that Jess Conrad is versatile enough to get away from his sixties icon persona and perform to the highest standards.

Jess Conrad has regularly toured with Jim Davidson in the adult pantomime 'Sinderella' and is an accomplished after dinner speaker. Add to this Jess's regular appearances on the golf course for charity events and other fund raising activities it is of course no surprise that he remains one of the hardest working men in show business.

On a personal note Jess Conrad has been married to his beautiful wife Renee, the original Miss Camay in the soap advert, for nearly fifty-eight years at the time of writing. They have two lovely daughters Sasha and Natalie. Jess Conrad is an outspoken and forthright man and he certainly doesn't suffer fools gladly this being the case I was doubly pleased when attending the Variety Club Dinner in Liverpool not so long ago, Jess spoke to me and said that he felt I was never offended by anything he said to me because I am his mate and therefore I realise when he is in character and when he is not. Having known him for nearly thirty years, I have to say being his mate is a privilege and I value the privilege of his friendship very highly.

Whilst I was writing this book Jess Conrad told me that he had been cast in the role of Larry Parnes for the film Telstar about the life of Joe Meek. That is an achievement and recognition of his talent. Jess Conrad's contribution to that remarkable time, the sixties really is iconic so it is no surprise that the producer and casting director made a point of casting the celebrated stage and television actor Nigel Harmon in the role of Jess Conrad in this film.

A fine accolade to Jess a man who says he is just a poseur not a singer, we know he is much more. A whole new generation of fans will see just how special Jess Conrad really was and indeed still is.

So there he is, my mate Jess Conrad, undeniably the golden boy of the sixties, while he remains brash and seemingly arrogant, Jess is simply larger than life, indeed he is everything a star should be. This was confirmed more than ever when he was presented in 2011 with an OBE for services to charity by Princess Anne.

Jess Conrad gets the joke better than anyone, when he ends his show with the song *It's Only Make Believe* Jess is telling us that he knows, laughing with us and showing his outrageous talent. Those of us who are very lucky have been privileged to see and get to know the wonderful man behind the star. Jess has deservedly gone on to be King Rat, showing that his peers recognise him for the fine entertainer and ambassador for the business that he really is.

SEVEN

VINCE HILL

Born in Holbrooks, a district of Coventry, on the 16th of April 1937 Vince Hill has always been one of the most popular performers in British show business. He first sang professionally in a pub at the early age of fifteen. This has continued the case right through from the time when he sang with vocal quartet The Raindrops till the present day. From Vince's earliest performances he has been loved, not only by the British public, but also by audiences worldwide.

Vince Hill

Starting his career in the fifties Vince Hill worked semi-professionally singing in the working men's clubs around and about his hometown of Coventry. Vince's career was interrupted when he was called up to do his National Service. However after he had done his basic training he was soon singing again with a dance band – the members being serving soldiers with The Royal Signal Corp.

After Vince Hill was de-mobbed he broadened his already considerable entertainment skills by working in musical comedy. During this period he also appeared in the Musical 'Floradora'. Living in London at this time Vince was also the resident vocalist with *The Teddy Foster Big Band*. Deciding to move on with his career Vince then went on to become part of *The Four Others*, The Four Others were a very successful stage and cabaret act and he really excelled in his time with them. I believe following his time with The Four Others Vince went on to be part of the formation of a new vocal group, which would be called 'The Raindrops'. Other members of this group who went on to have great success in the music business were Jackie Lee, famous for her recording of *White Horses* theme for the television show of the same name and 'Rupert' and Johnny Worth who wrote successful songs for Adam Faith and Eden Kane while using the name Les Van Dyke.

Vince Hill spent more than three years with The Raindrops before he decided to make the break from them and in the mid-sixties he embarked on a solo career. This proved to be the defining moment in his career. People in high places heard him sing and before long he was working on radio and television. It did not take many appearances before Vince Hill became a great favourite with the television and radio audiences of the day. So great was Vince Hill's popularity with those audiences that he went on to make more than three hundred appearances during a four year period, singing on such programs as the BBC's Parade of the Pops and ITV's popular weekly show Stars and Garters. In Stars and Garters he performed weekly alongside alongside other popular artistes of the day. The most notable of these included vocalists Kathy Kirby, Tommy Bruce, Clinton Ford and Comedian Ray Martine.

In 1962 Vince Hill released his first record *The River's Run Dry*. Inexplicably this song did not sell well enough to make the Top Twenty. Having looked at this problem which affected many of Vince's contemporaries, to a lesser, or in some cases greater, degree including Ricky Valance, Tommy Bruce and Dave Sampson I have to say that all of the sixties artistes would have benefited from better promotion of their records. Having said that in those days sales of more than one hundred thousand would not ensure that an artiste would get into the top twenty. How different from today when less than half that number of sales can see an artiste at the top of the charts.

In 1963 Vince Hill participated in '*A Song For Europe*', the heats of '*The Eurovision Song Contest*' Vince sang a song called *A day at the Seaside* and although it did not take him to the top in the competition it did become popular with his fans. In spite of his universal popularity Vince Hill would have to wait until 1966 for chart success with *Take Me To Your Heart Again* quickly followed by two other successful recordings *Heartaches* and *Merci Cheri*. However in 1967 Vince recorded the song that would take his popularity to a new and what has proved to be a lasting level, it was called *Edelweiss* – it reached number two and spent seventeen weeks in the charts.

The cruise ships have benefited from Vince Hill's talent over the years. Vince has worked on them since the late sixties and I have spoken to many people whose choice of cruise was made on the basis that Vince Hill would be performing for them. Performing in the USA on many occasions helped Vince widen his audience as he continues to enjoy great popularity there and I hear that a tour over there may be a strong possibility in the near future. Vince Hill has always appeared at prestigious venues, indeed many of his performances have seen him backed by *The Florida Symphony Orchestra;* It is true say that whenever and wherever he appears Vince Hill is as much admired for his warm and charismatic personality as he is for his wonderful voice. There is no doubt that Vince Hill is a consummate artiste, he is the complete professional and is always well worth the admission fee.

Vince Hill has been married to his lovely wife Annie for fifty years and he couldn't have chosen a better companion to share his life; Annie has been his constant companion and supported him in every way that a wife possibly could. Annie has stayed by his side on all the cruises and tours that Vince has undertaken in his career, helping to make his work a pleasure which in turn makes sure that they both get the most out of life.

In conclusion to my reminisces about this great and charming man's career, I will just say that I am sure that Vince Hill's many fans join me in wishing both Anne and Vince continued health and happiness, along with the fervent wish that 'the singer who was born to sing' continues to entertain us and bring us even more pleasure through his music and his friendship for many more years to come.

Eight
Vince Eager

Vince Eager is remembered by all of the people who avidly watched television music programs like *Drumbeat* and *Six Five Special* in the late fifties and early sixties. Because even back then Vince Eager's vocal range and power not to mention his stage presence marked him out to be one of the success stories of the late fifties and early sixties. But his life as an entertainer began even earlier.

Vince Eager with Dave Lodge

Vince Eager was christened Roy Taylor and his vocal talent would first come to light while he was singing in his local church choir. The choir mistress at St Johns Parish Church Grantham Lincolnshire soon realised that here was a boy who was something special and was worthy of her personal attention. Under her guidance Roy Taylor became a leading boy soprano. He went on to achieve national recognition, the highlight of his youthful singing career was being chosen to perform at Westminster Abbey. However as they say all good things must come to an end and inevitably Roy Taylor's voice broke. Now for many young lads this brings about the end of their vocal career but unusually in Roy's case it would just be the beginning of an international career.

Very keen to forge a career in the music business Roy and two friends formed a harmonica trio. They called themselves *The Harmonica Vagabonds*, incidentally although one of these friends Roy Clarke, subsequently left show business to pursue a successful career in engineering, the other, Brian Locking went on to achieve fame as Brian 'Liquorice' Locking who all now know as the bass player with *The*

Shadows, another example of the phrase from small beginnings come great things.

However going back to Roy – in his eagerness to become a more rounded entertainer he found that just playing the harmonica in itself would not be enough to fulfil his musical ambitions. That being the case the name *The Harmonica Vagabonds* would be short lived in the annals of show business because soon as Roy's voice had settled into its lower register, the boys decided to augment the act with skiffle songs.

Roy and the other lads were all greatly influenced by the one of the big names of the day, one time king of skiffle Lonnie Donnegan. Lonnie Donnegan is sadly no longer with us but he is still regarded as one of the great British entertainers and songwriters.

After they had changed the groups name to the *Vagabonds Skiffle Group* the lads achieved great success in talent competitions. When they came runner up in the televised World Skiffle Championship Roy, Brian and Roy Clarke were catapulted to national and international prominence causing them great excitement and raising their hopes for the future.

The success the three lads had achieved in the competition led to the Vagabonds Skiffle Group being booked for a six-month residency as the house band at the now legendary 2i's Coffee Bar in London. While they were appearing at the 2i's they came to the attention of famous pop guru Larry Parnes. Larry Parnes was so impressed by their act that he booked them to appear in a Sunday night concert at The Gaumont in Coventry. This show was headlined by Marty Wilde and such was the success of The Vagabonds Skiffle Group's performance that only a matter of hours after the end of the show

Big Jim Sullivan, the Author and Liqourice Locking

Roy Taylor had became Vince Eager the latest member of Larry Parnes's stable of Pop singers.

A recording contract with Decca was soon forthcoming for Vince Eager and the release of his subsequent records introduced Vince to a legion of fans who still support him today.

In fact the number of new fans continues to grow each time a new generation hear and see Vince Eager perform. Vince Eager performed on all the music shows of the day and before long he was given a six month contract at the prestigious Churchill's Night Club in New Bond Street, London. All these things added together would ensure that the tall good looking and extremely likeable young man from Grantham would become a household name.

Charismatic, dynamic, powerful and talented are just a few of the words used to describe Vince Eager at that time and they are as true a description now as they have ever been. Over the years Vince Eager has shown himself to be the complete all round entertainer, always improving every aspect of his performance since those early days when he started playing the harmonica.

An example of this was shown in 1980 when he played the role of the mature Elvis Presley in the West End production of Elvis the Musical, Vince then toured the world reprising that role for six years always receiving rave reviews. With his powerful and emotive interpretation of a variety of wonderful songs he has made himself a truly international entertainer, who is welcome in cities across the globe from Sydney to Toronto, and all points in-between.

Vince Eager based himself in Florida for eleven years, during this time he also entertained on cruise ships, earning his living in

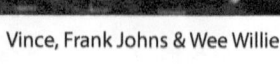
Vince, Frank Johns & Wee Willie

this way kept Vince away from his British fans for far to long. When Vince Eager finally returned to this country and started performing here on a regular basis the fans welcomed him home with open arms. This welcome ensured that he now plays to the packed houses that he deserves. A few years ago I had the privilege of being in the wings on three consecutive nights as Vince Eager and Tommy Bruce performed Rock and Roll as it should be performed.

Vince with Rockola

As I listened to the rapturous applause from the packed auditorium I felt that I recognised what Larry Parnes knew all those years ago when he set Vince Eager on his way. Vince Eager is naturally talented man whose rapport with his audience makes everyone in it feel that he is putting on a special performance just for them. It may appear that all aspects of his performance are natural and to some extent of course it is but I have to tell you that he really works hard in his preparation for the show and he continues to work hard when he gets on stage.

If you want to be guaranteed an enjoyable evening's entertainment I strongly recommend that you go and see Vince Eager, you will not be disappointed because Vince Eager is everything you would expect a top line entertainer to be, he is totally professional, he has a warm and welcoming personality and to top it all off Vince is the complete master of his craft. Vince Eager has proved that he is also a reliable friend who has shown over the years that he remembers the people who treat him well.

Once again I have to say Vince Eager is a man who I am proud to count as my friend.

Nine

Danny Williams

Preface by Danny Williams
When Dave told me that he was writing the first draft of his book 'The Long Road' and that I had a chapter in it I was both surprised and pleased. Dave Lodge and his wife Margaret are two of the most loyal friends I could wish for. They never let you down I have spent many happy hours in their company and hope to spend many more. There are a couple things you can be sure of this book, Dave won't exaggerate or try to make cheap points from his friends and that is what we are Dave and Margaret's friends, I look forward to reading the book.

Danny Williams International Recording Star.

Danny Williams

Authors note: Sadly Danny died before publication but I hope his son, the actor Anthony Barclay, enjoys reading what we thought of his dad.

One of the first things we all noticed about Danny Williams, apart from his wonderful voice was the courtesy he showed to others. He always conducted himself with great charm and humility he was a true gentleman whose demeanour never gave a clue to his great talent.

Danny Williams was born in Port Elizabeth and sang as a boy soprano in his local church choir, to such effect that he may well have gone on to great things in this field of music. If it had it not been for the fact that at the age of thirteen he entered and won an open talent contest we may well have been talking about Danny Williams as a classically singer. Winning the talent contest gave Danny the opportunity to work on the international tour, featuring the renowned vocal group The Golden

City Dixie's. This tour was instrumental in opening up a potentially very exciting future to the shy and vocally gifted Danny.

The tour brought Danny to London where he was noticed by among others record producer Norman Newell, who quickly realised that Danny Williams, was some thing special and had no hesitation in signing him up to the HMV label. Chart hits such as *We will never be as young as this Again* and *The Miracle of You* made Danny successful in the UK but international success with the 1961 recording of *Moon River,* theme song from the film *Breakfast at Tiffany's*, made Danny the house hold name he remained until his sad death.

Other hits recorded by Danny are *Jeannie, Wonderful world of the Young, Tears* and *My own true Love*. Very few people of our generation that I have met on my travels do not possess at least one recording by Danny Williams in their record collection.

Danny's recording of *More* was a huge success in the American charts, to the extent that this recording is now regarded among the great standards. Other hits on the American continent have been *White on White* and *A little toy Balloon*.

Danny always toured extensively, in the early days of his career he worked with the Beatles, Helen Shapiro, Matt Monroe, The Four Freshmen, The Shadows and Eartha Kitt. He appeared on all the popular radio and TV shows of the day. Probably the major television show of the day was the legendary Sunday Night at the London Palladium and of course Danny made appearances on that.

Prominent musical arrangers of the day such as the late great Nelson Riddle were delighted to work with Danny. The benefits of working with people like Nelson Riddle was something that Danny regarded as a privilege throughout his life. The album produced by this association was entitled 'Danny Williams' and was an immense success, the result being that Danny went on to have his own BBC TV show.

During the Seventies and Eighties Danny was touring almost worldwide, recording with all the top arrangers including, Geoff Love, Roger Webb and Nick Ingman. Chart success came Danny's way again; with a song inspired by the Martini TV commercial *Dancing Easy* making the top twenty. Danny recorded an album with musical arrangements by Roger Webb; *The Gentle Touch* showing once again that Danny Williams was a master of his craft and had become an artiste of distinction. In fact it seemed as the decades past that the record buying public had taken Danny to their hearts although success in the singles charts was not happening Danny's albums continued to sell well. Although for a brief period in the eighties Danny wasn't performing for while choosing to stay at home to nurse his sick wife to the end of her life.

After her death a mutual friend of ours Graham Bodman became Danny's manager and set about raising Danny's profile again. It was in the mid eighties that Danny and I became friends. This came about because at the time Danny often worked on shows with Tommy Bruce, with me as the compère and we always had a great time. I well remember one show in particular at the Aylesbury Civic Centre where I was treated to my first real taste on stage, of Danny wonderful sense of humour. It was an excellent show put together by our previously mentioned friend and at that time soon to be business partner Graham Bodman. The line up included Danny, Ricky Valance and Tommy Bruce, the excellent Paul Roberts Band, Flying High, backed everyone and I was the compère.

Danny finished his show and the audience were as usual shouting for more and I was encouraging him to come back on stage. I kept looking stage left, but Danny had sneaked back from stage right and had sneaked up behind me. The audience was laughing loudly by this time as I was starting to panic, as he had not sung *Moon River*. Eventually Danny tapped me on the shoulder and I turned to find him grinning broadly. Great times and great laughs and I really wish Danny was still here so we could share more good times.

In the early nineties under the auspices of his manager Graham Bodman and with my input Danny began touring his Nat King Cole Tribute Show. This was to some degree completing a circle that began in Danny's childhood back in South Africa. Nat King Cole was the man who inspired

Danny to start singing, as he used to sing along while listening to Nat's great recordings;

Danny had always listened to them on his grandmother's wind-up gramophone and said that Nat's voice was at that time the best he had ever heard. Strangely enough, Nat King Cole would later be heard to say in his own expression of respect for Danny Williams, when he was asked to record *Moon River*, I couldn't do a better job than Danny Williams. It just goes to show that while Nat and Danny never met, great artistes always recognise quality in other performers.

We presented the show for the first time at Birmingham Town Hall and Ed Stewart was the narrator. It was a great success and we embarked on a national tour. However due to problems unfortunately of his own making Graham upset Ed Stewart and we needed to find a new narrator. We were fortunate to secure the services of Elliott Brooks who apart from doing an excellent job as narrator became a friend to Danny and myself.

The tour had its ups and downs logistically because the first signs of cracks in Graham's financial empire were starting to show. To the extent that I actually became a lighting technician for the show at Middleton Civic Centre. However in spite of everything Danny continued to give outstanding performances everywhere he appeared.

Our friendship grew and Danny would often stay with Margaret and I when he appeared in the North of England. That said I know that Danny would not mind me telling you that he had two unfortunate weaknesses in his talented make up. One was a weak bladder and the other was absolutely no sense of direction. This combination resulted in Danny often finding himself miles from anywhere and bursting for a pee. These weaknesses manifested themselves on many occasions but one we both thought quite humorous springs to my mind at this time. I had booked Danny for a gig in Manchester and he said he would drive up from London in his pride and joy a big red sports car. Knowing how difficult it would be for him to actually complete this journey successfully.

I devised what I thought was a foolproof plan. I should have known that with Danny and his complete lack of a sense of direction there was no such thing as foolproof. Part of the plan included Danny coming off the M1 at junction 35a. We were to meet a mile from there on a straight road, at a roadside café at approximately 3.30pm. This I assured myself was definitely a foolproof plan absolutely nothing could go wrong.

How wrong I could be! 3.30, 4 o'clock and 4.30 all came and went with no sign of Danny, I tried his mobile but it was turned off. By 5 o'clock I was really worried as Danny was due on stage at 7.30pm in the centre of Manchester. At 5.15 a red blur hurtled down the road towards me coming to a halt with a squeal of tyres and a cloud of dust.

As the dust cleared a very flustered Danny leapt out of the car and broke into a run, as he sprinted past me he shouted, "I can't stop because I'm bursting for a pee". When he emerged from the facilities I asked him where he had been. "Oh" he replied smiling, "I got confused and came off at junction 25a and then I got lost when I couldn't find you".

"Well" I thought "We are together now, nothing more can go wrong, Danny just has to follow me". I was wrong again, all went well until we got to Glossop when I went straight on ... and Danny turned LEFT. As I drove on I looked in my rear view mirror and saw him do this, I swore and pulled over naturally expecting him to turn round and come back. After a few minutes I realised this wasn't going to happen. As we were both hands free I decided to call him on his mobile, this time it was turned on and he answered. "Where are you" I asked? "I don't know" he replied "OK no problem" I said, "Just turn round and come back to the junction where you turned left and I will be waiting for you". "I can't do that he said", "Why?" I asked, "Because I have made two left turns and three right since then" Danny replied. I sat in stunned silence while I gathered my thoughts, then I said "OK keep driving and when you see a sign for a town tell me what it is and I will meet you there".

There was silence for a while and then Danny said, "I've seen a sign – Hyde two miles", "Right" I replied, "You go to Hyde and find a big store and park on the car park, I will meet you there". I hung up and made my way to Hyde. I found an Asda store and parked on the car park, I couldn't see Danny so I phoned him saying, "I am in Hyde on Asda car park ... where are you?" "I'm in Hyde on the B&Q car park" replied Danny, "Right" I said, "Just wait there for me." I found B&Q without any difficulty, drove in and parked next to Danny's car. I got out of my car took my suit bag out of it, locked it and got in next to Danny, saying 'that is the last time I let you out of my sight. We were giggling like a couple of schoolboys as we drove along, it was just impossible to be annoyed with Danny, his persona was so endearing

After all the excitement we arrived at the gig ten minutes before the show was due to start. I felt ten years older, but the relaxed Danny once again excelled giving a relaxed and professional performance. Happy days.

Incidentally, speaking of Danny's red flying machine of a car it came to an unfortunate end. One morning Danny had arrived back from a gig in the early hours and parked in the street outside his house. He went inside feeling tired and emotionally drained sat in quiet reflection with a drink. Looking through the window he saw the car and thought he'd better put it in the garage. He went out, got in the car, and in the space of couple of minutes somehow managed to hit two or three of the neighbours cars before planting it firmly in the wall of his garage ... leaving it a total write-off.

He went back in the house and phoned me at about 4am to ask me if I understood the vagaries of automatic transmission, as he needed an explanation for the catastrophe. This incident resulted in another friend, Maggie Stredder's, husband Jim, kindly driving Danny to and from gigs for a while.

As we approached the end of the nineties Graham Bodman my friend, and by this time business partner, sadly died having by this time lost his own money and mine following a series of financial reversals, a story which is all to common in show business.

This left Danny needing to look for new management. Which he found with another great friend of mine, Johnny Mans. Johnny was able to tour Danny as part of the Johnny Mans production 'Back to Bacharach' with Bobby Crush, Linda Nolan and Susan Maughan. Danny showing once again the wonderful versatility and vocal skill for which he became famous. At the same time Johnny continued to tour Danny in 'The Nat King Cole Story'. He also kept the services of our other friend Elliott Brooks as narrator for the show.

As I continue to record my knowledge of Danny's life it seems incredible that he made his way during his childhood by collecting empty pop bottles between performances at the local theatre in Port Elizabeth using the money he got on the returns to help support his family. The theatre manager heard Danny singing to himself while collecting the bottles and could not believe how good he was.

Having heard Danny singing to himself the theatre manager encouraged Danny to enter the next talent contest that was put on at the theatre and as previously told Danny won.

So this theatre manager, sadly Danny did not tell me the man's name, was the man who gave us all the chance to enjoy Danny Williams's wonderful voice. It has to be said that Danny's success came from his wonderful voice and personality, if he had never made a penny these things would have shone through.

Of course I can't continue without telling as Danny told me the little known story of his entry into this country on false papers. He was in no way embarrassed by this as he only found out what had happened later. When the Golden City Dixie's got the opportunity to tour the United Kingdom

Danny was only fourteen years old, too young to come on the tour. The management of the tour realised that without Danny's voice the group would not have the same impact so he `was issued with false papers stating he was sixteen.

Danny always made the joke that this made him an illegal immigrant. Of course this situation couldn't last and after a few months the deception was discovered and Danny was sent back to South Africa.

Luckily for Danny and us he was not sent back before he had made his mark on British television, notably on 'Drumbeat' where compère and song writer Trevor Peacock had made the comment that defined Danny Williams's performances for the rest of his career, Trevor said 'Danny Williams didn't just sing a song, he seemed to get inside it and move around. Certainly Danny had an incredible vocal range, I just wish I had the foresight to describe him that way.. Trevor would later become famous for his portrayal of *'No No No Yes'*, Jim Trott in the Vicar of Dibley.

Because of Danny's remarkable talent and popularity Norman Newell was instrumental in bringing him back to this country legally and the rest as they say is history. This led to something of an anomaly in connection with his great recording *'Moon River'*, publicity at the time would have us believe that Danny was eighteen when he had this hit, Danny himself assured me he was only sixteen at the time, whatever his age it was a truly remarkable recording which has stood the test of time.

Danny Williams's talent was not limited to his singing; he was a skilful martial arts exponent and a fine tennis player. Indeed his love of the game of tennis was shown when I arranged an interview for him with the famous GMR broadcaster Fred Fielder, Danny agreed to do the interview but only in the last hour of the show because that would give him time to play three sets of tennis.

Fred kindly re-jigged his show to accommodate Danny and the interview was done with Danny in tennis kit with a towel round his neck. Danny Williams was a man who lived his life to the full that I was lucky enough to share that life brings me great joy.

Danny honoured me with his friendship and before his death asked if I would write the sleeve note for his next album, which was to be released by EMI. I had already agreed to do this and I was very proud and moved when after Danny's death his son Tony repeated the request. I am doubly honoured and privileged that Danny's son thought, indeed thinks of me in the same way his father did, as a true friend.

Although he would actually die before Tommy, Danny proved his friendship to Tommy and I. This came about because Tommy was seriously ill and I phoned Danny to ask him to appear in a benefit show for Tommy, Danny said yes straight away. Little did we know that Danny would die himself before the show. However thanks to Danny's son Tony giving me permission to show a DVD of his dad's performance of 'Moon River' with Henry Mancini and Johnny Dankworth accompanying him, Amazingly Danny Williams was given a standing ovation that night and I'm not ashamed to say that not for the only time that night, I was moved to tears. The other occasions were due to the support Tommy's fellow performers gave me in my efforts to do the right thing for Tommy.

Danny Williams was a great performer but more importantly he was a wonderful human being and I am proud to have spent time in his company and got to know him.

In spite of his poor sense of direction I do not think Danny Williams would get lost on his way to heaven. God will have known about Danny's terrible sense of direction and so will have sent an angel to guide him straight to Heaven's Gate where Danny will have been made most welcome.

Danny Williams was one of life's gentlemen, like the rest of us he was not perfect. Indeed at times he could be infuriating and the cause of great frustration but Danny made the world a better place with his presence and the fact that he was my friend makes for many happy memories.

Sadly as I have said Danny passed away in 2005 and Margaret and I personally lost a very good friend. However I am pleased to say that the friendship Margaret and shared with Danny continues through our friendship with his son, the actor Anthony Barclay, who has inherited his father's wonderful voice and may well have a successful musical career underway himself by the time this book is published.

Anthony Barclay

Ten

Billie Davis

Preface by Billie Davis.

What can I say about David Lodge? Well, I recall my first meeting with David, I was doing a theatre show and the compère had not turned up. I was in my dressing room getting ready when I heard a knock on the door, I opened it to find a well dressed and very fit looking young man, looking at me with a smile on his face, it was David, He said how pleased he was to meet me and that he could not, indeed would not let me walk out on stage without a proper introduction, so he was going to do it himself.

Billie Davie - our angel of the morning!

Well he gave me a really warm introduction ending with the words Ladies and gentlemen please welcome on stage, the very lovely talents of my angel of this of this or any other morning, the one, the only Miss Billie Davis. It was only afterwards that he told me that my recording of 'Angel of the Morning' is one of his all time favourite records. I also didn't know at this point who David Lodge was, when he appeared out of nowhere in my dressing room the way he did. It turned out that David was looking after business for Tommy Bruce and when I say looking after him I mean that he moved mountains to get what was best for Tommy's career.

We have shared many happy and also sad moments together since that first meeting. The saddest I think was having to say goodbye to Tommy when he died in 2006 because David and Tommy loved each other like brothers.

Behind David and helping him in all he does is a sweet and lovely lady, his wife Margaret. I would just like to say David and Margaret I love you very much and I look forward to spending many more fun times together with you in song and in friendship. Your 'Angel of the Morning' Billie xxxxxxxxxxxxxxxx.

Billie Davis. Hit recording artiste and world renowned entertainer

Billie Davis is one of show business's great survivors, and to quote the title of the B-side of her first hit, *'I'm Thankful'* is a sentiment shared by Billie's fans everywhere. A lot has happened since a very pretty girl called Carol Hedges became a beautiful woman with a sexy and soulful voice.

It was early in 1962 when Carol entered a talent contest at Southall Community Centre, actually had it not been for her friend Sue pushing her on stage we would not have been privileged to see and hear the many wonderful performances she has given over the years. With backing provided by Cliff Bennett's Rebel Rousers her rendition of Connie Francis's *'Many Tears Ago'* won the competition and a very impressed Cliff Bennett suggested that she go and see Joe Meek.

After ringing for an appointment, borrowing bus fare from her grandmother, with whom she lived, Carol set off from her home in Egham Surrey on a journey to Holloway Road in North London that would change her life.

Joe Meek gave her the opportunity to learn about her voice and it's capabilities, whilst testing out sounds in his now famous bathroom studio. He also gave her acetates of several songs to take home and listen to. Two of these songs *'Merry Go Round'* and *'Mister Right'* were her first recordings, incidentally backed by the Tornados, sadly they were never released and are now lost.

Billie at the time she was recording with Joe Meek

At this point Robert Stigwood came into her life; in terms of a future in show business his arrival would be most significant.

Carol told Stiggy as she called him that she was a fan of the early Sammy Davis and Billie Holiday and so as he had already noted that Carol was a bit of a tomboy Stiggy decided her stage name would be Billie Davis. Robert Stigwood gave Billie a thorough grounding in show business, arranging two classes a day with a drama teacher. He also enrolled her at a fashion school; this grooming allied to her natural charm this added confidence and poise giving her an image and stage presence that many of today's artistes would do well to emulate. Billie also appeared in some cinema ads for Pepsi that were arranged for her through Robert Stigwood's Agency.

The next stage in the building of Billie Davis's career was for her to perform live. With this in mind Robert Stigwood decided that Billie would appear on John Leyton's current tour. John Leyton was also managed by Robert Stigwood and recording for the same record producer as Billie Joe Meek.

It has to be said that Robert Stigwood was a very astute manager and he showed this when he linked Billie with Mike Sarne for live performances of Mike's novelty hit with Wendy Richard 'Come Outside'. Wendy Richard was a very busy and successful actress and she did not want to tour with Mike Sarne just to speak a few lines of one song, where as Billie could sing her own recordings on tour and just support Mike when needed. Mike's follow up recording '*Will I What*' featured Billie's voice on the record and it went on to be a hit in its own right. Next on the agenda for Billie would of course be solo recordings.

It was Robert Stigwood's intention that Billie Davis should release a version of Little Eva's hit recording 'The Locomotion' however Billie was not happy about this and refused to record it. Billie felt that Little Eva had sung the song as well as it could be sung, therefore she would not be able to put her own mark on it.

Luckily Robert Stigwood had heard the Exciters recording of '*Tell Him*' while abroad with John Leyton who was on a tour of various countries to promote his most recent film 'The Great Escape' Robert and John just knew that this song was ideally suited to Billie's voice and would defiantly be the one to bring Billie Davis to prominence in her own right,

In spite of another much-loved performer and indeed favourite of mine, Alma Cogan releasing '*Tell Him*', Robert and John were proved right. The British record buying public took Billie a truly lovely girl with a sultry and sexy voice to their hearts and in early February 1963 the record was in the top five of the British hit parade, Billie Davis had arrived.

Nationwide and world tours plus many Television appearances followed hard on the heels of Billie's chart success. Of course it is no surprise that, inevitably with such an attractive girl there would be romantic attachments. Billie Davis's always attracted the media's attention so it was inevitable, that her relationships were carried out under the glare of the media spotlight. During the early days of her relationship with Jet Harris, Bass player with The Shadows, Billie and Jet were involved in a car crash Billie sustaining a broken jaw. This might have been to much of a set back for some singers to overcome so early in a career but Billie Davis showed the fighting spirit that has sustained her throughout her career and when she recovered, Billie came back stronger than ever.

Many more recordings followed with success and distinction and while I do not intend this to be a discography, rather an appreciation

of a very talented lady. I will just mention *'I Want You To be My Baby'*, No.1 in Spain for over a year in spite of poor distribution, is recognised as one of Billie's finest recordings by the public and the recording industry alike, and my personal favourite, 'Angel Of The Morning'. Billie gives this song a haunting quality so that once you have heard it you never forget it. This song was a hit for Billie in Europe and with the right publicity behind it I feel could still be a worldwide hit if the record company re-released it.

Speaking of Billie Davis's success in Europe, Billie lived there for some fifteen years. Her home during that time was in Barcelona to be precise, and she achieved great success during her time there. Billie was voted Best International Artiste of the Year winning again in 1969 when she shared it with Julio Iglesias. South America is another part of the word that has succumbed to Billie's talent and charm.

So although she was still enjoying great success abroad, Billie like many other sixties artistes Billie struggled to come to terms with the punk era that existed during the seventies, at times in the UK work was difficult to come by. But it would only be a matter of time before this determined and talented lady would find her performances back in demand with the public.

Helped by her prodigious talent as a songwriter and a new association with Albert Lee the talented country rock guitarist, Billie Davis began to attract new and wider audiences. Albert Lee's musical collaboration on Billie's songs resulted in the highly acclaimed album 'Stormy' being recorded in London and Nashville. This album along an upsurge in the public's interest in sixties music led to Billie Davis making many appearances on sixties revival shows. This renewed interest in her music made sure that Billie Davis was back where she belonged, in the limelight.

In more recent times Billie Davis has toured successfully with PJ Proby another of her paramours from the sixties, who hasn't fallen in love with this beautiful lady at some time? Billie Davis is a hard working lady and she has formidable work ethic, this means that instead of sitting at home waiting for the phone ring she promotes shows.

Through her continued hard work Billie has made a success of promoting and appearing on Me and my Shadows tour, with Jet Harris, this show, which also features The Rapiers, was one of the most popular shows on the road at that time. Billie Davis whilst being inescapably bound to the sixties will be remembered for much more, for me and countless other people Billie will be remembered for her talent as a songwriter her, willingness to diversify, and the quality of her voice not to mention her loving and giving nature.

Through sheer determination and hard work Billie Davis has achieved a place in her chosen profession that is timeless. Because of these things Billie Davis will continue, and her talent will charm new generations of fans as long as she continues to perform.

Go and see Billie Davis perform whenever you can you are sure to have a good time. For my own part I look forward to phone calls from Billie with her sultry husky and sexy voice opening the conversation with the words "Hello Sexy" before dissolving into a fit of the giggles. When we are together Billie will often look at me very seriously when I am trying to be sensible and saying, "Oh David you are funny" always prompting more laughter. The world is a much better place and Margaret and I enjoy it more with Billie Davis in it. Billie has endured great sadness in recent times, but as always her courage and caring nature continue to shine through. We love you Billie.

Dave, Billie Davis & Margaret Lodge

Eleven

Danny Rivers

Preface by Danny and Emily Rivers.

We first met Dave Lodge at the Ace Café when Tommy Bruce was doing a gig there. We had decided to go because Danny had worked with Tommy Bruce on package tours and shows back in the sixties and as it had been many years since they had seen each other we thought it would be a nice surprise to for Tommy to see Danny again.

Danny Rivers.
One of Joe Meek's recording artistes.

When Tommy Bruce came on stage he saw Danny in the audience and said 'Hi Dan' then he went on to say 'ladies and gentlemen there is a really good friend of mine from the sixties in the audience, you remember him Danny Rivers, give him a round of applause.' Dave heard Tommy say this from the side of the stage and when the show was over he came over to speak to us and we exchanged phone numbers. From then on we have become good friends with Dave and his lovely wife Margaret.

Dave has booked Danny on a few occasions since then and our experience of working with him has shown us that he is the most genuine and honest person you could ever wish to meet. Dave can not do enough for you and will always help you if he can.

Over the years he and Margaret have become our great friends and are two people we think very highly of. Dave Lodge is highly respected in show business circles for all the hard work and the loyalty he has given to Tommy Bruce and to many other artistes. Dave Lodge always wants us to be part of show business events and gives us an open invitation to go, when ever where ever we want to attend.

Danny and Emily Rivers.

One of the most handsome young men to come on to the Rock and Roll scene in the early days was the shy and unassuming Danny Rivers. With his good looks and powerful voice Danny seemed destined for the very top.

Born in Liverpool on January 24th 1942 and christened David Lee Baker, if it had not been for his father moving the family south when he was two years old there is no doubt we would have been referring to Danny as one of the legends of the early Mersey Beat, he would surely have come to fame at the same time as Billy Fury and been carried along in the wave of excitement created by the arrival of the Larry Parnes shows in Liverpool.

However in spite of Danny having left Liverpool at such a young age his date with musical destiny would not be missed because Danny would still come Parne's attention. There was no way this talented young man could be denied his taste of stardom it seemed to be written in the stars. His parents had always encouraged Danny's love of music and helped him learn his musical parts when he was chosen to sing in the school choir. It was natural that when Danny left school that he would start work in his father's carpentry shop and this happened as expected.

However at this time the Skiffle craze was at it's height and the exciting new music of the young people, Rock 'n' Roll was just starting to take off. Danny knew that the music scene was something that h he wanted to be a part of.

There was a local group called Peter Raymond and the Stormers, and they invited Danny, still known as Dave at this time, to perform with them. And when they entered a talent contest at The Majestic Ballroom Finsbury Park in North London no one could have been ready for the reaction that Danny's voice received, not only did the audience go crazy about him but he found that he had record company scouts clamouring to sign him up. So after changing his name to Danny Rivers, he chose this name because he was an Elvis Presley fan and having seen and been inspired by two characters played by Elvis in films he liked the idea of

113

combining the two. One of the characters being Danny Fisher from the film King Creole and the other being Deke Rivers from the film Loving You. Then Danny made his decision to sign a recording contract with Top Rank records, there was no doubt that the 18 year old Danny Rivers vocal career was on it's way.

Danny River's first single release *Hawk/ I've Got* had all the music publications of the day raving about him. It was no wonder really because with his dark hair and flashing smile there were inevitable comparisons to Elvis. Danny Rivers glowing press reviews drew him to the attention of the legendary Jack Good who had no hesitation in putting him in the successful TV show of the day, Wham. Danny Rivers was an instant success with the viewers.

Looking back this success comes as no surprise, because Danny Rivers with his good looks and powerful voice was driving the girls wild. Danny quite simply drove them into a frenzy, They screamed and shouted his name at every performance, Danny Rivers name had become a solid gold certainty to sell tickets for any show, he really was a promoters dream. So much so that press reports at the time had Jack Good saying 'Danny Rivers is the boy to watch, he is the greatest discovery since Cliff Richard'. Things just got better because after being signed up for all the Wham shows Danny Rivers then had the good fortune to be given a contract by Larry Parnes for the Rock and Trad tour. This meant Danny would be appearing with the other teen sensations of the day Marty Wilde, Billy Fury, Tommy Bruce, Nelson Keene, Lance Fortune, Peter Wynne and Joe Brown to name but a few. There is no doubt that everything was going great for Danny Rivers, nothing it seemed could prevent him from hitting the heights in show business.

Danny Rivers, Tommy Bruce and Dave Lodge

Danny Rivers was right there at the top of the popular entertainment tree, added to names already mentioned he was on the bill with Dickie Pride, Cuddly Dudley and the Vernon Girls, Danny could be forgiven for thinking he had it all So it came as real shock when the record company Danny Rivers was signed to, Top Rank, went out of business.

Sadly this was the start of worrying changes for Danny Rivers who wondered what would become of his recording career and if it ended would promoters' sill want to book him for live performances.

Jack Good, producer of 6-5 special, Tommy Bruce and Danny Rivers

Initially Danny found he did not have to worry but this setback showed him how precarious a career in show business could be.

Danny Rivers was on a tour of the Granada circuit and while appearing at the State Ballroom, Kilburn record producer Joe Meek Came to see him. Joe had been knocked out with Danny's performance and good to his word soon had Danny signed to a deal with Decca records. Danny's first release for Decca was *I'm Waiting for Tomorrow/ Can't You Hear My Heart* in November 1960, this just making the top 40 a very poor return in terms of chart success for what I feel were excellent recordings by a very talented artiste.

Danny's voice is so good that he even toured as resident vocalist with Cyril Stapleton's Orchestra and how this gig did not lead to even greater success is a mystery to me. One of the great tours that Danny Rivers would also appear on was George Cooper's promotion which would see him

Danny and Dave

115

starring alongside great American performers of the calibre of Johnny Burnette, Gene McDaniels and Gary US Bonds.

While Danny Rivers got on very well with Johnny Burnette in particular and treasures his memories of the man and the autograph that Johnny signed for him to this day. Unfortunately from a recording point of view Danny's career was not going as well as the live performances. Danny made more recordings with Joe Meek, *Once Upon A Time/ My Baby's Gone Away and We're Gonna Dance/ Movin' In*, all well performed and produced. It has to be said that *Movin' In* is a fabulous number which for some strange reason just failed to chart; perhaps it just needed more promotion.

However undaunted by his disappointments and encouraged by Joe Meek, Danny River's recorded *There Will Never Be / I Don't Think You Know* in 1964, once again these songs failed to make the anticipated impact on the charts.

In spite of the lack of record sales Danny Rivers continued to make successful appearances George Cooper's tours during this time. He was performing with the likes of Marty Wilde, Heinz and The Tornados always continuing receive rave reviews. The popularity that Danny enjoyed with audiences should have led to chart success, but as said previously this success inexplicably eluded Danny who as a result was becoming disillusioned with show business. After all he kept hearing what a wonderful voice he possessed but his records would not sell in sufficient quantities to provide him with a hit. Danny continued to sing as a guest on various shows for a while but eventually he decided to leave the business so that he could pursue other interests.

Danny River fans however have never forgotten about him and were delighted when he appeared again in the nineties at a Billy Fury Tribute Show. Buoyed by the success of his return, Danny began making guest appearances on sixties revival shows.

Having had the pleasure of meeting Danny at the Ace Café when he and his wife Emily came to see Tommy Bruce perform at Mark Wilsmore's Ace Café in London I was delighted, because I had been a fan since seeing perform in the sixties, when he agreed to appear in a show I promoted at New Brighton's Floral Pavilion on the 5th July '03. On this show Danny once again performed with Tommy Bruce, Marty Wilde, Dave Sampson, Terry Dene and Johnny Gentle who had all been part of the Larry Parnes era with him.

Also at this point I would like to mention Lance Fortune who in spite of ill health agreed to turn up for me on that occasion so that he could be part of what turned out to be a great evening's entertainment.

From my point of view on that and all the other occasions I had the pleasure of seeing him perform, Danny Rivers fully lived up to his reputation as a powerful singer and entertainer. I have to say that Danny's performance of *'Little Sister'* was one of the highlights of the show.

At this point I would like to thank Wirral entrepreneur Doug Darroch and Operation Big Beat for giving me the opportunity to bring together more of the Larry Parnes performers than had been on stage together at any one time since the Rock and Trad tour. I have to tell you that time has not diminished the voice or the talent of this intelligent and likeable man, who still looks good and sounds better. If you see Danny Rivers advertised go and see him you won't be disappointed. Make a point of speaking to him after the show; you will enjoy his conversation and his knowledge about the history of music is of course extensive. Whenever you meet Danny Rivers you will always find him in the company of his lovely wife Emily who is a lovely lady and has a delightful personality. Emily has her own history in show business because she was a talented dancer in the sixties, who has many credits to her name. Not the least of her credits was her appearance in the Cliff Richard film Summer Holiday.

Danny Rivers was one of the famous Parnes boys and that in it's self is a claim to fame but there is more to Danny than just being part of one of the great eras of entertainment. Danny Rivers is a charming and intelligent man who like so many of the performers from the sixties era has matured in to a great entertainer. Danny and Emily are two of our closest friends, they are lovely people and I hope our friendship will continue throughout, what I hope will be the many years ahead.

Twelve

Chas McDevitt

Chas McDevitt was born in Glasgow on the 4th of December 1934 he is one of the great performers of our time. Though he came to prominence during the Skiffle craze, one could almost say he started it for the British fans, he certainly was the first person I heard perform this music and his success with the recordings of *Freight Train / Cotton* definately got things going in a big way. In spite of this it is impossible to categorise Chas into one style of music.

Chas McDevitt
Pioneer of Skiffle

To start at the beginning of his musical career I need to go back to his college days when he played banjo in the local jazz band, this led to him joining the then renowned Crane River Jazz Band in 1954, within this band Chas featured in folk style group which evolved in 1956 into the Chas McDevitt Skiffle Group. The boys plied their trade in the coffee bars and jazz clubs of Soho until in 1957 their recording of the afore mentioned *Freight Train / Cotton Song* elevated them to West End theatres and the Royal Festival Hall.

Freight Train topped the Hit Parade and entered the charts worldwide. This led to a trip to the United States and an appearance on The Ed Sullivan Show, being one of the first popular music groups to do this.

On their return to the UK Nancy Whiskey the featured vocalist left the band to get married, Chas brought in Shirley Douglas as a replacement and Shirley sang with them until Chas disbanded the group. He then worked with Shirley as a duo for a while until they also split up as they both wished to have solo careers.

In between 1959 and 1976 Chas began to show a wider audience how diverse his talents are In order to continue his career he embarked on a series of cabaret and concert appearances. During this time Chas appeared with such sixties luminaries as The Beatles and the Shadows. His travels took him world wide to locations as diverse as Rhodesia and Reykjavik. Chas McDermott has entertained the UK and US forces at bases everywhere and is welcome back wherever he performs.

In 1978 Chas reformed the Skiffle group with some of the original members and included his daughter Kerry on washboard. His skiffle group has continued to tour worldwide right up to the present day with great success.

Chas McDevitt has received the recognition and respect of his peers, not just for his undoubted talent but also for his good works for charity. Chas is an active member of the Grand Order of Water Rats and in 1980 he became Rat of the year. He has had the honour of serving as King Rat on more than one occasion.

Chas McDevitt is still performing to a high standard but many people may not be aware that he is also recognised for his song writing talent. Among the artistes who have recorded his songs are Cliff Richard, Chet Atkins and Peter Paul and Mary. I have to say that Chas McDevitt's modesty belies his musical talent and from my point of view he can only be described as a lovely man who is a pleasure to talk to and spend time with. Chas has earned a place in the hearts of the world's music loving people; he is at home performing Jazz, Skiffle, Folk, indeed all forms of pop and contemporary music. His skill in playing Guitar, Banjo, Autoharp and Flute is universally recognised. It is with good reason that Chas McDevitt is thought of by many as a true Legend of the music industry and perhaps of equal importance he is a good and loyal friend to many of us.

Thirteen

Heinz

Heinz Burt was in his lifetime many thing to many people, indeed there were those who made no secret of the fact that they disliked him intensely, with very valid reasons.

However to my wife Margaret and I he was just our mate.

Heinz lived in our home as guest for the better part of twelve months and during that time and since Margaret has often been heard to say that Heinz was the perfect house guest.

Heinz Burt

An example of the person he could be is shown by his behaviour when ever we had been out. We would come back into the house to hear Heinz saying put your feet up I'll make a brew, there's a meal in the oven Heinz really was a most domesticated man.

While he was living with us Heinz made a determined and successful attempt to get fit. We went running and swimming together and always had a laugh as his competitive nature would make him cut corners on our runs in an effort to get home before me. At the time I was still competing in triathlons and therefore I had a high level of fitness so on the longer runs I would pull ahead of him only to find myself turning a corner after a couple of miles to see Heinz ahead of me.

I would chase him down as if it were true run race and as I went past him he would jump on me and wrestle me to the ground and then run off in an effort to get home first. When we got back he would run down the path laughing and telling Margaret that he had beaten me again.

However there was no need for him to cut corners when we swam because he was an excellent swimmer and it was all I could do to keep up with him.

One of the things that Heinz really loved was going to car boot sales and he and Margaret would wander round them looking for bargains, we still have ornaments that he bought for her.

Heinz was a great supporter of my athletic endeavours and often travelled with Margaret and I to events I was taking part in. He used to roar his encouragement and loudly proclaim to all the people around that's my mate, he's good isn't he? People did not realise that my noisy mate was in fact the same Heinz who had topped the charts on both sides of the Atlantic while in the Tornados, with *Telstar* and had his own top five solo hit with *Just like Eddie*. It is a real shame that happy times like that were rare in Heinz's life as he would sadly die at the relatively young age of Fifty seven.

Heinz at the Napoleon

Born in 1942 Heinz was discovered by the legendary Joe Meek, who brought him up to London from Eastleigh just outside Southampton. Joe thought that Heinz, whose father had been a German prisoner of war and married a local girl, had the looks that could help him to succeed in show business.

Joe had ideas Heinz that initially involved putting him into a group he had an interest in called The Tornados. The plan being that Heinz would replace the much better known Brian Gregg as the bass player. The group went on to be the first British group to top the charts on both sides of the Atlantic with their hit recording of *Telstar*.

More recording followed but none had the chart success of *Telstar*. The group also went on tour backing the sensational Billy Fury. Their live performances were a great success and Joe Meek could see that the good-looking young Heinz was getting a great deal of attention from the girl fans.

With this in mind Joe decided to take Heinz out of the band and promote him as a solo act. Heinz's first solo record was a tribute to Eddie Cochrane the American performer who was tragically killed in a car crash near Chippenham while on tour in Great Britain. Instant chart success followed with a top five hit for Heinz. Unfortunately his subsequent solo recording just as with the Tornados did not achieve the same success as his first disc.

Unfortunately the publicity surrounding Joe Meeks subsequent death was not helpful to Heinz's career. Also he found that the life he had been living was provided by credit and was not funded as he thought by performance and record success. For example the house Heinz naively thought had been a gift from Joe Meek turned out to be rented and the rent was in arrears so he was soon evicted.

His car was leased and was repossessed because the payments on it ceased with Joe's death, similarly the boat which was Heinz's pride and joy was reposed for the same reason. Basically Joe's death left Heinz penniless and with little to show for his brief time at the top of the entertainment ladder.

Added to this being questioned by the police about the fact that his shotgun had been used in Joe's suicide and the Death of the landlady caused Heinz to have a breakdown that he never fully recovered from, indeed this traumatic experience would certainly impact on his health and well being throughout his life.

Heinz, Alan 'Fluff' Freeman and Tommy Bruce

Heinz remained a popular performer appearing at Butlin's Camps like Barry Island and Bognor Regis as part of sixties shows and Rock 'n' Roll weekends. Difficult financial circumstances meant that he did take employment outside the entertainment industry.

Some of the jobs included among things being a track layer for British Rail and more fulfilling from a personal point of view Heinz spent time spent as a graphic designer this gave free rein to Heinz's obvious artistic talent. Over the years he appeared on many sixties revival and package tours, one of these being 'The Way it Was' a show that I promoted and toured from the mid eighties to the early nineties.

This show starred Tommy Bruce and Heinz, backed by Manchester band Wall Street. This was by far the most successful and easy to sell of the shows I have been involved in. This success was due in no small part to Heinz's continued popularity with the ladies and the on stage rapport between Tommy and himself. From time to time venue managers would ask for other artistes to be brought in and we would call on the services of other performers like, Jess Conrad, Wee Willie Harris, Screamin' Lord Sutch, Dave Sampson, Billie Davis and Ricky Valance

During this period as previously mentioned Heinz lived with my wife Margaret and I and we became very good friends. Heinz began to suffer with ill health after he moved back to Eastleigh and as I said died sadly and somewhat ironically at the relatively young age of fifty-seven. Strangely enough Heinz always predicted that his life would end at this age.

We always had great fun on the road and Heinz was frequently the victim of humorous misfortune. One time I remember he fell off the stage due to a dramatic entry. Heinz decided that with the band already playing he would run on stage from the wings on my left when I introduced him, drop to his knees, and slide cross the stage snatching the microphone from me on the way past. It all went badly wrong, he got the mic alright but then as he stumbled out of the slide and tried to get to his feet he tumbled into the orchestra pit. The crowd cheered wildly as he climbed back on stage, head bleeding and with the knees torn out of the trousers of the white suit he was wearing that night. He didn't try that entrance again!

The other occasion that stands out was when in full teddy boy regalia including crepe soled boppers he jumped from a speaker onto a grand piano only to find when he landed that it had no lid. Heinz ever the professional kept singing as he tried to free himself from the strings. He finally got free minus his shoes and finished his act in fluorescent yellow socks, the piano players language cannot be repeated here.

There was another occasion were a piano featured was at a theatre in St Helens, Lancashire. The contract had been sent in and one of the riders was that a grand piano should be available. When we arrived at the theatre the manager greeted us and told us the piano had been tuned and took us to the stage and showed us proudly that it had been French polished. Who will play it he asked, oh replied Heinz it's not for playing I just want to dance on the lid. The theatre manager's face was like stone as he had the piano was wheeled into the wings. It was never dull on the road with Heinz.

Heinz with Margaret Lodge

Heinz is still fondly remembered and spoken of by performers and fans alike and for my part I lost a dear friend when he died. As a performer Heinz was someone who in company with Tommy Bruce provided me with only show that I ever promoted that literally sold itself, 'The Way It Was'. Margaret and I will always miss him.

Fourteen

Wee Willie Harris

Preface by Wee Willie Harris.

Wee Willie Harris (courtesy of Wee Willie)

Dave Lodge is one of the people in show business who has always treated me right. Ever since Dave came on to the scene nearly forty years ago as Tommy Bruce's friend and manager he has always been fair in the way he treats me and the other guys. My wife Sheila always used to say 'I wish you had some one like Dave, Willie he would make sure you were looked after on the gigs' I would have liked him to be my manager but he was and still is always loyal to Tommy and I don't think he will do individual management again, but if he did I know he would want to be my manager as Tommy always said Dave's a hard worker. Incidentally I used to like to phone Dave up late at night and say the words, 'allo my son what's happenin' I would always make him think it was Tommy Bruce calling. That is what rock and roll is about, having a laugh with your mates, I am sure Dave and I will always be mates and I look forward to seeing him on the next gig.
       Wee Willie Harris. Recording Star and Entertainer.

Wee Willie Harris is as his name might suggest is a five foot two-inch ball of fire. Even after over fifty years in show business Willie still explodes on to the stage with the same enthusiasm for Rock'n'Roll that he has been showing since he started out way back in the fifties. Willie's live show is as volatile as a tube of nitroglycerin.

  Willie, so he told me was the resident piano player at the legendary 2i's coffee bar located in London's Old Compton Street. Many of the young

125

Rock 'n' Roll hopefuls performed there in those days Cliff Richard, Adam Faith and Screamin' Lord Sutch to name just three so it was a good place to get noticed if you wanted to get a break into the world of show business.

Around this time Jack Good was looking for acts to appear on his exciting new TV show Six Five Special so Willie decided to go along to the BBC studios at Shepherds Bush for an audition. As soon as Jack Good heard Wee Willie Harris he had no hesitation in booking him for five shows.

Because Willie was loud, exciting and had his hair dyed green the fans were knocked out by this flamboyant rock'n'roller and his popularity with them soon ensured he was working in theatres and clubs up and down the country.

Not that Willie always pleased everybody, appearing in a show in Liverpool one night he hurtled out on to the stage clad in a leopard skin only for the local watch committee to close the curtains on him on the grounds that his performance was in bad taste.

That small set back has not prevented Wee Willie Harris from becoming one of the most popular and enduring entertainers both in the UK and abroad for almost fifty years. I often hear Willie say the words "I've worked everywhere you know" followed by a short pause and then he says "Including Finland".

I have had the pleasure of knowing Willie and his lovely wife Sheila for over forty years and his dry humour never ceases to amuse me. Willie can eat for England and the word's 'I'll have that' are often heard in the dressing room when one of us decides we don't fancy the sandwich or the pie that we were going to eat.

Wee Willie & Liqourice Locking

Dave and Wee Willie

Although Wee Willie Harris has not yet had a chart topping record the will to succeed has never left him. I have to say yet because if determination has anything to do with it Willie is definitely going to have one if it takes him till he is ninety. No one I have ever met in show business has put the effort into gaining that elusive hit in the way that Willie has. The fans of course love Willie's live shows and buy the self produced CDs that he sells afterwards in great quantities. Although Willie is a great Rock and Roller he also shows his versatility with his highly entertaining and amusing cabaret show. Whenever and wherever he appears Willie only has to give his little cough followed by the words, "I've not been well" to have the audience in fits of laughter.

When you book him for a show Willie is always heard to say, "I don't mind closing the first half, I can sell my CD's in the interval". If the powers that be counted the tapes and CD's he has sold in the interval during the last fifty years Willie would have had his hit record long ago. In spite of the absence of a hit record Willie does have the distinction of having recorded *Rockin' at the 2i's* a song which for many people encapsulates the feeling of fun that the music of the late fifties and early sixties brought to a whole generation.

Wee Willie Harris may not put his flamboyant wigs on and wear his leopard skin anymore but he still gives great value for money every single time he performs. If there is a British Rock and Roll Hall of Fame then Willie has rightful place in it along side people like Marty Wilde, Joe Brown, Vince Taylor, Tommy Bruce and all the rest.

Wee Willie Harris continues to stand the test of time with the same qualities that endeared him to his many fans all those years ago still in evidence today. Long may he continue to give his own inimitable performance of songs like *Cell Block No 9*.

Willie and his wife Shelia are valued friends and Margaret and I always enjoy the time we spend in their company.

Fifteen

Norman Wisdom

Norman Wisdom was an outstanding example of the very best that British entertainment had to offer. With his natural enthusiasm and an eagerness to learn, Norman put his time as bandsman in the British Army to very good use. He learned the discipline of mind and body required to make a good musician. Also he was the undisputed Flyweight Champion of the British Army in India.

Norman Wisdom made some wonderful and classic British films including *Trouble in Store, Follow a Star,* and *The Square Peg* to name but three. His comic timing was second to none. He had a wonderful singing voice and was a charming and delightful man.

Norman Wisdom receiving his Knighthood

It is clear that Norman's live performances have that same touch of sadness and joy that we see in his films. Sadly at times this has been reflected in his life but the Norman Wisdom I was privileged to get to know is a man who possessed great stoicism and personal courage – these qualities always saw him through.

Norman's support of charitable organisations included being the patron of International Aid Services, the Norman Wisdom Children's Hospice in Mayak near Odessa and he actively supported everything he believed in. So much so that he went with a truck convey to Chernobyl, living rough and enduring the same hardships as the other volunteers.

Norman was always a delight to accompany on the road and I often made trips to Granada for him to film episodes of *Coronation Street*. Incidentally it was on Norman's last appearance of *Coronation Street* that I had pleasure of spending a short time in the company of Bradley Walsh, Bradley is a very talented and versatile entertainer and I feel very fortunate to have had my photograph taken with him and Norman on the cobbles outside The Rovers Return, a splendid memory of a wonderful day spent in the company of two remarkable men. I also met among others the very talented Eileen Derbyshire a lovely lady who has devoted her career to making Emily Bishop one of the most endearing characters on British television and the incredibly beautiful Jane Danson, who is quite simply a truly lovely girl and a fine actress.

Norman Wisdom, Bradley Walsh & Dave Lodge on the set of Coronation Street

I enjoyed taking Norman on the outdoor set of *Last of the Summer Wine* and meeting Peter Sallis in his professional surrounding having only previously met him at The Grosvenor House Hotel during Heritage Foundation Functions. I also took great pleasure in our trips to Durham to play charity golf, on any and all of these occasions Norman's company has been splendid. More personal occasions such as sitting drinking coffee with Norman in his flat in Epsom, or dining together in restaurants have just been too wonderful for words.

One special memory is of the time Norman got down on one knee in a restaurant in Manchester and sang *Don't Laugh At Me* to my wife Margaret, there wasn't a dry eye in the place. Or when he signed his autobiography to us with the words, 'To my dear friends David and Margaret', going on to say 'with a big kiss for Margaret but only a little one for Dave, because we are not puffs!' These memories are priceless and irreplaceable; they are forever in my heart and will remain with me always.

Of course I can not leave my memories of Norman with reference to aspects of his humour and star quality. The happy journeys we spent together in many

Norman Wisdom in Last of the Summer Wine
Photo courtesy of Michael Howarth BBC TV

cases came about because of his love of cars. We could not pass a car showroom without Norman wanting to stop and look at the cars even if it made us late for an engagement, how could I refuse him when he gave me that little boy lost look that he used to such effect through out his career? Or the countess times on the motorway when Norman would notice a car ahead of and say me Dave, can you speed up because I want to look at the car in front.

Then as I drew alongside the car in question he would say, slow down I want to have a proper look at it. Norman would look at the car while all the time waving and smiling at the driver and any other occupants of the car in currently in view. Then he would say to me overtake it now and then pull in and slow down so that they will have to overtake us and I will be able to look at it from the other side. I must have happily upset half the motorway drivers in Britain in order to make sure Norman enjoyed his journey.

Of course as I have said before Norman Wisdom has great star quality and he never forgets his public. This was always proved when ever we stopped anywhere during a journey he would always make time for the people. For example on the motorway services, a crowd would always gather round him asking him for his autograph or to have their photo taken in his company. Norman would always sign every autograph, pose for their photos and generally entertain everybody with his charm making sure that no one ever left feeling disappointed. When all the autographs were signed Norman would invariably put on an impromptu show. These shows would always end with a little song written by Norman himself, about having a small house and a pension, going on with a verse saying if any of the ladies were interested they should get in touch. Norman would then leave everyone laughing, departing with a salute accompanied by his trademark pratt fall.

Norman Wisdom has a little foible that if you have ever served him in a shop, you will recognise, he always signs his credit card slips, Sir Norman Wisdom. As Norman says he was given this honour late in life and he intends to get full use from it. Norman Wisdom is more than just a great entertainer is, he is a great man and I am privileged to call him my friend.

He lives happily in the Isle of Man and no one has earned or deserved that happiness more. I hope to spend more time in his company in the future.

Whilst writing this book Norman's family made me aware of his problems with Alzheimer's disease and sadly this great entertainer will be unable to perform in theatres or on film again.

Although Norman, because performing is as natural to him as breathing will always give impromptu little shows anytime people are around him as up to this date he still remembers his entire act and always delivers it with perfect timing. Having said how sad this news makes me, this unfortunate turn of events does give me the opportunity to mention Norman's family who have responded to his downturn in health with great courage and fortitude, sacrificing there time to help and support him, in a little more detail. I have to say that I liked Norman's daughter, Jacquie the moment I met and spoke to her, she is to me a feisty lady with a great sense of humour who certainly doesn't suffer fools gladly. Norman's son Nick appears to me to be a quiet and thoughtful man who cares deeply for his family, he is a gentleman in the truest sense of the word. Nick's wife, Kym who I have come to know quite well in recent years is a fantastic lady who whose courage is immense and whose devotion to her family and those around her is a credit to her. We are all lucky if we have somebody like Kym in our circle of family or friends as they make difficult days easier.

My wife Margaret and I consider ourselves blessed by Kym's friendship and we are pleased to know her. We look on our contact with Kym, Nick and Jacquie as a blessing and a gift bestowed on us by Norman.

There are many people at this sad time in Norman's life who think they are entitled to voice their opinion on Norman and his family. Not only are they wrong to think they are entitled to air this opinion in the media, they are also invariably completely wrong in their opinion. Personally I have no opinion save to say that I do think I know that whatever decisions Norman's family make on his behalf they are made out of love and respect for Norman and that is all the public need to know.

While I am talking of the people who have come into my life that are associated with Norman I feel that here is the best place to mention

Johnny Mans, Johnny is above all else a fine family man and a good and loyal friend. He has lovely wife, Becky and two wonderful and talented children, Lucy and Elliott. It is because of my friendship with Johnny that I was able to meet Norman Wisdom in the first place. This came about because Johnny had been unable to arrange transport for Norman on one of his trips up north and phoned me to see if I could help. He offered to pay me but naturally I refused, all payment – what an opportunity he was giving me! On that occasion I could not get to the airport quickly enough, after all I was going to meet a man who I had admired since I saw his film *Trouble in Store* in the fifties. On top of this *Don't Laugh At Me* was one of the first records I ever bought, indeed having read the early part of this book you may even understand why I consider it to be my theme tune. Johnny Mans was a talented entertainer in his own right who toured the world presenting his own brand of humour to the masses. Johnny Mans has gone on to become one of the most respected managers in show business. The artistes he represents include Norman Wisdom, Max Bygraves, Rose Marie and Ronnie Ronalde and the reason why they and many others have stayed with Johnny is because of the respect he commands through out the business and the loyalty he gives to them. Johnny Mans is also a very astute show promoter, a man who other would be promoters including me come to for advice, which incidentally has always been freely given. I have to say Johnny Mans is a fine man who has given me gift of his friendship and I will always value it, added to that he allowed me to meet Norman Wisdom and through that meeting a friendship ensued that has greatly enhanced my life. Sadly Norman passed away before this book was completed, Margaret and I mourn his loss as our friend but take great joy in the memory of his company. He was simply the best.

Dave Lodge, Norman Wisdom & Margaret Lodge relax after a nice lunch together.

Sixteen

Billy Fury

I only met Billy on a couple of occasions, but those occasions were always a great pleasure. As always it was thanks to Tommy Bruce that we met and the conversations always ran to talk of the old days, on the Larry Parnes shows. Sadly Billy died too soon and my chance of knowing him better passed. However I did know him long enough to meet his brother Albie and their mother Jean.

Billy Fury (Courtesy of Chris Ely)

Many of you will remember Albie as Jason Eddie a fine performer in his own right. We became close friends, partly because we were born on the same day. Born Ronald Wycherley, Billy Fury was destined to become one of this countries biggest musical stars, sadly although his star burned brightly, it burned for too short a time.

Although I cannot claim to known Billy well he did influence me with his music and personality and I liked him immensely. The stories I tell about are from his memories and those of Tommy Bruce. For these reasons Billy belongs in this book. Billy Fury and Tommy Bruce were great mates; He never tired of his company or of his stage performances. He had a great sense of humour and in Tommy's eyes Billy was a real gentleman. Apart from the Rock and Trad Spectacular, they did hundreds of gigs together – with long summer seasons in Great Yarmouth and Blackpool. To him they were just two young guys having a great time.

Tommy recalled how Billy would duck out of travelling on the tour bus whenever he could and on one occasion he crashed his car and was lucky he didn't finish up in hospital. He ended up with a badly bruised forehead, the bruise shows quite clearly on one of our photographs. Then he decided he wanted to go up to Liverpool and see his Mum but didn't feel up to the drive, so he asked Tommy to drive, what a journey that was, the steering wheel from the damaged car was nearly lined up with the passenger seat but they laughed all the way. Happy days.

We all loved Billy and we wish he was still with us, sharing the laughs on the road and singing as only he could. Tommy remained popular with Billy's family to the end of his life and through that I was able to form my own friend ship with Billy's mum Jean and his Brother, Albie.

Having retired from the business to indulge in his love of the countryside and animals Billy lived on his farm in Wales, but there were plenty of people in show business not to mention his fans who wanted him back. He resisted for some time but in-spite of his ill health he still felt the pull of the crowd. Billy did make an ill-fated comeback and the fans turned out to see him perform in theatres throughout the British Isles. He collapsed and subsequently died on stage at the Beck Theatre Middlesex.

It was very poignant for Tommy and I when he later appeared at the theatre which has a Brass plate erected to his memory.

Billy Fury may have missed out on a No.1 record but he will always be No.1 in the hearts of his many thousands of fans, including Margaret and I.

A statue, made by sculptor Tom Murphy, was erected of Billy Fury in his home City of Liverpool in 2003. The statue now stands outside Piermaster's House in the Albert Dock

Albie Wycherley (Billy's Brother), Jean Wycherley (Billy's mother), Jack Good, Tommy Bruce & Danny Rivers at the unveiling of Billy Fury's statue. This statue, made by Liverpool sculptor Tom Murphy in 2003 and stands outside Piermaster's House in the Albert Dock

SEVENTEEN

CRAIG DOUGLAS

Preface By Craig Douglas

David Lodge and I met many years ago when he started managing our good friend Tommy Bruce. It was clear from the very start that he cared about Tommy and looked after him like a father.

Because of our friendship I asked David to write the sleeve notes for my 50th anniversary CD and believe me he has done a wonderful job. Over the last fifty years I have made many acquaintances in show business, but very few good friends. I am delighted to say that David and his lovely wife Margaret are included among my very good friends.

Craig Douglas with Dave Lodge

Craig Douglas International Recording Star.

Perfect timing and phrasing, and a warm but polished delivery all combine to make Craig Douglas the ultimate cabaret entertainer. He has travelled along way from the oft times mentioned milk round on the Isle of Wight. More importantly Craig Douglas is the perfect gentleman, a loyal and true friend who would never let you down. Craig has impeccable manners and is the most courteous man you could ever wish to meet.

If you are lucky you will have seen Craig Douglas in one of the fabulous nightspots around the world places that conjure up images of a Millionaires Paradise. Audiences at Caesars Palace Las Vegas, Le Chateau Supper Club Nairobi, The Mandarin Hotel Hong Kong, have all been thrilled by his incomparable voice and humorous asides making every one feel as though they have known him all their lives.

An evening with Craig Douglas is just that, a gathering of friends. Whether it happens to be on a balmy evening in Kuala Lumpur or Hong

Kong, be it on board a sumptuous cruise ship like the Oriana, or on cold and wet winter's night in Manchester or Leeds. The warmth and pleasure he brings to your company is just the same. This is just a small measure of what he brings to his audience so imagine the joy that can be experienced in his company when he really is your friend. I think Craig was born to be an entertainer, his instant rapport with an audience comes naturally; it cannot be learnt or taught. Craig's ability to think on his feet and provide the right performance at the right time was shown when he toured with *The Solid Gold Rock and Roll Show*. Being the relaxed ballad singer that he is would have pleased the audience but would not have provided the excitement that the other artistes like Freddie Cannon and John Leyton create.

So Craig gave a virtuoso performance, singing the wonderful ballads which provided his hits, then at various points swivelling his hips, unbuttoning his shirt and whirling his tie around above his head to accompanying screams from the ladies in the audience. These performances brought rave reviews from Rock and Roll magazines every where he appeared at he time when he could have been forgiven for just resting on his laurels. Not Craig Douglas he took the risk, pushed the envelope, call it what you will and reaped the rewards as he took his career forward in the new century.

So how did it all begin? How did a likeable young lad who was far from the bright lights of show business find his way to stardom and more importantly longevity in his chosen career? It began with Craig, who had been interested in music and singing from early childhood, winning a local talent contest singing *Mary's Boy Child*. His pleasure at winning the £5.00 first prize was increased many fold, when he discovered that his remarkable natural singing talent had drawn the attention of the renowned Bunny Lewis who would go on to become his manager, indeed his friend. Within a few short months Bunny had negotiated a Decca recording contract for Craig and arranged his appearance on television. In No time at all Craig was starring in shows such as 'Six-Five Special'.

Bunny Lewis was a very astute man and before long he changed Craig's recording contract from Decca to Top Rank this change showed the business acumen that allied to Craig's talent would bring the success and stardom that for most people is only a dream.

Craig's first single for Top Rank *A Teenager in Love* climbed to number 13 in the charts in the summer of 1959 and the follow up *Only Sixteen* went to No.1 in the Autumn of the same year. This was followed by fantastic recording success, Pretty Blues Eyes, *The Heart of a Teenage Girl, Time* and *A Hundred Pounds of Clay* (unbelievably banned by the BBC For suggestive lyrics).The list of Craig's successes is endless.

His recording success was enhanced by film and stage work. Craig's films have included *Climb up the Wall, The Painted Smile* and *It's Trad Dad*. Success continued for Craig with his nationally acclaimed stage performances, *No No Nanette, Lock up your Daughters, Wait til Dark* – a dramatic none singing role, *And then I Wrote*. A list that many of his contemporaries would find enviable. His television appearances included, *Sunday night at the London Palladium, Thank Your Lucky Stars* and *Juke Box Jury*; Thirty six weeks as compère on *Five 'o'clock Club* and more recently *Time of Your Life, Night of A 100 Stars, Unforgettable, Greatest Hits* and *Surprise Surprise*. The wonderful 'Fairy Snow' adverts have made Craig a household name.

Gold and Silver Discs came Craig's way both the recording industry and the general public were quick to recognise his talent. Craig Douglas has performed before Her Majesty The Queen and other members of the Royal Family, he is still touring regularly throughout Great Britain and the World after more than fifty years in the business he can claim to have kept his old fans and unusually I think, continues to attract new generations to his music with his easy going and relaxed style.

For some of the stars of the fifties and sixties the arrival of the Beatles caused a dip in popularity and even brought

137

about the end of some careers. Not so with Craig Douglas his talent flourished as he became the complete all-round entertainer, with his relaxed charm wonderful voice and wry sense of humour, he has become the very best that a British entertainer can be because of this he is loved where ever he appears.

In summary I have to say that as an entertainer Craig Douglas has undoubted talent, class and vocal ability. Craig also has charisma in abundance and because of these things is a truly exceptional performer. From a personal point of view; I have to say that over many years Craig Douglas has proved to be is a real gentleman, a man who is a true and loyal friend, not just to Margaret and I but to many of the other people who know him. Tommy Bruce who introduced Craig to me said that Craig Douglas was simply the best as always Tommy's judgment was spot on. Long may Craig continue to thrive in his life and career. All our futures will be better and brighter with people like Craig Douglas in our lives.

In recent times Craig's health has not been to good, but he still finds time to show how he cares for Margaret and I during what has been a very difficult time. He remains a very special man whose friendship enhances our lives.

Eighteen
Lynn Alice

When Lynn Alice lost her brave fight for life in January 2001 those of us who knew her lost more than her talent, we lost a much loved friend. That was how it was with Lynnie, if you met her you knew her and if you knew her you loved her. She had a great sense of humour and she filled our lives with her infectious enthusiasm. She was vivacious and bubbly, a lovely girl whose beauty and charm shone from within. Lynn Alice was special and we were all privileged to have spent time in her company. One of the really special things about Lynn was that because she was so modest she didn't realise how talented and lovely she was.

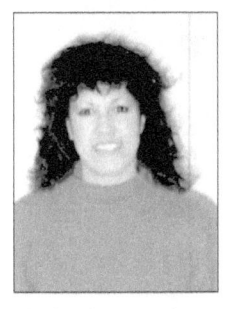

The lovely Lynn Alice

Lynn Alice started her career in the entertainment business as a Blue Coat at the Pontins Holiday Camps. There is no doubt that Lynn was adored by all the holiday makers young and old who came to the camp because Lynn Alice was a rare person, a person who had so much generosity of spirit that it was simply impossible not to like her. Add to that her wonderful charismatic talent and singing voice and any holiday would be twice the fun with Lynn Alice around.

Lynn Alice went on to tour the continent with various rock bands and pop groups always enhancing the shows she appeared on with her presence. Lynn was also very popular with the people in the audience at the Kings nightclub in Ilford and at the Ilford Palace. Always in great demand to appear in venues, Lynn Alice was the featured singer with the Ross Mitchell Band and was also the very popular resident singer at Caesars Palace in Luton until the venue ceased to provide live entertainment.

In 1989 Clem Cattinni made the decision to reform his highly successful band The Tornados. Clem wanted to provide a complete show this time around as The Tornados had made their reputation as an instrumental band. That being the case he made the decision to include a girl singer in the line up.

He auditioned quite a few girls for the job as I recall, but none of them had the special qualities that Lynn Alice possessed. Lynn proved to be an inspired choice she was sensational and had no trouble winning over any of the traditional sixties fans who might have thought Clem should have stuck to an Instrumental line up. Even though Lynn's star shone brightly for entire world to see, in her own mind she was just an ordinary girl singer, Lynn simply didn't realise how highly thought of she was by her many fans. More than that Lynn Alice had the admiration and respect of her fellow entertainers.

I first met Lynn at the Beck Theatre when Graham Cole booked Tommy Bruce to be part of his show. Graham was kind enough to book me as the compère and it really was a great show to be part of. Also on the bill were the Tornados, Cliff Bennett, The Honeycombs and John Leyton. Everybody gave great performances, notably John Leyton who was making his theatre comeback as a singer. I am pleased to say John and I became friends that night, a friendship I value, he is the best of men. For me the stand-out performer on the night was Lynn. The power of Lynn's performance, her infectious humour allied to her enthusiasm and fabulous voice just blew me away. That night we also started a friendship of great warmth, which included Margaret, as do all these friendships.

When Lynn first became ill we in the business would have done anything for her. Typically in spite of her illness and the setbacks involved she still thought of others. Lynn put herself in the frontline by performing in several concerts for cancer charities, always thinking of others Lynn Alice really was a wonderful lady.

Clem and the guys in the Tornados are always going to miss her more than any of us, because they knew her best. But everyone in the business who knew her, realised they had lost a special friend when she passed away. Tommy and I often spoke of her as we travelled round the theatres and worked with other artistes. Those artistes may perform songs that Lynn sang, but they can never put her interpretation on them but when we heard the songs our memory of Lynn was stronger.

One of the Theatres where our thoughts of Lynn were more poignant than usual was Leeds City Varieties. The reason for this was that when we, Tommy and I that is, were appearing with Mike Berry, The Honeycombs, Cliff Bennett and the Rebel Rousers and The Tornados at that theatre. Tommy and I, like The Tornados, were using the dressing rooms on the top floor.

There is a steep staircase and at that time there was an old carpet with holes that had worn in over the years on some of the steps. That worn carpet was the cause of one of my fondest memories of Lynn. I was coming back up the steps having been on the stage introducing one of the other acts as Lynn started to come down. Unfortunately after only a few steps she caught her heel in a hole in the carpet and started to fall. Hearing her cry out I looked up to see her falling down towards me head first. Somehow I caught her, without falling myself. So there it is – my truthful claim about how one of the most beautiful girls in show business fell for me! As she thanked me for catching her I was struck by how special she was. As always, Lynn's reaction was the opposite of what people might have expected. She just gave me her radiant smile and said, "It's a good thing you caught me, because Clem would have been awfully upset if I had hurt myself." Lynn, showed once again that she was a special lady who always thought of others first.

Tommy and I were last at The Leeds City Varieties on September 10th 2004. We talked about Lynn and said how much we missed her. I remember thinking there could never be better time to say, as I stood on the stairs that I caught her on "Thank you Lynn for sharing your talent, wonderful personality and friendship with us we are all better for having known you and we will always miss you". It appears to me to be one of life's ironies that little did I know then that by the time I came to write this book I would have had to say goodbye to Tommy as well as Lynn. I am sure that they are together with all our other friends in heaven.

Nineteen

Karl Denver

Karl Denver

Karl Denver was born in Glasgow on December 16th 1931 and christened, so he told me, Angus Murdo McKenzie. Karl was one of the most talented men I have ever met. Having said that he was modest about his talent but he knew his worth and he never suffered fools gladly.

I first became aware of Karl in the late fifties as he was starting to make and impression on the Manchester entertainment scene. Friends of mine who where a couple of years older than me talked having seen this wonderful entertainer with a fabulous voice who was appearing at a venue in Wythenshawe Manchester Called The Yew Tree. I decided I wanted to go and see him as soon as possible.

When I did see Karl I was absolutely knocked out by the breathtaking speed at which he and his trio were able to perform even what seemed to me the most difficult musical manoeuvres with what he termed his African music. Then just when you thought you knew what his music was about Karl would surprise you with his` renditions of soulful country ballads. It was plain that Karl Denver really was something special a man with a remarkable talent.

Surprising as it may seem Karl was a very approachable man, a man who took time to speak and listen to his fans. I went up and spoke to him after the show and so began a friendship that lasted right through to the end his life.

It seems to me if my memory serves me well although I am going back forty years or more that his appearances at The Yew Tree overlapped his initial recording success. I do remember discussing his recording contract with him and I think it was after a performance at The Yew Tree. If that were the case it would be in keeping with the kind of person he always was with me, loyal to those who cared about him. If he was booked to appear somewhere, it was no good promoters offering him more money, he would always honour his bookings.

Karl Denver made many recording and to his fans they are all wonderful 'Marcheta', 'Wimoweh', 'And Never Say Goodbye' all spring easily to mind but my personal favourites were 'Pastures of Plenty' 'Still', and 'Dry Tears'. I am sure all the fans have their favourites. One thing is sure Karl Denver never made a forgettable record; each one was touched with his special magic.

When Karl was on stage with Kevin Neill and Gerry Cottrell making up The Karl Denver Trio the impact was electrifying, it seemed that Karl's voice was enhanced by Gerry and Kevin's musical ability the overall sound was second to none. The Karl Denver Trio toured the country receiving rave reviews, wherever they appeared. Cruel as it may seem even at the height of Karl's success sadness was never far away.

Karl Denver had three really bad car crashes in the early days of his career. One of them was very serious to the extent that I remember Karl actually performed with his jaw wired up. As always he gave a great performance for the fans ignoring the pain while he was on stage. When he came off he literally collapsed in agony as he reached the wings as he came off stage.

The Karl Denver Trio

But the worst of all the things that happen to Karl was something, which I felt affected Karl all his life. Karl's young son also named Karl was, killed in a street accident in Glasgow. Karl was naturally devastated at the time. Throughout the remainder of his life that was a tragedy I am sure from a similar personal experience, was never far from his mind.

Because of Karl's success in show business and the vagaries of life in general took Karl and I in very different directions and we did not see each other for long periods. As we made our journey along life's highway we would bump into one another at various times and these occasions the warmth of his friendship was always evident.

One these occasions occurred back in the Eighties, I noticed in the local paper that Karl was appearing in a Venue called The Napoleon in Cornwall Street, Manchester, so I decided to take my wife Margaret to see him. At this point in time I was looking after business for Tommy, it was unusual he wasn't gigging that night, so I suppose Karl and I were fated to meet up again. After the show ended I said to Margaret we will wait until Karl has signed autographs and then have a word with him. I thought it was only right to let the fans have the opportunity to speak with him.

When we went into the dressing room Karl and I talked for while, Margaret who had seen Karl handing out photographs to the fans asked if she could have a photo, Karl smiled and said no. Margaret looked crestfallen but Karl continued saying "I can't give you of these, because you are Dave's wife you are entitled to a special one. I'll tell you what, we will meet up again tomorrow night and I will bring you a really nice photo".

Karl was, as I knew he would be, good to his word – but in that moment I knew that a friendship that he had started more than twenty years before with young teenager meant as much to him as it always had to me.

During the next few years, because we were on the same entertainment circuit I saw more of Karl than I had since the early sixties. Because of this I became friendly with a member of his new backing group Keith Elliott, who I came to respect greatly. Keith is a man who I feel did more to help Karl extend his career in his later years than any of us. I also came to know Keith's brother Peter Elliott at the same time and he turned out to be one of the most talented and unique entertainers I have ever met.

Tommy Bruce also liked and admired Karl and often took the opportunity to see him perform, particularly when then they where both appearing in Spain. They would often meet up and go for a meal and a drink on the occasions they weren't performing.

It is worth mentioning that unfortunately Karl's record company did not treat the other two members of the trio, Kevin Neill and Gerry Cottrell as well as they treated Karl. In the early days when Karl was given cars to travel to gigs Kevin and Gerry were still traveling to them on the bus (not the only group who travelled this way). When you think they had to carry their instruments with them and that Gerry played a double bass, it would not have been surprising to find that there was some resentment.

To this day Gerry Cottrell and Kevin Neill have not received the recognition or the recompense that their contributions to the Karl Denver sound, their talent deserved. Having said that I also know that Karl did not get anywhere near the amount of money that it was rumoured that he did. In later years Kevin Neal carved a new and successful career with 'The New Bachelors'. Both Kevin and Gerry were fine musicians who helped Karl create one of the most exciting sounds in popular music.

We will all miss Karl Denver not just because of his great talent because he was a good friend. Even more important is the fact that like so many of our talented friends we will always remember you.

Sadly Gerry and Kevin both passed away before I completed this book.

Fans gather to pay respects at Karl's grave

Twenty

Carl Wayne

I sat down to write this chapter full of joy at the prospect of describing my dear friend Carl, the radio was on and I heard the awful news that he had passed away. I am continuing to write this chapter with a heavy heart knowing that he will never now how much Margaret and I liked and admired him, not just for his talent but also for his personality, the man he was. When Carl Wayne sadly passed away he was just 61 years old. He had been fighting cancer of the oesophagus for some considerable time. He faced his illness with courage and a generosity of spirit that showed itself in his continuing work for charity.

To say that Carl Wayne was just a pop singer would diminish his contribution to entertainment. From the very beginning of his career he was striving to make memorable music. One of his early bands, the Vikings were an outstanding example of the quality of musical talent coming out of the Midland area in the sixties having honed their craft in Germany Carl and the other boys hoped for success with record releases unfortunately it didn't transpire.

With Mike Pinder, Carl Wayne decided to form the M & B Five named after their sponsor's, local brewery Mitchells and Butlers. However things did not go as he had hoped so he left. Incidentally other members of the Group reformed as The Moody Blues.

His next band would bring the success his talent deserved joining up with Roy Wood in The Move and in spite of problems caused by there manager to do with the government of the day their recordings were successful. *'Flowers in the Rain'* was the first record played by Radio 1 when they began broadcasting in 1967. When The Move split Carl returned to the cabaret scene to great success and acclaim. But in spite of continuing his association with Roy Wood further success with recordings was not to be. Although, he is still remembered for TV's New Faces theme.

Carl's development as an entertainer continued as he performed on children's TV shows appeared in pantomime even at one point doing several commercials. He also played the part of the milkman in the long running TV show Crossroads. During this time he met and in 1974 married the lovely actress, Sue Hanson.

Carl and wife Sue
Courtesy of Weekend Magazine 1984

Moving into musical theatre he was in many productions but is perhaps best remembered for his role of narrator in the West End production of Blood Brothers. He also recorded CD's of songs from the shows.

Joining The Hollies as their lead singer in succession to Allan Clarke in the year 2000 he thrilled us once again with his soaring voice as he toured the country thrilling new fans as well as old. Survived by Susan and their son Jack he has left us all with a legacy of professionalism and quality of performance in many and diverse recordings. He was a gentleman in every sense of the word, my friend and he will be missed by us all.

TWENTY-ONE

MAC POOLE

Preface by Mac Poole

Mac Poole

Dave Lodge and I met and subsequently became friends because of his friendship with and management of Tommy Bruce. Right from the start I knew Dave was different, unlike many who come into show business late Dave is always prepared to listen and learn from those of us who have long experience in the business. Added to that he has great determination to get the best for his friends, he has unbelievable stamina, this a legacy from his days as a triathlete.

This was shown on one occasion when he made a four hundred mile trip to get Tommy Bruce to a gig at The Orchard Theatre, he had no right to succeed in the journey. Let alone make it on time, that he did is testimony to his loyalty, commitment and friendship for Tommy Bruce. He tries to always support his friends in times of trouble and he has always supported me, they say I am the most talkative man in show business but the many long phone calls Dave and I have shared prove that he is a serious rival for that title I am proud to say that Dave and his wife Margaret are my mates, the best I can say about Dave is that he is a good northern lad with strong northern values. Keep on Rockin' we all Love you. Mac Poole.

Mac Poole started his career in the early sixties playing in local bands in the Birmingham area, Mac brought his special mix of talent, enthusiasm and sheer hard work to The Mark V, Derrie Ryan and the Ravens, The Way of Life, Chucks, Locomotive and the band in which he first came to my attention Young Blood, although twenty five years would pass before

I would be privileged to call Mac Poole my friend. Mac is that rare breed of entertainer who excels with Drums and Vocals. This talent keeps him in popular demand with fans and artistes who choose to have him as a part of their shows.

In 1967 Mac found himself playing on the Isle of White with some success but it wasn't long before the bright lights of London were calling, and after working with Jimmy Saville at the Radio Luxembourg studios in Hertford Street he found the time opportune to form his own band Hush with producer Albert Hammond, (who wrote *the Air That I Breathe*) this combination recorded *Elephant Rider / Grey* a single much sought after as a collectors item today.

Hush had notable success as live performers and regular bookings came in but chart success eluded them, until the opportunity to work with Marsha Hunt star of the hit musical *Hair* who was at that time Mick Jagger's girlfriend, this association resulted in Mac being part of a chart hit *Walk on Gilded Splinters* this success was not to continue as Marsha became pregnant and retired.

Undaunted Mac formed Warhorse with such musical luminaries as Nick Simper (Bass) Ged Peck (Guitar) Frank Wilson (Organ and Piano) and Ashley Holt (Lead Vocal) The band recorded a few singles and two successful albums, Warhorse and Red Sea, both of which are now considered collector's items. This band toured extensively and helped to enhance Mac's growing stature in the Business.

1972 would find Mac living in France and touring with the band Gong. This experience helping to make the complete entertainer we see today. On his return to England he played with a variety of bands including Brett Marvin and the Thunderbolts (aka Terrydactyl and the

Warhorse

Dinosaurs) and had a hit with *Seaside Shuffle*, *Becket* (with Paul Kossoff from Free), *Broken Glass* (Chicken Shack),

Then Mac became house drummer for BearsVille (Bob Dylan's manager's label) in 1976, there he played on many albums and singles most notably Billy Oceans hit *Love Really Hurts Without You*. In the late seventies he worked with artistes such as Hazel O'Connor, Ian Hunter, Helen Terry and George Hatcher he also played drums for Mickey Jupp on the Stiff tour.

Tommy Bruce and Mac Poole with Tommy's platinum disc

In 1980 Mac was touring America with Jack Green who had a top ten album over there, on his return to England he recorded and toured with various bands before forming Orkestra with ex ELO members.

At the beginning of the Eighties Mac became involved with the revival of sixties music, being instrumental in helping get many of the names from the sixties back on the road, and keeping them there. He has been Musical director for P J Proby, the late Lonnie Donnegan, Billie Davis, Susan Maughan, Danny Williams, Craig Douglas, Ricky Valance, Jess Conrad, two more of our dear departed friends Screamin' Lord Sutch and Heinz, Mike Berry, Eden Kane, John Leyton, The Vernon Girls and significantly for me Tommy Bruce.

As Tommy's manager I am only too aware that without Mac's friendship and help, all that Tommy and I were achieved over the last twenty years or so, including Tommy's last appearance at the London Palladium, would have been doubly difficult.

None of us who aspire to keep sixties music alive could ever under estimate the contribution made to our efforts by Mac Poole. He has been a mainstay of The Solid Gold Rock and Roll show, which has been touring since 1995 featuring Marty Wilde, Joe Brown, Eden Kane, John Leyton and The Vernon Girls.

Other branches of the entertainment world benefit from Mac's musical abilities, Max Bygraves, Russ Conway, Ted Rogers, Ken Goodwin, Shane Richie and Joe Pasquali are just a few of the people he has backed in the country's most prestigious Cabaret Venues. He performed at St James's Palace with Norman Wisdom; he is always in demand to MD Pantomimes and just to keep things interesting he performs in a cockney duo act with a keyboard-playing partner, Mac on drums and vocals keeping up a stream of quick fire gags.

Over the years he has appeared in West End Musicals including Hair and Jesus Christ Superstar, He has also had walk on parts in television dramas such as, Dangerfield, Casualty, and Tom Jones. TV adverts have come his way Pepsi Cola being just one.

People in the business have a high regard for Mac, but one of the most complimentary and descriptive comments I have heard recently came from Jess Conrad. He said to me that Mac Poole is one of a kind and that we are so used to his professionalism and enthusiasm that we some times forget to show our appreciation. I am grateful for the opportunity in this book to put that right, if only in a small way.

In these politically correct times it may not be fashionable to say it but Mac is a wonderful family man a loyal friend and a true Christian who cares more for the well being of others than himself. This is doubly true at this time as Mac fight a real battle with ill health. God Bless you Mac we all love you man, you are not just a true hero of the sixties, but of any time.

Twenty-Two

Dave Sampson

Preface by Dave Sampson

I have known Dave Lodge for the past twenty five years, as a loyal friend, agent and a very honest person.

Let's deal with Dave as a friend first, along with his wife Margaret, he is one of the nicest people you could wish to meet. An example of this is during the late nineties I had a lot of health and personal problems, Dave and Margaret stood by me during this period consoling me, telling me to hold my head up and that the situation I was in was not the end of the world, if you know Dave you will understand what I am saying, because if he is anything, he is certainly a good talker!

Dave Sampson, Goffs Oak 1959

As an Agent he is second to none, he drives a hard bargain and gets what he wants in the end. I have seen him after a gig paying artistes out of his own pocket, when something has financially gone wrong: the venue knowing nothing about paying out on the night. (Boy haven't we all come up against that one!) There are certainly not many people who will do that for an Artiste, But Dave is a man of principle and as honest as the day is long.

Dave was the perfect man to look after Tommy Bruce, I knew and worked with Tommy for forty six years and he was one of the loveliest people in showbiz, but also one of the biggest worriers as well. Dave's cool guiding approach was the best thing that ever happened to Tommy... They were friends and soul-mates to the end.

Dave it is a pleasure to have Margaret and yourself as friends, Thanks for your loyalty, this comes from my wife Wendy as well, keep up the good work.

Dave Sampson Colombia Recording Artiste.

Dave Sampson to some degree qualifies as one of the unsung heroes of the sixties. He is a talented performer with an excellent voice, well respected by his peers. But, fate has somehow conspired to deny him the universal recognition that those who know him feel he has deserved. It should

Dave and Dave

be said that, with different management choices in the early days he might well have had a very different career in the business. From my point of view over and above his great talent he is a good and loyal friend.

Like many of his contemporaries in the late fifties Dave found himself drawn to the 2i's Coffee Bar here he was able to meet and mix with many of the performers who like himself would go on to be part of the exciting and new British Rock n' Roll scene.

The power and range of Dave's voice created a lot of interest and before long he attracted the attention of one of the finest exponents of the guitar the late and much missed Brian Parker. Brian had a band, The Parker Royal Five and when his lead singer decided to leave there was no hesitation in asking Dave to replace him. Easily combining Rock n' Roll with lovely ballads.

Dave's voice became very well known in his local Chingford area allied with Brian Parker's brilliant lead guitar, Norman Sheffield on drums, the late John Rogers on bass and Henry Stracey on rhythm the whole band had a very professional approach and it soon became apparent that the boys were destined for big things. A change of name for the group to Dave Sampson and the Hunters only helped confirm this. Having discovered his ability to write songs Dave seemed to have it all going for him.

A young man who was to become a friend of Dave's was just coming to the fore at this time, Cliff Richard. Cliff was enjoying the public acclaim and chart success that would continue to the present day, so it was only natural that knowing him, it was to Cliff he took one of his songs realising that if Cliff recorded it and had a hit with it his own success would be assured. Cliff listened to the song, liked it and took the tape to his recording manager Norrie Paramour.

Dave & Hunters 1959

Norrie liked the song but instead of letting Cliff record it liked Dave's voice enough to let him record the song the song himself and give him a recording contract, that sadly did not include The Hunters, the song was 'Sweet Dreams', it was a hit and Dave Sampson had a career. The Hunters continued to work with Dave and also went on to a successful career in their own right recording for the Fontana Label Brian Parkers composition 'The Storm' now regarded, as a classic was their most successful disc.

Dave Sampson & Cliff Richard

The top music television shows of the day saw Dave become part of the teen scene as it was known, Six Five Special, Wham, for which Dave was coached by the legendary Jack Good to whom Dave attributes everything good in his career and Oh Boy giving him the opportunity to work with Cliff Richard, Vince Eager, Marty Wilde, Terry Dene and his great friend Tommy Bruce to name just a few. He toured on the Larry Parnes shows appearing with another good friend The late great Billy Fury other record releases followed, *'If You Need Me'*, *'It's Lonesome'*, *'Easy To Dream'* all receiving critical acclaim and high praise from the likes of DJ and presenter Pete Murray but none as successful as his first release.

Dave Sampson with Clem Cattinni on drums

One of the highlights of Dave's career was appearing at The Royal Albert Hall with Jerry Lee Lewis another was meeting and becoming friendly with Ricky Nelson a friendship based on mutual respect for each other as performers, which lasted until Ricky's untimely death. It has been noticeable throughout Dave's career that other artistes recognise his talent and some have even found him to be an inspiration.

With the benefit of hindsight Dave has commented to me that it might have been better for him, to have approached another record label, there were others showing an interest at the time and not had the same manager as Cliff because of the similarities between them picked up on by the media, but how many young men would have turned down what was being offered? It must have seemed that all his dreams had come true.

Dave continues to work combining his love of Rock n' Roll with ballads; his rendition of Billy Fury's *Wondrous Place* has to be heard to be believed. He still has his Fans both here and in Europe a fact recognised by RPM in releasing his Album on CD. Twenty great tracks on RPM180 demonstrate the depth and versatility of Dave's talent. He appeared for me with Marty Wilde and Tommy Bruce the 5th July 03 at The Floral Pavilion, New Brighton and he says these shows

Clem Cattinni, Dave Chevron, Dave Sampson

were just like the ones that Larry Parnes put on and the guys still liked to have fun and entertain the crowd.

It is fair to say that Dave Sampson's relationship with his fellow artistes and the fans is a continuing success. He has recently worked with such luminaries of the music world as Clem Cattinni, Ray Fenwick and the legendary James Burton appearing once again at The Floral Pavilion in front of a packed audience, singing the songs of the late great Ricky Nelson, James Burton who as you will know played on Ricky Nelson's records and backed him when not working with another guy who was pretty good, Elvis Presley has been heard to say that Dave Sampson's vocal performance and professionalism is right up there with that of Ricky and Elvis, praise indeed, but no surprise to those of us who have followed Dave's career over the last fifty years.

I must mention Perry Smith who was a good and loyal friend to Dave throughout his lifetime, always there for him. Perry has been a good friend to me as well, indeed he provided some of the photos for this book.

Dave Sampson's associations with The Hunters have ensured that as long as there are Rock and Roll Societies around the world Dave will be held in high regard. Quite simply Dave is a great vocal entertainer, one who I hoped would continue to grace our stages for many more years. Sadly Dave passed away while I was editing this book. I wish his time had been longer as I had recently heard the news that he would have joined forces with two of Johnny Kidd's original Pirates, Clem Cattinni and Brian Grieg in a new band at some time in the future.

Dave, you and your wife Wendy were our true friends and Margaret and I loved you.

L to R - Pete Langford, Dave Sampson, Tommy Bruce, Dave Lodge & Tony Harte

Twenty Three

Lee Curtis

Mention Peter Flannery to sixties fans and you are unlikely to receive much of a response but if you refer to his alter ego Lee Curtis you will receive a very different response. Lee Curtis was right there at the outset of the beat revolution in Liverpool. In fact, but for the hand of fate in the shape of his brother he could very well have hit the big time before the Beatles. Brian Epstein was keen to sign Lee just before he linked up with The Fab 4.

Dave Lodge and Lee Curtis

However Lee's brother who had his own agency felt he had more chance of success with Lee's career than the then relatively unknown Epstein. Initially it looked as though he had made the right decision succeeding in securing a recording contract with Decca. At this point Lee Curtis's show looked to be well and truly on the road.

We need to backtrack to discover how the transition from Peter Flannery to Lee Curtis came about. On a night out with friends having his first drink and generally having a good time, it was suggested Peter get up to sing with the band. When he came off stage he was approached by some other young guys who were looking for a lead singer for their band, he had enjoyed performing so he thought it would be a good idea to give it a try. Peter's brother Joseph, Joe as he was and is known took a hand at this point because he was busy setting up an agency.

Joe suggested that the band should be called Pete Keen & the Keenmen Peter did not like this so the band kept the name they had at this time The Teenage Rebels fronted by Pete Keen this still did not really suit. So one of the band said what do you think of this, there is an American guy called Curtis Lee how about turning it round and calling yourself Lee Curtis? I like it said Peter and so Lee Curtis was born.

However Joe Flannery was determined to have some say in the group's name and after an initial suggestion of The Detours finally came up with the All-Stars. Although Lee thought it sounded a bit like a basket ball team, he could see some merit in the name particularly when Pete Best previously with The Beatles was brought in on drums.

Incidentally Glenda Collins was in Joe's agency and it should be remembered that when he turned down Brian Epstein Joe Flannery was an important figure on the Liverpool entertainment scene and could reasonably have expected to bring great success to his brother.

However life has away of slapping you in the face just when you think things are going well. Just as being turned down by Decca would turn out to be a good thing for the Beatles, conversely the contract for Lee would actually put his career into reverse. Recordings that showed great promise such as *'Lets Stomp'*, *'Little Girl'* and *'What About Me'* failed to chart and Decca showed a reluctance to keep up Lee's contract.

As Lee said to me recently the recordings were a couple of years behind the selling market something not realised at the time. Another thing that didn't help was that Lee and his brother lacked experience at this level of the business and never questioned the choice of material being recorded.

Although Lee was developing into an exciting stage performer, in fact I had the pleasure of seeing him at the Northwich Victoria Halls where he appeared on the bill alongside Tommy Bruce and The Rolling Stones around this period. I was knocked out by his performance. It was difficult to see how Lee's career could be taken forward at this time.

Pete Best had what seemed to be the answer; he had appeared with The Beatles at the famous Star Club in Hamburg so he suggested they go there. Lee Curtis & The All –Stars were at that time the only band to appear at the Star Club without being auditioned, which speaks volumes for Pete Best's reputation over there. A reputation that would soon to be equalled by Lee Curtis.

However the journey was not with out incident, all the guys in the band were arrested at the Dutch border because their visas were one day out of date. Held over night although the cell doors were not locked, and sent on their return journey the next the next day. Having run out of money so with out a penny to their name their plans of success once again on hold.

However visa and money problems solved they finally arrived in Hamburg and Lee became what he remains to this day, a rock & roll legend. His success was unequalled making more than seven thousand appearances at the Star Club in the company of great American stars such as Jerry Lee Lewis and little Richard.

During the years he spent in Germany he was perhaps forgotten to large extent in the UK apart from a flurry of excitement caused by a record made whilst in Germany. Having made what could be called a Star Club album plus a single *Ecstasy / Shot of Rhythm and Blues* he sent a few copies home to his family in Liverpool.

Brother Joe never one to miss an opportunity, sent his copy to the Pirate station Radio Caroline and it made a great impact becoming record of the week fans requesting plays and also wanting to buy it. Once again Brian Epstein still with NEMS at the time, phoned Joe to find out how to get copies of the record, Joe contacted Lee who in turn through his sources in Germany found out it was Phillips who had the rights to the Star Club label.

They in turn rushed through a supply of the disc to the UK sadly it was to late, by the time all this had been done music fans of the day had moved on to something else. With hindsight it might have been a good idea to relaunch the single with label backing as the recording still creates interest to this day. I have been involved in the release of a CD for Lee, called The Two Sides of Lee Curtis, writing the sleeve note, and when news of it's impending arrival got out several Emails and letters arrived welcoming the idea and all insisting that Ecstasy be included.

Now Lee's career in the UK is moving again, he once again starts out on Merseyside, working with the guys who were around when he first exploded on the Liverpool scene all those years ago. He takes part in the efforts of two excellent charitable organisations, The Mersey Cats and Sounds of the Sixties performing with such luminaries of the Liverpool beat generation as King Size Taylor & the Dominoes, Farrons Flamingos, Karl Terry and the Cruisers, Nicky Crouch's Mojos to name but a few.

He came back into my life when he appeared on the bill with Bobby Vee at The Floral Pavilion New Brighton letting me and many others see that the power of his performance is undiminished. In fact I had no hesitation in booking him to appear with Tommy Bruce at The Leeds City Varieties as part of a show were the proceeds went to Breast Cancer Research. He recently appeared On Del Richardson's Good Rockin' Tonight show on Radio Caroline and also Mike Adams Record Collector show to great listener acclaim.

Lee Curtis is right up there with the best of British performers if you see him advertised go and see him if you love Rock & Roll you won't be disappointed.

Twenty-Four

Ricky Valance

Preface by Ricky Valance.

I first met Dave Lodge more than thirty years ago, he was working in his capacity as personal manager to the late and much missed Tommy Bruce. Tommy was of course a colleague, friend and fellow recording star of the sixties. It was obvious from the start that there was a tremendous bond of friendship between Tommy and Dave. It was also clear that Dave was fairly new to the business in fact as Tommy put it "a little bit green". That being the case, what impressed me most about Dave was his down to earth sincerity and determination to learn what being a good professional artistes manager was all about.

Ricky Valance

I am happy to be able to say that I watched Dave grow into the man and manager he became over the years. He did this despite many pitfalls both personal and professional and has become, in my opinion having spent the best part of fifty years in show business one of the best managers in the business. There are very few people I can honestly say I respect, but Dave Lodge is one of them and I am proud to be his friend. Enjoy his story of the friends he has made along the way.

Ricky Valance International Recording Star.

Ricky Valance has had a diverse and interesting life to date. His life has been filled with success in the entertainment field and more importantly he has enjoyed a happy and successful marriage to his wife Evelyn. Ricky Valance has without doubt been one of the most successful artistes to have been born and started their career in Wales. In his capacity as a Columbia recording artiste, Ricky Valance has achieved No.1 status in the charts and in the process he has been awarded Silver, Gold and Platinum records in recognition of his success. Perhaps his greatest achievement has been the longevity of his marriage to his lovely wife Evelyn. In a business were marriages fail with an alarming regularity theirs has stood firm. Ricky Valance is a good family man and in my experience a devout Christian.

Things could have been very different, as Ricky was a bit of a tearaway in his youth. Nothing serious but like some other wild teenagers, my self included his escapades could have got him in to trouble with the law.

Ricky surrounded by admirers

However this inherently decent young man realised like many of us that there is a time when we should grow up. So Ricky left the foolishness of youth behind and took the opportunity to volunteer to serve in the RAF.

That sensible decision led to problems though. As when he was enjoying a little rest and recuperation while stationed in Singapore Ricky went swimming. At one point he dived into the pool striking his head on the bottom jarring his neck. Although he did not realise it at the time he had actually broken his neck. This would result in Ricky being airlifted to hospital more than forty-five years later in 2007. Ricky was involved in a car crash when travelling back from a gig with wife Evelyn. When the paramedics arrived they thought he had broken his neck and so called for the air ambulance. It was only on arrival at the hospital it was discovered that thankfully, although he had severe case of whiplash, his neck was not broken – it was the combination of the whiplash and the old injury that had given that impression.

Ricky's wild time as a youth was not forgotten by him. He feels that he was fortunate to put this start to his adult life behind him without serious problems and would like to think he would be able to prevent others making any silly mistakes. He is always happy to speak of that time at youth groups, in the hope that he can help them follow the right path.

Ricky Valance was very successful in putting the foolishness of youth behind him and so achieve a recording career. A massive hit *'Tell Laura I Love Her'* was merely the foundation stone that his longevity in the business has been built on.

Although his career has been to a large extent musical Ricky Valance has also excelled in the acting field. During a period between 1963 and 1965 Ricky studied his craft during two terms at The Actors Forum. Ricky then went on to appear with distinction in Television series such as *The Plane Makers, No hiding Place* and *Maigret* to name just three.

In 1967 Ricky moved to Ireland for a while to front a show band called 'The Chessmen' with great success. During this period he re-recorded *'Tell Laura I Love Her'* with his own definitive version of *'Twenty Four Hours From Tulsa'* on the B-side. In 1969 Ricky's vocal talents drew him to the attention of Decca who recorded a track called *'Six Boys'* with him. This song featured prominently in the top 100 best selling singles reminding the record buying public once again of his remarkable vocal skills.

In the period between 1970 and 1974 while continuing to perform in the UK Ricky Valance took his talents to the international stage. Cabaret engagements in Singapore, Tehran and Poland ensured that new audiences appreciated his vocal and stage skills.

In 1975 Ricky Valance made a strong move in a new direction touring with

Margaret, Ricky, Dave and Evelyn

his own country band. After touring for a couple of years establishing a new following, in 1978 Ricky made his first Country Music Album on the Tank label. Titled *'Rainbows'* this established him as a British country music star.

In 1975 because he was still keen to diversify and show his talent for acting Ricky played the role of Hindley Earnshaw to great acclaim in the classic tale of *Wuthering Heights,* appearing at The Richmond Theatre Yorkshire and The Bournemouth Playhouse. He also played the lead role in Ken Lees' famous production *'Leave Him To Heaven'* at The Connaught Theatre Worthing.

In 1980 Ricky started his successful American country music career in San Antonio Texas working in the top country music venues. Also he appeared on TV singing a new song titled *'Time After Time'*.

His career in Europe continued to go from strength to strength appearing in Cabaret in Holland, Germany including TV appearances, and Belgium. His popularity also extended to West Africa.

In 1989 he appeared by special invitation on the top rated American TV show, Nashville Now, achieving an audience rating of over 70,000,000 viewers.

In 1990 Ricky showed yet another side to his talent when presenting his own radio show on Chiltern Radio Supergold it was called The Ricky Valance Magic Music show it became very popular and ran for two years.

In a six-year period during 1990 to 1996 Ricky Valance was picking up nominations and awards in recognition of his talent. These included the top male vocalist award and the audience nominated best solo artiste at the memories of music club festival. Also in recognition of his contribution to popular music The Variety Club of Great Britain gave Ricky a prestigious award.

In 2001 Ricky recorded his first American Album in Nashville, It was titled *'One Of The Best'* the success this album had prompted the release of a single titled *'Mother Loves Another Man'* this got into the Nashville charts making Ricky the first British performer to achieve this.

In 2005 Ricky was given the opportunity to present his own TV chat show in Spain this showed once again that he is not just a one dimensional performer. Ricky Valance is a multi talented and multi skilled artiste.

Just to show that his talent is physical as well as cerebral Ricky is a fine golfer and he won The Dunhill Masters Celebrity Pro Am on no less than three occasions with three different partners. First in 1987 with Ken Brown, 1988 with Jose Riviera and then he succeeded again in 1992 with Jeff Hawkes.

Ricky Valance and his wife Evelyn are two of our most valued friends Margaret and I hope to spend more time in their company.

Not for the first time or the last in my life, I am very grateful to Tommy Bruce for introducing Margaret and I to so many wonderful people.

Recently Ricky received a lifetime achievement award at the Millennium Centre in Cardiff, where he was recognised as the first Welshman to have a number one record in the charts in 1960 with *Tell Laura I love her*. This recognition is long overdue.

Ricky has experienced some ill health recently, but with the love and care of his lovely wife Evelyn, he is out on the road performing again. So his fans will be enjoying his talent for some time to come.

Twenty-Five

Ronnie Carroll

Ronnie Carroll made his first public appearance at the Ulster hall in Belfast, where he appeared with Ruby Murray having been booked by Ruby's father for the splendid fee of two guineas. At the time I was working for thirty shilling a week, he liked the idea of show business because he had previously worked for five and a half days for that sort of wage. More to the point that first performance showed that the public liked him.

Ronnie Carroll

Nat King Cole influenced Ronnie Carroll vocally during the early days of his career. He loved Nat's relaxed style. His initial success as a singer meant that he had to make a hard choice. Ronnie was a very talented footballer and several of the clubs in his native country Ireland, wanted him to sign professional forms with them.

On the day he got a really lucrative offer by telegram to join *The Hollywood Doubles* He also received a telegram From Portadown Football Club offering him a contract for exactly the same amount – £8.00. This of course was an awful lot of money back then. He decided that he would enjoy a longer career as a singer and not have to get kicked around the park every week. So thankfully for his many fans Ronnie's vocal career took off.

A very personable and likeable man Ronnie Carroll has enjoyed a career that has been full of highlights. He has sung at Windsor Castle for the Royal Family, taken part in to Eurovision Song Contests and saw his recording of *Roses Are Red* go to the top three in the charts. Although for him the two songs that he enjoyed recording the most were *The Very Thought of You* and *Maria*.

While Ronnie is happy to have enjoyed success in the sixties because it was a wonderful era, with a marvellous atmosphere and people seemed happier and enjoyed life, believing anything was possible. He also still hankers after the music of the big bands from the thirties, forties and fifties. Hopefully by the time this book has been published he will have achieved his ambition to live in a cottage with the waves of a rough sea breaking on a beach close his front door. Once there he will take quiet walks with his dog Meg and reflect on his successful career.

Danny Rivers, Ronnie Carroll and Mike Willets

Sadly that was not to be as Ronnie passed away in 2015 depriving us of his great talent and his warm friendship.

Twenty-six

Pete Oakman

Another man for whom I have great respect is Tommy's longtime friend Pete Oakman. As Tommy always said Pete is one of the good guys, probably best remembered for being one of The Bruvvers Joe Brown's backing group, Pete deserves to be remembered in his own right. He wrote the song that more than any other, in the opinion of millions of fans is the most identifiable number of Joe Brown's sixties recording career. That song written in conjunction with Johnny Beveridge called *Picture of You* was not just a hit it also changed the musical direction that Joe and The Bruvvers were taking.

Pete Oakman

Pete and his older brother Tony were there right from the very beginning, together they started a skiffle group in 1957 called The Spacemen. The line up underwent a few changes but by the end of 1958 the group consisted of Pete on bass, brother Tony banjo, George Staff rhythm, Sid Rodwell washboard with Joe Brown on lead guitar. In 1959 this line up came to the attention of the afore mentioned impresario Larry Parnes who was looking for talented musicians to be a backing band for a forth coming tour. The line up consisting of Sally Kelly, The Viscounts, Gerry Dorsey (Later to become Englebert Humperdick under the auspices of Gordon Mills, at that time one of The Viscounts) and Marty Wilde.

Pete recalls that the change name came about due to the influence of Jack Good innovative producer of the now legendary 'Oh Boy' show on television.

As he says Jack also produced our first record and thought we needed a new name. In conversation Joe said well we are like bruvvers, so we became Joe Brown and the Bruvvers. As the Joe Brown and the Bruvvers they would also go on to support Gene Vincent the great American rock and Roller.

Tommy Bruce, unknown, Frankie Connor Mike Berry, unknown, Pete Oakman & Son, Steven

The Bruvvers

Pete Oakman continues to perform with The Bruvvers and as a guest in other bands to this day, It has to be said that his musicianship is second to none and it is worth mentioning that his son Steven has inherited Pete's musical talent and is much in demand.

Twenty-Seven

Don Lang

Don Lang

Although Dong Lang was not destined to be one of the people who I can claim as my friend I did I am pleased to say come into contact with him a few times. He was though a great friend of Tommy Bruce and conversations with Tommy about the wonderful man that Don was added to the short time spent in his company made me feel that we were friends. The first of the occasions I spent in his company was on 'The Legends of The Sixties' Tour organised by Chris Black and Didi Melba and then on a Six-Five Special tour in the early nineties sadly during that tour Don went into hospital and died. He had previously told Tommy, that he was suffering from incurable cancer when on a plane coming back from Spain.

That did not stop this remarkable man performing right to the very end.

Don Lang was a special man and a special musician, born in Yorkshire and christened Gordon Langhorn he found fame playing Trombone and singing in dance bands. Whilst still performing under his given name he began to be recognised for his trombone playing with bands led by the great band-leaders of the day like Teddy Foster and Vic Lewis. He was recognised for the vocal talent he also possessed by Ken Mackintosh and he would be credited as such on the label of the bands records.

Musically Don had ambitions to play Jazz in his own style so he decided on a solo career in the mid fifties. During this period he recorded for Decca records and then in 1955 he signed for HMV making a fabulous recording of *Cloudburst* with a great rendition of scat singing. In 1956 Skiffle was the musical craze in Great Britain Don now with his own

Band the Frantic Five began to make an impact in Skiffle music and then in the follow on Rock 'n' Roll.

A really big break came for Don and his band when the legendary Jack Good came up with the innovative new television show Six-Five Special Don recorded the shows theme song and it instantly became his defining song. Even now fourteen years after his death people can't mention one without the other. Although that said getting Don Lang and The Frantic Five into the charts did not prove easy in spite of the regular television appearances.

That changed in 1957 when Don and the band got into the charts with *School Day* which was a cover of a Chuck Berry song. Then he stormed the British top ten with a song written by David Seville, *Witch Doctor*. Incidentally David Seville went on to create those delightful characters Alvin and the Chipmunks.

Although chart success again eluded Don after that he and The Frantic Five went back to jazz / pop music on the Dance Hall circuit having a successful career right through the sixties. He was also in great demand as musician for recording sessions and in 1968 Don was chosen as one of four trombonists to play on the Beatles song *Revolution 1* for the groups' *White Album*.

Don played on the sixties revival circuit right up to his sad death in 1992. He also continued to perform and play Jazz right through the seventies and eighties. More importantly Don Lang was quite

Heinz and Don Lang

171

simply a lovely man with a great outlook on life. He was as likely to be seen driving his pink Vauxhall Cresta as he went down to buy out-of-season strawberries from his local shop, Cullens, in Wimbledon for impoverished school children, as he was to be seen playing with the great bands of his day. We will all miss Don and I often listen to his recordings and remember the quietly spoken kind man, who was our friend,

It is worth mentioning that Don's musical talent lives on in his son Brad Lang, who is an accomplished bass player. Brad's career has seen him play in bands such as ABC, Jade Warrior, Wham and Wisbone Ash.

Like his father he will be well remembered by the record-buying public. It is fitting that I should end this chapter with the words that Tommy said to me before I met Don; "Don Lang is a lovely man". He was and that is how I shall remember him.

Twenty-Eight

Brian Poole

Preface by Brian Poole.
Over my years in the Rock and Roll business, I have had the pleasure of meeting and working with many of the R&R gentry who preceded the bands of the sixties. People like Billy Fury, Cliff Richard, Eden Kane, Marty Wilde, 60's icon Jess Conrad, (I know he's an icon because he told me to call him that), Sounds Incorporated and of course the inimitable Tommy Bruce. As the years went by Tommy introduced his manager and friend Dave Lodge to me. We in turn formed our own friendship and when Tommy sadly died I was able to talk to and help Dave, who was devastated at the loss of his best friend.

Brian Poole with the author

I said to Dave then and I still believe it now, that his book about Tommy, 'Have Gravel will Travel' would be a fine tribute to our old mate. Indeed I believe it will eventually come to be regarded as a piece of history. As will I believe Dave's current book 'The Long Road' in which we all get a mention. When the Tremeloes and I got together again after a gap of forty years for our recent tour I invited Dave and his wife Margaret along to see the show and Dave kindly reciprocated by reviewing the show for The Beat Goes On. Once again Dave 'wrote as he saw it'. It was refreshing to actually talk to the person who was reviewing the show and as always have another pleasant meeting with Dave.
Last year I attended a memorial dinner given for Tommy Bruce and although Dave was still upset at the death of his best friend Tommy he organised the afternoon and evening at The Grosvenor House Hotel immaculately. Everybody from our era was there and speeches were made by many including Dave. If Tommy had seen this, (he probably did) he would have been proud

of his friend Dave, who to this day keeps the memory of Tommy Bruce alive. So on Tommy's behalf I will just say, Dave Lodge was a fine friend to Tommy and continues to be a good friend to many more of us old rockers. Thanks Dave! Brian Poole and Family.

When Brian Poole phoned me at the time of Tommy Bruce's death to offer his condolences and remind me of his is continuing friendship. I was pleased also to also be asked by him to come out with my wife Margaret and see him whilst he was on tour with the Tremeloes. When we did go along and see the show it was at The Burnley Mechanics Institute.

That night not only did Brian show me the depth of his friendship for me he along with the guys in the band brought back my love of the music which seemed to have died when Tommy passed away. Because I thought that for me, without Tommy the fun had gone from the entertainment industry. But as the show progressed and we were being treated to all the hits. Including *Here comes my Baby, Suddenly you love Me, Me and my Life, Call me Number One and Silence is Golden.* These songs performed to such a high standard and Margaret and I came to realise that we were actually enjoying ourselves. In fact I found myself being carried along by an irresistible wave of audience participation. So much so that with the song *Hellula Hellula* the seats in the auditorium became a nuisance as we all bopped, sang and waved their arms in any space we could make.

Brian and Pam

It would be impossible to write about Brian's early life without mentioning a least three other people his wife Pam who he married in 1968, Pam, has been there for Brian in all he tries to do, Dave Munden a kind and thoughtful man, who was with Brian from the very beginning as the Tremeloes drummer, Dave has recently been in hospital for operations to have both hips replaced. I hope he is fully recovered by now and of course Alan Blakely an extremely gifted musician and song writer who sadly is no longer with us. The band was formed in the late fifties after Brian and Alan had been working as a duo during 1956/57. The lads actually came together after having known each other while still attending school, Park Modern School in fact. Incidentally Brian excelled at playing rugby union while still at school he was selected for his county, Essex in the same position I played, wing forward. In his younger Brian was an excellent all-round athlete playing football and basketball as well as rugby.

Brian Poole with the Tremeloes

When the boys first put the band together they just called themselves the Tremeloes and did not have a lead singer. Brian has since been known to say that it was just because he wore the same glasses as their idol Buddy Holly that he was picked to be lead singer. Personally as someone who wore the same glasses, (see the picture of me standing beside my speedway bike) I know that it would have more to do with the quality Brian's voice and that rare commodity charisma that he got the job. Brian's real gift is that his fans love him because they feel he is just the same as them, always one of the boys. Artistes of his calibre, have a unique gift, the gift of being natural in all they do. Brian fills the stage with his presence and these days doesn't need to sing, although he does, because the audience are so moved in his presence that the sing every song for him as soon as the opening bars are heard.

There is no one like Brian Poole in this respect; I have often seen audiences sing along but not while their idol just stands and smiles at them. Brian's performance is simply best that British entertainment has to offer and people love him for himself. Of course Brian doesn't spend all his time on stage just letting the audience sing he always gives his all with his performance and rendition of the hit songs we love to hear. Songs such as *Do You Love Me, I want Candy, The Three Bells, Candy Man, Twist and Shout* and of course a special favourite, *Someone Someone.*

However I should mention that Brian's success is not just limited to being a performer he has also became a successful businessman during the period when he was retired from performing. During this time he ran the family butcher's shops and his own record company, Outlook Records. He is also a published author. One of his books entitled *Talkback* about Cockney Rhyming slang is a delightful reading experience. It is very humorous with a laugh on every page. In 2008 Brian also recorded a very fine solo album *Antique Gold*

I remember that in 1988 Brian as part of 'The Corporation' also affectionately known as 'The Travelling Wrinkles' the members of the band were, Brian, Tony Crane from the Merseybeats, Reg Presley The Troggs,Clem Curtis The Foundations and Mike Pender The Searchers. This was a great line up and I recall that they recorded a very exciting version The Showstoppers *Ain't Nothin' But A House Party.*

Brian was drawn back to performing by the sixties revival movement which started nearly thirty years ago. I think all the Tremeloes can thank Chip Hawks for deciding the band should get back together in 1979. Indeed at time of writing Brian appearing regularly on the Reelinanarockin' tours with other sixties luminaries such as Tony Crane and Dave Dee.

Brian is not just loved by the fans he also has the respect and love of his fellow performers, people like the late Tommy Bruce, Brian's fellow Tremelo Len 'Chip' Hawks, Tony Crane of The Merseybeats and Dave Dee are just a few of the many who have all had long held affection for this lovely man. Brian has an inherent goodness and love of his fellow man that you can only be born with. Indeed it has to be said that we all have the benefit of something truly wonderful when we say Brain Poole, oh yes he is friend of mine. Margaret and I are very glad that many years ago Tommy Bruce gave us the chance to get to know Brian and his beautiful wife Pam.

I think this would be a good time to draw attention to the fact that many of the guys from the fifties and sixties had offspring who would go on to be talented entertainers in their own right. Take the examples of Marty Wilde and his daughter Kim who had great success in the seventies. Tommy Bruce's daughter Lorraine is one of this countries finest actresses and his son Thom is a fine singer songwriter. Joe Brown's daughter Sam enjoyed chart success. The list goes on and Brian and Pam Poole's daughters are no exception. Michelle, known as Shelly to family and friends and her sister Karen enjoyed great chart success as 'Alisha's Attic'. Both of these young ladies are excellent songwriters – their song *I Feel* was nominated for an Ivor Novello award in the best lyrical, and melodic composition category in 1997. They both continue to be musically creative; for instance Shelly, who is married to Texas guitarist Ali McErlaine, has I believe written songs for Westlife, Boyzone and the alternative country band 'Red Sky July' with whom she also continuing her singing career.

Karen who is married to fellow songwriter David Etherington has written songs for Kylie Minnogue, Will Young and Annie Lennox.

Brian has been very ill recently following an aneurysm. Thankfully when I spoke to Brian and his wife Pam recently he assured me he is well on the

Brian Poole with the Tremeloes

road to recovery and will have been out on tour again by the time this book is published, sharing the stage with two of his oldest friends - Dave Munden who has I believe added knee surgery to his previous operations and Len 'Chip' Hawkes who has recovered from previous health problems. Margaret and I are glad to hear this good news because we need good friends like Brian Poole around us, he really is the best of men.

Twenty-Nine
Len (Chip) Hawkes

I cannot say that I know very much about Len Hawkes or that I have any interesting stories to tell about him. That said he finds his way into this book because of the kindness and consideration he showed me, someone he had only met briefly on a couple of occasions, after Tommy Bruce's death. He spoke of Tommy with great respect and I appreciated that, it was one of the things that helped me get back on track as it were. Therefore it is only right that I pay some small tribute to him here. I only wish I had the ability to truly make you aware of the remarkable man he truly is.

Len Hawkes

Len 'Chip' Hawkes that has already had many great things said about him and his talent, by people who know him better than I do. He is quite simply unique, his abilities as a songwriter are legendary his musicianship is of the highest calibre and his voice is a joy to listen to. He fills the stage with his presence and his evident joy at performing is shared by his audience.

Len Hawkes, as far as I am aware, started playing music in 1962 with The Horizons. This band also had as far as I know a guy called Rod Evans in the line up – who if I am not mistaken went on to become the original singer with Deep Purple. The Horizons like many other bands in the early sixties went to Germany to ply their trade and hone their skills.

In 1965 Chip made a great career move by joining Brian Poole and the Tremeloes. However Brian Poole would leave the group about two to three years months after Len joined to try a solo career. So Chip and Alan Blakley looked for and found a song called *Here comes my Baby* which proved to the group's first world wide hit. Over next few years

The Tremeloes enjoyed constant chart success with some great songs including *Silence is Golden* which was a No.1 hit and sold one million copies globally. Just to really boost the group's prestige in Chip Hawkes they had really great song writer at the very height of his abilities.

Never one to stand still musically Len Hawkes took the decision to leave The Tremeloes and move with his family to the USA. He signed for RCA and began recording in Nashville Tennessee. Over a period of five years Len worked with many of the top country artistes of the day, enhancing his own reputation in the process.

Returning to the UK Len decided to reform the original Tremeloes in 1979, going on to successfully tour the UK and the rest of Europe until 1988. At this point Len's son Chesney had a massive hit with *The One and Only*. This success prompted Len to leave the group again to look after business for Chesney.

After a couple of years it seems that Chip was missing performing so he went back to touring with the Chip Hawks band, following that incarnation with the great band The Class Of 64. This group featured Chip, Mick Avery (The Kinks), Eric Haydock (The Hollies) and another friend of ours, Alan Lovell,

Quite simply Len is the best at what he does the way he does it. He adds a great sense of humour to his vocal and musical talent when he performs. Putting his show together a with timing and panache that is rare among the modern crop of performers, Len makes sure that the sheer joy and sense of fun coming from the stage is so infectious so that you can't help joining in.

At this point I feel I should mention Chip's lovely wife Carol who is a talented actress and game show hostess in her own right. She is a great mum to sons Jodie and Chesney and is clearly the reason that Chip Hawkes gets up in the morning and plays such wonderful music.

Brian Poole and Len Hawkes

From a personal point of view Margaret and I found that being in Chip's company was a pleasure that leaves you looking forward to the next time. Like another of our friends Chris Eyre, Chip has the gift of making you feel that you were the person he most wanted to speak to. He really is a thoughtful and considerate man.

Chip Hawkes list of achievements is endless. He is worthy of a book all to himself as that would be the only way to do proper credit to him. Therefore my efforts to describe him are totally inadequate. I can only hope that my brief words encourage you to go out and see him perform, because he is quite simply one of the most charismatic and talented performers around today. He is always worth the admission fee and on top of that he is a really nice guy who thinks of others. Not a bad combination when you come to think about it.

Thirty

Terry Dene

One of the most pleasant people that Tommy introduced me to is Terry Dene. Terry is a far greater talent than has been recognised and had it not been for his sensitive and to some extent nervous disposition he would have spent more time at the top of the entertainment ladder.

He was born Terrence Williams in 1938 in the Elephant and Castle area and worked after leaving school as a record packer at a pressing plant. He liked listening to the American artistes of the

Terry Dene with Dave Lodge

fifties and fancied he could probably sing as well as they did. So he started playing at the 2i's Coffee Bar in Wardour Street London and soon showed that vocally he was going to be a sensation.

Before long he had come to the notice of Jack Good the man responsible for discovering and nurturing many of the exciting young stars of the Fifties and sixties. After appearing on Six-Five Special Terry signed and recorded for Dick Rowe at Decca and had his first hit with *A White Sports Coat* this recording sold 300,000 copies in the first seven weeks after it's release. Other hits included *Stairway of Love* and *Start Movin*.

He also starred in the film *The Golden Disc* which was a biopic of his rise to fame.

However as successful as Terry was becoming, and although the fans loved the sound and the look of him, Terry was a little disappointed. This was because he wanted to perform songs in the style of the Americans he had been listening to because he wanted to known as a real Rock and

Roll singer. He need not have worried to this day he is still regarded by many, as Great Britain's best rock and roll performer

His feeling of frustration were to become even greater. Although *The Golden Disc* was a great success and he had the adulation of the young people of Britain, who were proudly wearing badges proclaiming that they were 'Deneagers'. Terry's career was about to be interrupted by his call up for National Service. This would be a disaster, as he was unable to complete his service due to medical reasons. The newspaper reports at the time vilified him when he was found unfit to complete his service as they thought it was just a cop out. This turned many of the fans against him. To my mind this was totally unjustified as Terry appeared to be on the verge of a nervous breakdown at the time so he should never have been called up in the first place.

I can state quite categorically that he did not bale out of his National Service in an attempt to keep his career going, as many people wrongly assumed. It was simply the fact that at the time he simply wasn't well enough to undergo the physical and mental ardours of basic training. In point of fact the effect on his career in the short term was catastrophic. As Terry has said to me on more one occasion the Ted's simply turned against him. Most of them had done their National service and took the newspaper reports about him getting out of the army to continue his career quite literally and so vilified him for being unpatriotic, this was never the case. Also during this time thanks to the media, Terry's relationship and breakup with Edna Savage was being carried out in the public eye. Terry's health suffered and his nerves became so bad that he actually went into a monastic retreat.

Terry Dene with Chris Black

He did attempt to come back onto the music scene during the sixties with varying degrees of success but never achieved the recognition his talent deserved. That that said he did enjoy a very successful period in the seventies as a gospel singer.

I first met him in the late seventies and then worked with him as with many of the sixties guys during the Legends of the Sixties tours. These tours were on the road in the late eighties and early nineties. It was plain even by the time we got into the nineties more than forty years after recording *A White Sports Coat* that he still suffered from nerves about every aspect of his performance. There was no need for him to feel that way because, his voice and performance made him a total success on the tour and in every show I have seen him in.

Terry Dene on stage

Since then we have bumped into each other, several times and I have even booked him on shows with Tommy on quite a few occasions and I am always pleased to see him because I have always found him to be a warm hearted and generous human being.

As I write this book I am pleased to say that Terry's life and career have taken on new meaning and direction, which I think is wonderful. This is largely due to him having a wonderful lady called Lucia in his life. I have to say that above all else Terry Dene is the ultimate survivor, long may he continue to have the life and career he deserves.

Terry Dene, Tommy Bruce, Brian Gregg & Dave Lodge at the Elvis Museum Lliverpool Docks

183

Thirty-One

Freddie Garrity

Freddie Garrity
Courtesy of Freddie Garrity

Freddie Garrity a good friend too many people including me passed away on Friday the 19th of May 2006 after a long and courageous battle with illness. Because Freddie was only 65, having been born on the 14th November 1940, he left those of us who knew him feeling not just a sense of loss but also a sense that he had shown us all what having a good time was all about. Freddie was because of his seemingly perpetual sense of fun and good humour was one of sixties music's most loveable performers.

I was very fortunate to know Freddie during different times in his life, starting way back when he was doing variety of jobs selling shoes and then brushes before finishing up as a driving a milk truck. At that time having been singing with Skiffle group the Red Sox which also I believe included his bother Derek. Thinking back I remember that Freddie joined a band called The Kingfishers who would later rename themselves Freddie and the Dreamers.

There have been few British performers who enjoyed the success on both sides of the Atlantic that Freddie and his band The Dreamers achieved. His was a special talent that brought him not just the admiration but the love of his fans. He made great recording that brought him into our homes through the medium of radio and also TV. They included *If You Gotta Make A Fool of Somebody*, *You Were Made For Me* and *I'm Telling You Now*.

His stage performances for those of us privileged to see him were frenetic to say the least. I defy anyone who saw him as I did jumping up and down singing *Who Wears Short Shorts*, with his trousers round his ankles with his boxer shorts on display, after as I recall, running round dropping the trousers of the band while they were playing, not to have been in tears of laughter. Then there would be tears of a different emotion in the audience as he sang the lovely ballad *I Understand*.

Freddie and the Dreamers
Courtesy of Freddie Garrity

During the Eighties and Nineties Freddie came back into my life when he appeared on shows with Tommy Bruce. The last of these shows being at Birmingham Town Hall around 1992. Though we had both changed physically over the years I found Freddie to be the same likeable guy he had been before he achieved his great fame. We then went our separate ways until he spoke to me on the phone after his heart attack in 2001. We remained in contact after that and seen each other from time to time. Most recently in the company of another friend and supporter of Freddie, BBC Broadcaster Fred Fielder.

I spoke to Freddie on a few occasions and we often discussed his successful career both here and in America and how life had treated him. It was always a pleasure to speak to him and I am glad to have had that last conversation with him. Although I would have wished for many more conversations and more time in his company.

To my mind the things that stood out about him indeed defined him even more than being a hugely successful entertainer were his humour and the incredible courage he showed during his illness. Whenever we

Courtesy of Freddie Garrity

spoke there was laughter as he told me jokes and even read excerpts from what he told me was his funeral speech full of anecdotes about death and Viagra and coffin lids.

Freddie also spoke to me on many occasions of his love for his wife Christine and of the love and support given to him by her. She was with him he said at a time in his life when he had to take more than he could give. Having spoken to Christine on several occasions and had the pleasure of meeting her I feel that is not how she saw things.

There is no doubt that Chrissie and Freddie were a great team and I feel that at a time in his life when he might have known nothing but despair, Chrissie gave him all the love and support that he needed to make his life worthwhile. Freddie Garrity was the father of four children and a friend as I have said too many people, he was my friend and I will miss him because of his warm sense of humour and love of life.

Thirty-Two

Jet Harris

One very special and talented man that Tommy Bruce introduced me to was Jet Harris. Born Terrence Harris on the 6th July 1939 in Kingsbury North London. Terry was known to his school friends so he tells me as Jet because he was a speedy runner who raced around everywhere. Terry or Jet as we have all come to know him started work as an apprentice welder making milk churns.

Jet Harris
Courtesy of Jet Harris

Jet Harris played in several bands before meeting Hank Marvin, Bruce Welch and Tony Mehan. As a result of this meeting he would become a member of The Drifters – Cliff Richard's backing band. This association would lead to Jet Harris becoming one of the most iconic musicians of his generation. At some point it was realised that there might be some confusion with an American group also called The Drifters, so it was decided that the group change it's name to Cliff Richard and The Shadows. Incidentally Jet told me that he was the one who came up with the name, if that was the case and I have no reason to doubt that it was, it was an inspired idea. In any event as a member of The Shadows Jet Harris was destined to be a part of some of the most exciting music to be created in the sixties.

The Shadows
Courtesy of Jet Harris

Because of their marvellous musical ability The Shadows were the biggest band in the country during the years 1959 to 1962.

How ever life has away of surprising us all and Jet Harris was no exception to that rule. Because he and Tony Mehan would not have the enduring success with the Shadows that Hank Marvin and Bruce Welch would go on to enjoy. Although they are both forever linked to The Shadows early and wonderful successes with recordings like *Apache*.

Initially when they left the band 1962 Jet and Tony very quickly achieved great success, forming a duo together and recording distinctive tunes like *Diamonds*. It is worthy of mention that Big Jim Sullivan helped Jet to master the 12 string Bass that he used on that recording with Tony Mehan. Incidentally some you may have forgotten as had I until Jet reminded that in 1963 *Diamonds* went to No.1 in the charts knocking The Shadows recording of *Dance On down* to No.2. As Jet put it when he reminded me, "Oh the sweet irony of it".

Working with Tony in the duo also gave Jet more opportunity to bring his natural if dry sense of humour to the stage. Having interviewed Jet for local radio I have experienced this humour first hand and I couldn't stop smiling all day. Jet did introduce me to Tony Mehan and I had the pleasure being in his company on a few occasions and found him to be a smashing bloke. Coincidently Tommy Bruce's son Thom played in a band with Tony's son for a while, it is quite amazing to think how different generations of artistes from the sixties find their way to performing together. Having just started to get to know Tony, I was very sad when I heard that he had passed away following an accident at home.

Unfortunately Jet was involved in a serious car crash when things were going rather well. In that crash he suffered serious head injuries and there were other problems the combination of these things caused Jet to disappear from the public eye.

Things were pretty bleak for a while with only a brief appearance in The Jeff Beck Group's line up in 1967 to show for his musical ability in this period. Jet Harris just dropped out of the music industry and found work where and when he could. During this time he found employment as a photographer, bricklayer, laborious, bus conductor and hospital porter. There was even a time when he sold cockles on the beach in Jersey.

It was as he said himself well known that he had a drink problem but he fought back from that affliction and took a prominent role on sixties revival shows. You will have read various reasons for his problems with drink and depression, I will not be adding anything about that, except to say it was disappointing that he was not invited to perform when Cliff Richard and The Shadows reunited to perform on The Royal Variety Performance in 2008, that being the same year he was starting his fight against throat cancer. I am pleased to say he was awarded a much deserved MBE in 2009, in the same year he was winning his battle with throat cancer.

On a happier note in more recent times I am pleased to say that Jet Harris has been working with Billie Davis and that excellent band The Rapiers performing on the highly successful Me and My Shadows tour.

Jet has endured many reversals of fortunes and difficulties in his life. For the most part undeserved so I am glad that he seems a last to have found contentment in both his life and career. This upturn is to a large extent due to having a lovely lady in his life, called Janet Hemmingway. I wish him well in his new lease of life and hope that this continues for many years. Jet Harris has also really benefited in recent times by having Peter Stockton looking after business for him. Peter is one of the good guys and he is taking a lot of the stress out of Jet's life.

Courtesy of Jet Harris

Fates hand strikes again and I find myself having to write the words, that sadly Jet Harris passed away on March the 18th 2011. Our hearts went out to Janet who I know cared deeply for him. Margaret and I mourn the loss of the lovely gentleman who was our friend. His many fans will also mourn his loss, once again we are thankful for the many recordings Jet has left behind.

Thirty-Three

Jean Vincent

Preface by Jean Vincent

Jean Vincent

If I am honest (which I have a bad habit of being!) I don't really recall when I first met Dave Lodge. That is because Dave is one of those people you feel you've known all your life. He is a naturally kind helpful man yet he never patronises or fusses, which for me in particular is a wonderful combination. Being a disabled woman in the predominantly male dominated world of rock 'n' roll it would be easy for people to either to smother me with kindness or ignore me completely. Dave has always managed to get it just right, lending a hand when needed and walking away when not. I remember being quite envious of dear Tommy (Bruce) because he had a Dave Lodge. Dave was Tommy's rock, never faltering in his support for all Tommy did. Their friendship both personal and professional was clearly built on the kind of mutual respect that can only be earned.

"Dave and his lovely wife Margaret are like family to me and I hope they are on the scene for along time to come…"

Jean Vincent International rock and roll artiste and recording star.

Jean Vincent is more than just a great entertainer, and simply awesome rock and roller. She is quite simply one of the most beautiful women I have ever met, her eyes sparkle and she has an inner glow that exudes from her in the form of her love of life and everything in it. She is a wonderful courageous lady who along with her husband Kerry, who is a hell of a guy, gives much of her energy to bring up the three marvellous children they have between them, Josh, Jamie and Rebecca.

It is difficult to know where to start with the story of Jean Vincent. Because she lives such a full life she seems to pack more in to one day than most people are able to pack into a month.

Jean spent much of her childhood in hospital being operated on and treated for a hip deformity (although you would never believe it when you see her). This problem was so severe that at one point there was a possibility that Jean might not be able to walk. Jean has never dwelt on this problem and I respect her far to much to do so now, as it says in the song she is *'a whole lot of woman'* and would not appreciate my even hinting that I felt sorry for her suffering.

Her passion for music was probably started by her Gran, who brought a radio into the hospital for her one day. As Jean told me she was just coming round from yet another anaesthetic when she saw her Gran, by her bed, holding out a radio. That radio was her constant companion bringing Dreamers, Dakotas, Drifters and hundreds of other visitors flooding into what she termed her 'cell'. That was when her dream of being an entertainer began; Jean wanted to be in that radio, making music, being in a band. To become part of the world of vocal entertainment. In effect to hold as she termed that magic wand that all singers posses.

Of course there was a long way to go before Jean would achieve her goal. She would encounter stupidity and prejudice along the way but the dream would continue to thrive. Once having got out of the prison she termed being in hospital her thoughts turned to how she was going to make a living. Writing was something she enjoyed and so journalism seemed a good option. By the time she was in her early twenties Jean was established on her local newspaper and they had recognised her forte for her abilities as a top line indepth interviewer.

However Jean's love of music was eating her up as she longed to perform. She would go along to audition for any band that advertised for a singer. Jean wouldn't say this (but I will) the people looking for a singer, were stupid, ignorant and prejudiced fools they never even allowed her to sing. Just because Jean limps they just said you wouldn't be able to dance so you won't do. What fools they were, that is probably why their bands never made it and what is more Jean can dance. I can honestly say that from the first day I met Jean I have never looked at Jean differently than I would any other women. She is a beautiful talented lady and the fact that these people could not see that astounds me.

However these set-backs could not dampen Jean's enthusiasm for the music and she was soon operating her own mobile disco, DJ-ing not just on gigs but for hospital radio. In the summer of 1977 still the local newspapers star reporter Jean would meet someone who she says made her the dynamic performer she is today. Billy J Kramer was due to appear in Dudley at a club called the Jodari.

The owner was described by Jean as a huge black man with a mouth full of big gold teeth, her friend Sam. After plugging the show on her hospital radio show, she turned up at the club to do the interview. When she did she met Johnny Miller, who was Billy J Kramer's drummer who became her friend and remains so to this day.

Through meeting Johnny Miller, Jean was drawn deeper into the music business as he introduced her to more musicians and that special breed in Jean's eyes – singers. Out of this came a sense of belonging, once again borrowing Jean's own words the kind of feeling you get when you smell your breakfast being cooked or you come home to find someone has warmed your slippers by the fire, in this company she really felt at home.

Through her friendship with John Jean met another musician, Chris who at that time was the bass player with Dave Berry and the Cruisers. Jean and Chris really hit it off and in 1981 he became her first husband.

Chris was and still is totally dedicated to his music. Jean's double life of day and night jobs fascinated him and as they grew closer Jean told of her dream; she wanted to be a singer. Chris turned her dream into his mission and on Jean's twenty first birthday he took her to a recording studio. Chris had brought along some of his musician friends to play for Jean and he had done arrangements for two songs that he and she had written together. The studio owner co-produced the tracks and said that Jean sounded a little like Melanie. He listened intently and said I like your voice Jean; he never once asked if she could dance.

By this time Chris had left the Cruisers and the record deals he had been offered had not come up to scratch. So he suggested that Jean formed a band with him. A friend, Harry, was asked to come along and take some publicity photos. When he turned up he looked at Jean and said, "Hello Jean Vincent", this puzzled Jean and she asked if Harry thought she sounded like Gene, "no" he replied, "but you walk like him!" Not at all offended Jean thought about his words and a four- piece skiffle-abilly band called Jean Vincent and the Nite Capz came into being. The Band featuring a very excited Jean on vocals recorded their first single. This single, a spoof version of Doris Day's recording *Deadwood Stage,* would become a cult hit and even to this day Jean is asked to sing it during her live performances. Their independent record company, Abacus, very astutely released the record at the beginning of December and put the band on an amazing tour of shopping centres. Traveling the country in a single decker bus attracting legions of new fans, Jean and the guys thought they had cracked it and a Christmas hit seemed assured.

Then the first sign of a problem appeared, when the fans went into the record shops, wanting to buy the recording, it wasn't there. An under the counter black list of singles to be held back until December the 28th was in force and *Deadwood Stage* was on it. The major players in the record business had intervened and the band's efforts had been in vain.

Jean Vincent and the Nite Capz tried to keep going but in the end having run out of money and being really disillusioned with the business, the band split up and they all went their separate ways.

But Jean Vincent would not be denied – she had her 'magic wand' and she knew that her adventure had only just begun. Looking in the Agents directory she picked the number of a man who is a giant of the business in more ways than one Paul Barrett. Paul Barrett is in my opinion one of the greats of the world of show business. Fierce and intimidating but always scrupulously fair, Jean could not have found a better agent. Paul soon launched Jean's career as a solo artiste in Europe and she was soon at home on her circuit. Working with people who in her mind were legends, like Marvin Rainwater, Joe 'Ducktail' Clay, Joe Brown, Marty

Wilde Graham Fenton and the irrepressible Wee Willie Harris, Jean was really living her dream.

Although she did not meet Paul Barrett for some time and all communication with him was carried out over the phone. This was put right on one the rock and roll weekenders that were held at holiday camps up and down the country. One night there was a knock on the door of Jean's caravan and standing there was the big man himself, Paul Barrett. He had a bottle of brandy in one hand and a tin of tuna fish in the other. "Dinner" he boomed, his powerful voice resonating in the air. At that moment Jean knew she had found a real friend for life.

Sadly Chris and Jean's marriage came to an end in the early nineties but they have remained good friends and they have a fine son, Josh, to remind them of the good times. Jean eventually found happiness with second husband Kerry, as I have already said is a hell of a guy. Jean met Kerry at a gig; this is a really romantic story that I am sure Jean will relate when she publishes her own book.

Jean is a favourite of all the many people in show business that know her, and she has favourites of her own. Some of them are mutual friends and some of them have, sadly passed away. People like Dave 'Screamin' Lord Sutch who made her laugh, indeed Dave told me on more than one occasion that he thought a lot of Jeannie both as a performer and as a person.

Then of course there was Tommy Bruce, Tommy made Jean feel safe and always looked out for her on gigs, Tommy, like me looked on Jeannie as we call her, like a daughter and had great admiration for her. What more can I say about Jean Vincent? Only that she is a very special lady who my wife Margaret and I feel blessed to know. How lucky we are that she likes us and counts us as her special friends.

Thirty-Four
Jean Fergusson

Jean Fergusson is one of those rare people who simply does not know how beautiful she is. With her sparkling eyes and captivating smile she has heads turning whenever she enters room. Jean has a youthful and vivacious persona, so the fact that she will always be remembered for being the most glamorous pensioner in the Dales, is a real testimony to her acting skills.

At this point I have to give Jean the credit she deserves for the sixteen years she spent researching the life of Hilda Baker. This research revealed a life so colourful that it just had to be turned into a play aptly titled *She Knows You Know*. By doing this Jean showed that her talent extends beyond being a fine actress.

Jean Fergusson

In due course, 1997 to be precise the play came to the stage with Jean in the leading role. Not just any stage but that of The Vaudeville Theatre in the West End, receiving rave reviews and being nominated for an Olivier Award for Best Entertainment. Radio 4 went on to commission Jean to adapt it for radio, then they transmitted it as a Saturday Playhouse.

There was more to come from this gifted lady was commissioned to write Hilda Bakers biography in 1997. By doing this Jean realised a long held ambition, as like me with Tommy Bruce's biography, Hilda's story was her first attempt at a book. Incredibly Jean may not have finished with Hilda Baker's life yet as she has written a screenplay which will hopefully be commission as a film or adapted for Television. Hilda Baker, I am sure could never have dreamed that some one would do so much to immortalise her life.

The depth of Jean Fergusson's talent as an actress is shown by the variety of roles she is cast in. Jean is the performer that all producers and directors must dream of when they come to into rehearsals. The reason for this because in Jean they have some one who will always gives one hundred and ten percent. This has been proved on the countless occasions, far more than I can hope to remember here, that Jean has captivated audiences with her interpretation of so many

Dave Lodge & Jean Fergusson

leading roles. Here from memory are just a few of the roles that Jean has played on National tour, Eva Reich in *Five Blue Haired Ladies sitting on a Green Park Bench*, Brenda in *Bed full of Foreigners*, Betty in *Breeze Block Park*, Maggie in *Suddenly at Home*, Ana Marten in *Maria Marten* – an incredible list. If that is not enough Jean did a variety tour with Jimmy Cricket and The Roly-Polys reprising her role as Hilda Baker. During this tour the Roly-Polys taught her how to tap dance, to me this once again shows Jean's appetite for hared work when it come to her profession.

It is very likely that Jean Fergusson has appeared in every theatre in every town and city in this country. If she hasn't it will certainly only be a matter of time. Just to show how Jean travels the length and breadth of the country I offer the following examples. Jean has taken the title roles in many of these plays, *The Prime of Miss Jean Brodie*, Linda in *Death of a Salesman*, Mrs Hardcastle in *She Stoops To Conquer*, Mrs Malaprop in *The Rivals* these roles where all at the West Yorkshire Playhouse. At Birmingham Rep Jean played the part of Mrs Northrop in *When we*

Lynda Baron, Jean Fergusson & Juliette Kaplan

are Married, Miss Marple at The Theatre Royal Windsor. Performances in the West End have been at The Whitehall where she took the part Mrs Cowper in *Cash on Delivery* and also the previously mention self penned work *She Knows You Know* at The Vaudeville Theatre. All this and I haven't even mentioned her television appearances yet.

Amazingly for one so young Jean even had the role of Caroline Herbert in *Crossroads*, it seems that there are few series and serials that have not had need of Jean's talent. As is shown by appearances in *Coronation Street*, as Helen Ashcroft and as Mrs Tremayne in *All Creatures Great and Small*. The list goes on Mrs Minton in *A Woman of Substance*, Mildred in *Lipstick On Your Collar*, Mary Newson in *Peak Practice*, Brenda Wallis in *Doctors*. Of course Coronation Street recognising that Jean's talent is such that it is impossible to typecast and so brought her back again to in the role of Mrs Mallet. The fact is that even though Jean continues to give outstanding performances as Marina in *Last of the Summer Wine* she is such a consummate professional that what ever role she plays you never feel confused as to who you are watching.

Robert Fyffe & Jean Fergusson
Photo courtesy of BBC

Time spent in Jean's company is a delight she has warmth of spirit that seems to welcome you as the most important person she has seen all day. In Jeans company sparkling conversation abounds, she really is the person you would most want to share a bottle of wine with. Her generosity is clear for to see in her kindness to her friends and her support of charitable functions.

Indeed some of my best times at The Heritage Foundation Lunches have been spent in the company of Jean and her Last of the Summer Wine co-star Juliette Kaplan who plays Pearl, Howard's long suffering wife. Juliette is an accomplished actress in her own right and I am sorry she doesn't get more television roles. In fact I think a spin off from *Last of the Summer Wine*, Featuring Jean, Juliette and the other outstanding member of the trio Robert Fyfe, who plays Howard, would make a splendid vehicle for their talents.

Quite apart from her acting talent Juliette is a fun lady and I have always enjoyed the times I have spent with her. She makes me laugh and knows how to enjoy herself; I really look forward to seeing more of her in the future and hopefully getting to know her better.

Juliette Kaplan, Dave Lodge and Jean Fergusson

Lynda Baron is another of the fine actresses that can be found in Jean's company and is another lady who casting directors should recognise as having immense popularity with the general public and bring her back to our television screens on a regular basis.

Returning to Jean, I have to say that Margaret and I think the world of this warm-hearted special lady and hope to enjoy many more years of friendship with her.

Thirty-Five

Mike Berry

Mike Berry

Those who think of Mike Berry as a Buddy Holly clone do him a great disservice because he is a multi-talented artiste who continues to enjoy success in all aspects of the many facets of his career. From a personal point of view I have witnessed first hand that Mike Berry is an exceptional talent and is someone who I am pleased to consider to be a friend of mine. Again it thanks to Tommy Bruce that I met Mike and like the other sixties entertainers he was one of the first to say he would perform in Tommy's benefit show at the Wyllyotts Centre. Mike is a quiet man who doesn't suffer fools gladly so I always appreciate time in his company and I have never known him to let his friends down.

Mike of course was one of the successful artistes to come out of the Joe Meek stable. He may not have had the biggest hits during his time with Joe Meek but his *Tribute to Buddy Holly* has to be one of the most memorable records to come out of the sixties.

Of course Mike is multi-talented having achieved success both as a musician vocalist, he is also an actor of some note having appeared in long running TV series like *Worzel Gummidge*. We also remember him taking over from Trevor Bannister as the long suffering junior member of staff, Bert Spooner in *Are You Being Served?* in which he appeared with another talented man who Margaret and I liked immensely John Inman. Other notable members of the cast included Arthur English who I had the pleasure of knowing all too briefly, Wendy Richard who I know slightly and admire greatly through our association with the Heritage Foundation, Molly Sugden and Frank Thornton who I met for the first time when I took my friend Norman Wisdom on to the outdoor set of *Last of the Summer Wine*.

Life started for Michael Bourne in September. 1942 and by the time he left school at the age of fifteen to become an apprentice compositor his vocal and musical skills were already in evidence.

Mike formed his own Skiffle band 'The Rebels' and apart from being the lead singer he augmented the sound on washboard. In a very short time he had progressed from Skiffle – with the improvised instruments of tea chest bass and washboard to a band with electric guitars and a drummer. This gave Mike the chance to put the washboard down and concentrate on vocals. After this change in style it wasn't long before people in the music business realised there was something special about Mike. The band made a demo disc in John Hawkins studio in South London. Mike took the demo to work with him and a colleague there said he knew a man in show business, Peter Raymond, who knew a record producer who might be interested in doing something with the band. After coming to see the lads perform Peter Raymond became Mike's manager. One of the first things he did was to contact Jack Good, producer of the '*OH BOY!* television show and then he followed up by speaking to the soon to be legendary independent record producer Joe Meek. This was probably upsetting for John Hawkins who had plans in mind for Mike and the band which included signing them up with West End recording studio IBC with a view to getting them a recording deal with Decca or EMI.

Although Mike went to see Jack Good he actually signed with Joe Meek which has since commentated was probably a mistake as the television exposure Jack could have given him a hit record in a fairly short space of time. As it turned out it took several months before Joe had a record ready for release the song, *Will You Still Love Me Tomorrow?* had been a hit for The Shirrelles, but I think Mike rightly as it turned out had his doubts about it's suitability.

Released on the Decca label as I recall the recording failed to make the top twenty, however at least Mike had achieved an ambition to have a record released. It would be almost a year before Joe finally came up with a recording that would bring Mike chart success.

Peter Raymond had by this time got Mike out on the road touring with the Outlaws as his backing band and Joe Meek's idea of Mike as Britain's Buddy Holly brought the haunting and melodic *A Tribute To Buddy Holly*, a song I believe was written by the talented Geoff Goddard, to fruition. This would be Mike's first hit and subsequently would be released giving him a No.1 hit in the Netherlands,

The song also enjoyed success with the fans in America and laid the foundation for the popularity he still enjoys there today. So much so that I remember Mike telling me once that Buddy Holly's parents wrote to him and thanked him for keeping their sons memory alive.

It was around this time that Mike came to the attention of Robert Stigwood the impressive young Australian manager who is mentioned in other chapters of this book. Stigwood was the first person of any note who recognised that Mike was more than just a pop singer. He identified Mike's versatility and realised that he had unique talent which he would seek to promote.

Mike's next recording *Every Little Kiss* just missed out on chart success, but the show was really on the road now and the follow up disc once again written by Geoff Goddard, *Don't You Think it's Time* literally flew into the top ten. With that success came bigger and better tours in which Mike appeared alongside American artistes of the calibre of Brenda Lee, Bobby Vee and the Crickets. The Rolling Stones and The Beatles also benefited from having Mike Berry on the bill with them and of course Mike was making television appearances by the score. However show business in for most artistes a bit of a roller coaster ride and by the seventies Mike was looking at other aspects of his life. At one period he indulged in his passion for motor racing but his interest in music never waned. Because of this he went back in the studios and recorded a country album entitled *Drift Away* which drew some interest from America and resulted in a tour of New Zealand.

Mike also had a top ten hit in the Netherlands at this time with *Don't be Cruel* which led to afore mentioned No.1 hit there with *A Tribute To Buddy Holly* While enjoying these successes Mike decided to make the move into photographic modelling and television commercials. He was very successful in this area and while filming a commercial he was asked by television director James Hill who asked Mike if he would like to play the part of Mr Peters in the forthcoming production of *Worzel Gummidge* which had Jon Pertwee in the title role.

Mike was a great success in the role and appeared in every episode. Incidentally in what was another good career move for Mike at Jon Pertwee's suggestion signed with Jon's agent Richard Stone. Always a loyal man in my experience and still with ambitions musically Mike then contacted long time friend Chas Hodges who had enjoyed his own success musically with another former Outlaw, Dave, as the popular due Chas and Dave.

They decided that Chas would produce Mike's next album – a wise choice not only did this liaison produce two successful albums. More importantly there were three successful singles on of which was Mike's fantastic rendition of *The Sunshine of Your Smile*. As Mike was then in great demand he was immediately signed up for a bill topping tour of Great Britain's theatres, appearing with another good friend of mine Jimmy Cricket, and Aiden J Harvey, the singer compère was Tommy Bruce and although I am not sure Mike remembers this during the Tour Tommy introduced me to Mike for the first time. Mike followed this successful tour up with among other things some pantomime work. His agent Richard Stone seeing that Mike had a gift for comedy acting put him forward to read for the part of Bert Spooner in the popular television series *Are You Being Served?* He was successful and appeared in the last three series not mention two Christmas specials.

Mike's acting career has seen him in theatres up and down the country in productions as diverse as *James and the Giant Peach* and *Pinocchio*.

Mike co-wrote and starred in a quite brilliant rock roll musical *Tutti Fruiti* from which ensued an equally successful sequel, *Great Balls Of Fire*

Mike Berry deserves all the success which has and will continue to come his way. He even delighted his fans by recording a Christmas single, *Hi There Darlin' Merry Christmas* under the name of his *Are You Being Served?* character Bert Spooner in 2007 showing that he is as innovative and creative as he was when he first stated out as teenager.

Tommy, Mike Berry, Pete Oakman & Son, Frankie Connor

When Tommy Bruce first told me about Mike Berry prior to introducing me to him he said, "Mike is a man who you will like and respect" Tommy wasn't wrong my respect for Mike grows more with each year I have known him. I wish Mike and his wife happiness and success throughout their lives.

Thirty-Six

Eden Kane

Eden Kane (Richard Graham Sarsted) was the first of the talented Sarsted Brothers to achieve chart success. Born in New Delhi India. In 1943 his mother and father decided to move the family to Kurseong near Darjeeling because his father had got a job managing a tea plantation. A few years later Richard and his younger brothers Peter and Clive were sent to various boarding schools. In 1947 the family moved again, this time to Calcutta. However due to India gaining independence Richards parents decided in 1954 that would be best for the family to move to England due to political unrest at the time.

Richard was an intelligent and articulate boy who also excelled on the sports field. He played a range of sports, including football, cricket and field hockey to a very high standard. Indeed such was his athletic prowess he achieved championship status in the High Jump. He had serious intentions to be an architect indeed on leaving school Richard worked in London as a trainee architect.

Richard came from a musical family, both his grandmother and mother had been trained in classical music and his father could play a variety of instruments, excelling on the banjo. He decided to learn the guitar after picking up one that belonged to a school friend.

Rock and Roll was in its early stages at this point and skiffle was very popular with the British youth at this time. Richard and his brothers formed the nucleus of a skiffle group called the Fabulous Five playing in Youth Clubs and Coffee Bars in the London area. In 1961 the Classic Cinema in Kings Road Chelsea put on a talent contest which Richard entered and won. Fortune smiled on Richard that day because to of the judges, Michael Barclay and Phillip Wadilowe were record producers who recognised that here was a good looking young man with talent. They signed Richard onto a management contract, which would put him on the road to stardom. Cadbury's Chocolate had put on the talent show to promote their drinking chocolate and sponsored Richard to make his first record. The song called *Hot Chocolate Crazy* was written by Richard and it was played as a jingle on Radio Luxembourg earning him the title of 'The Chocolate Troubadour'. When Decca Records heard the jingle the offered Richard a record deal, which he accepted. The first thing Decca did was change Richard's name to Eden Kane. The thinking behind the name was Eden sounded biblical and Kane was chosen by Michael Barclay because Citizen Kane was his favourite film. A new image was thought up, the immaculate white suit and Eden Kane was on his way.

Eden Kane hit the charts with a bullet; *'Well I Ask You'* went straight to number one in 1961 and was followed by a string of hits. *'Get Lost', 'Forget Me Not', 'I Don't Know Why'* and *'Boys Cry'* all made it in to the top five, the hits just wouldn't stop coming.

The big plus point for Eden Kane's management was that he was and still is a charismatic performer who wowed audiences wherever he performed. On the strength of his record sales and exciting performances Eden began to tour the UK with the top names of the day, people like Helen Shapiro, Dusty Springfield, Marty Wilde, Cliff Richard and Joe Brown to name but a few. Eden also toured the UK with his own band The 'Downbeats' the line of which was Roger Retting, Ben Steed, Roger Sinclair and Bugs Waddell. Sometimes the band included his brothers Peter and Clive (AKA Robin) who would go on to enjoy their own recording successes. Malcolm Cook who in later times would work with Eden's British Management Company, The Hal Carter Organisation was his Tour Management.

In 1964 at height of his career Eden recorded *'Boys Cry'* which gave new impetuous to his career at a time when some of the other solo artistes were suffering from the invasion of British groups, led by the Beatles, into the charts. The success of *'Boys Cry'* gave Eden the chance to tour Australia where he was already popular and New Zealand. He was so successful during the tour that Australian television gave him his own show. He also went to entertain the Australian troops in Vietnam this thoughtful act served to increase Eden's popularity over there even more. During this time Eden worked with Roy Orbison, Del Shannon, Peter and Gordon, The Searchers and PJ Proby. Naturally romance played a part in Eden's life and in 1969 having know her for about six years, he married one of America's leading showbusiness Journalists, Charlene Groman, sister of 'Hart to Hart' star Stephanie Powers. Following the marriage Eden decided to make his home in Los Angles where he continues to live today This has proved to be a long and happy marriage during which time the couple have had two children Ami and Robbie.

Dave, Dell Richardson and Eden Kane

Not having performed for a few years and living happily as Richard Sarsted again Eden was still an entertainer at heart and keen to get back on the stage. After recording the 'Worlds Apart Together' album which gave a musical chronology of the brothers life together starting from their days in India and continued through to their successful musical lives.

In 1989 Hal Carter invited Eden to tour the UK with Marty Wide and Brian Hyland. The tour was a great success and made Eden determined to return to the UK on a regular basis. In 1993 he flew in from the USA to appear on Capitol Gold's Anniversary concert at the Royal Albert Hall. Following his appearance there he joined Marty Wilde and John Leyton in great show entitled 'Oh Boy!' – the success of which prompted Hal Carter and Derek Nicol of Flying Music to tour a production called the 'Solid Gold Sixties Show'. It starred Eden Kane Marty Wilde and the Wildcats, John Leyton Joe Brown and The Bruvvers and The Vernon Girls. The show was so successful that there have been six nation wide tours to date.

Dave and Eden Kane

I met Eden Kane and his wife Charlene during that tour and I would like to think that we enjoy mutual respect.

My reason for this thought is that in 2007 following the death of my great friend Tommy Bruce in 2006 Eden Kane contacted me from his home in America and asked if I could help him to perform in the UK again. With this in mind he even flew over from the USA to Windsor so that we could meet up. He took took me out to lunch, during that lunch we agreed to give it a go.

The result of that we embarked on a short and enjoyable tour for Eden Kane and the Citizens in March and April 2008. We didn't play a lot of dates but the ones we did, delighted Eden's fans, As always he gave stellar performances and he took time to speak to his fans and sign autograhps

Margaret and I greatly admire Rick Sarsted (Eden Kane) and his music and I was grateful for the chance to spend time in his company. I would also like add that anyone would be lucky to work with Rick Sarsted, he is a true professional.

I end this chapter by saying that Margaret and I wish Rick and his wife Charlene long life, happiness and success in all they do.

Thirty-Seven
Julie Felix

I have to say that Julie Felix is a mystery and an enigma to many people as she has always seemed to disappear from view when she not performing. Nothing could be further from the truth, because Julie is always working tirelessly for other people, her efforts help to make the world a better place. I met Julie at the funeral of my dear and much loved friend Kay Garner and her innate goodness immediately came shining through. I think we both felt that we were destined to meet and I am very glad she took the time to speak to me.

Julie Felix

Julie Felix is an unusually attractive lady whose appearance belies her birth date. Julie was born on the 14th of June 1938 in Santa Barbara California. She is of Welsh, Mexican and American Indian descent. Julie brings a style and a flair to her music that moves her away from mainstream folk and indeed brings something special that is not found in any other musical genre.

I enjoy her music and her company; Julie cares for all things on the planet and works for the awareness that will bring about the preservation of all species of life.

It was a lucky day for British entertainment when Julie Felix landed in England during 1964. With all her worldly goods in a duffel bag and a Mexican guitar that had been a gift from her father Julie embarked on a continuing career that to date has lasted more than thirty five years.

Firsts have been the norm for this lady right from the start when she was the first solo folk artiste to be signed to a major record label when DECCA signed her. In 1965 she was voted Britain's First Lady of Folk by

The London Times. Incredibly in the same year Julie was the first British based folk singer to sell-out The Royal Albert Hall.

Being the resident singer on the popular Television show The Frost report in 1966 was instrumental in making Julie Felix a household name. Due to this fame she became the first popular singer to perform in Westminster Cathedral, she did this as part of the Cathedral's 900 Anniversary celebrations.

By 1967 Julie Felix's popularity was so great that Brian Epstein made her top of the bill for a week-long production alongside Georgie Fame at London's Saville Theatre. Incidentally newcomer Cat Stevens was the support act on that occasion.

Julie Felix was going from strength to strength; success followed success from the sixties through into the seventies. A hit on her own record label with *If I Could*, (*El Condor Paso*) in 1970 would lead to another decade of success. In December of 1971 Julie much to her great delight had a beautiful daughter, Tanit, However she was soon back in the studio and in 1972 Julie released her first LP *Clotho's Web* on the Mickie Most's RAK label. During the same year she appeared in New York on David Frost's US television show. Followed this success with her second hit the Hot Chocolate song *Heaven is here*. Julie has had hits in Norway and Sweden and I have no doubt her popularity will continue.

Julie Felix has wonderful philosophy on life, which she has been kind enough to share with us. Julie tells us that life is a journey, a journey that in her case and in common with the rest of us has been a journey filled with laughter and tears. As Julie says we should all help each other on that journey and Julie Felix helps others more than most.

It is our privilege to know Julie and enjoy her music and share in the good that she brings to the planet.

Thirty-Eight
Tony Dangerfield

On the morning that I heard Tony Dangerfield had died sitting in his chair reading a book, I had just finished writing the following chapter. That made the news an even greater shock to me. Tony knew I was including him in this book and with that slow smile of his had said I look forward to that Dave, sadly he will never read it and fully know what I thought of him.

The greatest shock about his death to me and I am sure many others was the manner of his passing. He lived his live in a way that epitomised the legendary rock and roll life style and I always thought of him going out in a blaze of glory. With his guitar in his hands lunging towards the audience, with his eyes sparkling and his teeth flashing, looking larger than life in a sleeveless T shirt with his biceps rippling. It just goes to show you never can tell what is waiting round the corner...

Tony Dangerfield was referred to by many as a rock and roll journeyman, but I found him to be an innovative musician who constantly strove to reinvent himself He was as much at home with the blues, ballads as he ever was with rock and roll. He first came to the notice of Joe Meek as part of Screamin' Lord Sutch's Savages. But Joe saw a front man when he looked at this good-looking and charismatic young man. Always in my experience a loyal friend Tony went back to the Midlands to get the guys in his previous band Gulliver's Travellers, Johnny Bedder on guitar and Neil Norman on drums so That they could share in what he hoped would be great success.

As soon as Joe Meek saw the band he changed the name to Tony Dangerfield and the Thrills, they added two other guys to the line up but sadly their names escape me. I know Tony told me the Bass player was nicknamed The Elf and that a guy called Mick played piano. If Tony was ever sober enough in our conversations to tell me their full names, I was never sober enough to remember. Sorry guys I am sure you know who are.

Although hit records eluded Tony there is no doubt that he achieved legendary status as a musician songwriter and as an exciting entertainer. The song that both describes his performance and I feel he is best remembered for was recorded on the Pye label and included two red hot solos played by Johnny Bedder, some of you may have heard that it was Ritchie Blackmore but Tony assured me it was Johnny. The song was called *'Too Way Out'* and I think it was a great number although it was intended to be the B-side. The A side was a soulful ballad called *'I've Seen Such Things'* a good song well sung and if Tony had written his own book as we discussed it would have made a very apt title for his biography, because Tony saw through the hype and found his way to the music.

Tony worked with great musicians throughout his time in the business and played in a great many bands most of which he fronted. Two things were always clear as he made his musical journey through bands like Gulliver's Travellers, the various line ups of The Savages, Tony Dangerfield and the Thrills, Circles, The Roman Empire, Crusaders, Ruperts People, Carl Douglas and The Big Stampede, Storm, Episode Six, Glass Menagerie, The Alan Bown Band, Black August, The Shakers The Dangerfield /Greenie Big Band, Flying Saucers and The Tony Dangerfield band, one was that Tony always enjoyed his music and at any given time knew what he was trying to achieve, even if others sometimes found it difficult to understand. The other was that he would never for any reason suffer fools gladly. We will always miss Tony but the memories and the music he left behind are his legacy to us, I am very proud and grateful that he made me his friend.

Thirty-Nine

Kathy Kirby

Kathy Kirby
Courtesy of James Harmon

Kathy Kirby will always have a place in hearts of any one who remembers the sixties. Particularly the hearts of those who knew her and her music. As Tommy Bruce's personal manager I can tell you that Tommy remembered Kathy Kirby with great affection. Tommy and I have often spoken of her during the time we have travelled together and at the time of his death we had been travelling together for more than thirty years, so that gives you some idea of the number of times her name came up.

Kathy Kirby, as I am sure many of you will remember, was discovered in her early teens by the famous band leader Bert Ambrose. Bert Ambrose brought Kathy great success in a musical sense because he recognised and nurtured her great talent. Indeed Bert went so far as to say she was the greatest talent he had worked with, even better than Vera Lynn and Ann Shelton in his opinion.

It seems that for all his show business acumen Bert Ambrose had a gambling addiction and as result of his gambling he lost all of Kathy's money. Added to that Ambrose's thoughtless treatment of Kathy, which he demonstrated by allowing her no freedom of thought or movement, meant that Kathy had no control of her own affairs. Although Kathy adored him and was never critical of him, Ambrose actually created a scenario that with his death would ruin not just Kathy's career but many aspects of her life as well. This story is told too much greater effect and with more clarity than I could hope to provide in James Harmon's biography of Kathy's life, entitled '*Secrets Lies and Lip Gloss*'. This book was

Kathy Kirby & Tommy Bruce

published by Graham and Margaret Smith at Media World Books. It would be well worth any fan of Kathy Kirby buying and reading this biography of Kathy Kirby's life.

By the time this book is published I know that a narrated tribute show with the very talented Suzi Jari singing Kathy's songs, produced by Graham Smith will have come to the stage. I am sure Kathy's fans will be interested to see the show and perhaps learn in some degree how such a wonderful talent drifted from the scene.

I for my part have always been a fan and although I only met her once, backstage, when she appeared with Tommy on Stuart Henry's 'Do You Remember?' concert. Always the perfect gentleman Tommy waited outside until her car arrived and then walked her to her dressing room. I got to know Kathy a little better later through phone conversations. Added to my splendid memory of meeting this lovely lady is my knowledge of her through my association with Tommy Bruce. I can tell you that in spite of having her own health problems, Kathy wrote to both Tommy and I when she learned that he was ill. She spoke to me on the phone a couple of times about Tommy's health and phoned him on a weekly basis until he became too ill to take her calls and finally passed away. Those calls meant a great deal to Tommy and I will always be grateful to Kathy for the pleasure the words she said brought him at the end of his life. Another reason for feeling close to Kathy is the fact that I enjoy the pleasure having Kathy's great friend and personal manager, James Harmon as one of my own dear friends.

It was because of all these things that when my friend Dave Chevron told me he had obtained an LP of Kathy's the following idea came up. The LP was in poor condition so we discussed the idea of him cleaning up the recordings in the studio and creating a CD based on the results Dave did this to great effect and when he came to me with the finished article, I provided a few archive photos from my own collection for the sleeve,

I then wrote a sleeve note. When the CD was finished we offered it to Kathy as our own small recognition of her talent. We also gave it to her with great affection and to express the pleasure the memory of her personality and voice still brings to us and all her fans. Kathy said she was pleased with the result and was gracious enough to accept the CD with her thanks. This CD is unavailable to anyone else as it was made as a limited edition that will never be for commercial sale, only Kathy, James Harmon and also those of us mentioned here making a total of five will ever have a copy. It is just a small thank you for the memories that Kathy Kirby as given to and shared with us. God bless you Kathy.

Tommy, Kathy & Clinton Ford

I really feel that I should mention in slightly more detail before ending this chapter the contribution James Harmon has made to Kathy's well being throughout what have been some very difficult years. James has done his best to support Kathy Kirby in every way possible on both a personal and professional level. Fortunately James has had the support of John Pugh in his endeavours. John devotes a great deal of his time on a daily basis to ensuring that Kathy has everything she needs, to enjoy her somewhat secluded life. I know she appreciates this and values John's friendship very highly. It is plain that between them James Harmon and John Pugh have succeeded in helping Kathy to enjoy her life. That life has sadly come to an end but Kathy's wonderful voice will endure for as long as people enjoy listening to music. A special lady who we all miss.

Kathy Kirby's Blue Plaque unveiling
Ernest Maxim, Anita Harris James Harmon and Paul O'Grady

Forty

Helen Shapiro

Preface By Helen Shapiro

Thank you Dave for the kind words have said about me in your book 'The Long Road'. My husband John has been banging on for years about how he has found a straight and honest guy in you and how helpful and supportive you have been in his long pursuit of some villains. John and I have also admired your determined fights for the rights of dear Tommy Bruce and others. We wish you every success with this book. Our love to you and dear Margaret.
Helen Shapiro. Colombia Recording Artiste

Helen Shapiro
Courtesy of Helen Shapiro

Helen Shapiro was born in 1946 and by 1961 had hit the British entertainment scene with such force that it was shaken to its very foundation. Helen had a voice of such maturity that the news that she was still at school was greeted with total disbelief. Of course Helen had been singing for a few years before she was discovered

Prior to being discovered as it were Helen was singing and playing banjo with a local skiffle group and having fun after all she was only about ten years old at the time so it should be fun at that age. The band members were Helen her brother Ron and a young lad called Mark Feld. He went on to be a great success with a band called T-rex he had changed his name by that time to Marc Bolan.

Once Helen had been discovered it has always been a complete mystery to me how Helen Shapiro with her wonderful and powerful voice allied to her warm and caring personality did not achieve world wide recognition and remain at the very top of her profession. Helen has qualities that many of today's vocalists can only dream of. The versatility of her voice is for me quite simply a miracle of sound. The fact that Helen and her husband actor John Judd regard Margaret and I as their friends is we feel, one of the greatest gifts life has bestowed on us. Incidentally I have to say at this point that John Judd is fine actor and several television productions for example The Sweeney, Juliet Bravo and course his well remembered role in BBC television's Jossey's Giants, Bob 'the gob' Nelson, have all benefited from his addition to the cast. He has also appeared on the big screen in films like Scum in 1979 in which he played Mr Sands

Going back to the beginning of Helen's career when Norrie Paramour, having had her brought to his attention by John Schroeder I believe, first heard her voice, he thought listening to the power and the timbre that she was a boy. As anyone who has seen her or been lucky enough to meet her can testify Helen is a gorgeous and feminine lady who lights up any room with her presence.

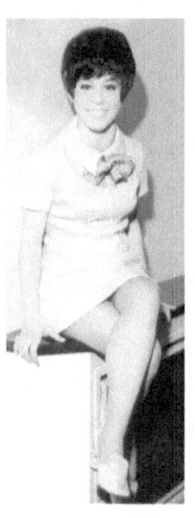

Ironically though the songs which first brought her to the British public's notice were not in the style which her voice is best suited to. Quite simply Helen Shapiro will be remembered as one of the worlds great Jazz singers.

However we have to thank Norrie Paramours perception of her as a bright and bubbly teenager for bringing her to our attention. I am sure her talent would have brought her to the fore at sometime, perhaps just not as quickly. I have to admit to loving all of Helen's early recordings, from the first hit *'Don't Treat Me Like A Child'*. Through *'You Don't Know'*, *'Walking Back to Happiness'* and my personal favourite of the pop songs she recorded *'Look Who It Is'*. When I bought Helen's recording of *'Fever'* in 1964 her voice, not for the first time simply blew me away

It is not surprising therefore that by the time she was sixteen years of age Helen Shapiro had already been voted Great Britain's Top Female Singer. These days the media talk about the success of other so called schoolgirl sensations, well in my opinion none of them can touch Helen Shapiro.

My reason for saying this is that the success of the girls who followed her is to some extent on media hype, whereas in Helen's case her success was built on her simply incredible voice. Helen Shapiro's talent and vocal ability are quite simply timeless. I just know that as long as people listen to music they will listen to Helen Shapiro and when they listen they will marvel at the quality of her voice. Helen Shapiro is incomparable because no one can do the things she does vocally in the way that she does them.

Helen's early career was fitted into a very short time frame, coming as it did between the out and out Rock and Rollers and solo ballad singers of the late fifties and early sixties and the emergence of the beat groups like The Beatles, The Searchers and The Merseybeats. Because of Helen's wonderful voice the beat groups who destroyed the careers of many of the artiste's would be unable to stop any aspect of Helen Shapiro's career and it's subsequent successful transition into the world of Jazz music.

Because of Helen's vocal talent she was able to make what appeared to be a seamless transition first into musicals and then she became, what I feel she was always destined to be, a queen of the jazz scene. Helen's fine musical performances would include her tour de force of a performance in the role of Nancy, heroine of Lionel Bart's musical Oliver, I have to say having seen other fine singers in this role Helen surpassed them all. As with every other aspect of her career Helen Shapiro is simply the best. Never having been a lady who would rest on her laurels Helen Shapiro made herself a star of the Jazz world singing with Humphrey Lyttleton's band.

Helen Shapiro has also proved her self to a consummate actress appearing on British television in programmes like the soap Albion Market.

From my point of view our friendship came about when Helen's husband John contacted me about trying to

Helen Shapiro and Norrie Paramour
Courtesy of Helen Shapiro

pursue an unscrupulous agent who had been ripping Helen and Tommy Bruce off for years. Indeed there where many artistes who had suffered at this agents hands, including Danny Williams. John has fought long and hard to put these injustices right and I like to think that I have helped him where I could.

The true value of John and Helen's friendship has been shown to me on at least two recent occasions. The first being when I asked them to come to Danny Williams funeral because I knew that many of his contemporaries were unable to attend. Tommy Bruce for example was just to ill and although we did not know it then would himself have died within six months. Helen and John did not hesitate to come and pay their respects, Craig Douglas another close friend also turned up when I asked him to, these are good people.

The other occasion was when with Mac Poole's help a benefit night was put on for Tommy Bruce and although Helen is now retired from singing she turned up with husband John and came on stage to say a few words about Tommy. Helen Shapiro is a very special lady and we all love her very much. As Helen travels round the country spreading her gospel and sharing her kindness with us all, we are reminded that good people come from all walks of life and that Helen Shapiro would be a good person even if fame had eluded her.

I still think Helen Shapiro has been cheated by show business, my reason for saying this is because I am sure that if Helen had better management in her early career the fame she achieved in this country and Europe would have seen her become famous on the world stage, Helen's exceptional voice should have seen her mentioned in the same breath as Peggy Lee Ella Fitzgerald and Sarah Vaughn. Of course Helen would never say anything like that herself, she is far to modest, it is just my opinion, one I think is shared by her legions of fans. Quite simply Helen Shapiro is the best of British entertainment and a wonderful ambassador for how we should all try to live our lives. It is a privilege to able to say that Helen and her husband John are friends to both Margaret and I. For my part I will do all I can to continue to be worthy of their friendship.

Forty-One

John Leyton

Preface By John Leyton.
Nelson Mandela said: "I have walked that long road, I have tried not to falter". Although Dave Lodge has walked a very different long road, rugby to athletics, to show business, to writer ... what next I wonder? He too has never faltered. Over the years Dave's integrity, generosity and friendship have been appreciated by so many of us. For example if you needed to be met at Heathrow Airport at five o'clock in the morning and then driven two hundred miles or more, Dave would be there, without you having to ask. For Dave and his wife Margaret may the long road continue to be happy and get longer for many years to come.

Dave & John Leyton

John Leyton Actor and Recording Star

John Dudley Leyton's thrilling and exciting journey to success took him from the place of his birth, Frinton on Sea, in 1939 to blitz-torn London in the forties. He then went on to being a hit recording artiste and Hollywood acting star in the sixties. That Margaret and I should have been privileged to become his friends and get to know, not just the star but the man, is one of the great gifts that life has bestowed on us.

I first met John Leyton at the Beck Theatre in Middlesex over twenty years ago when I compèred promoter Graham Cole's Telstar show. Graham, a likeable and fair man, had booked Tommy Bruce for the show and was kind enough to book me to compère it.

Unbelievably for me when I arrived at the theatre I was asked if I minded sharing my dressing room with John Leyton. As I look back now I still find it incredible that I was asked that question. It was unbelievable for two reasons: 1). That I was asked and 2). That an incredibly talented man like John Leyton would consider sharing a dressing room with me. Quite apart from John's chart success, adding to that he was one of the country's leading television actors ... and he had then become one of our greatest acting exports to Hollywood. On that evening we forged what has become one of my most valued friendships.

A young John Leyton

John made his first live performance as a singer in 1960 at The Colston Halls in Bristol; the backing band on that occasion was The Charles Blackwell Orchestra. This is where for me the story is quite uncanny. The man playing the drums on that occasion was our mutual friend Clem Cattini ... and also appearing that night was Tommy Bruce. Tommy recognised that John was really nervous about his transition from serious actor to popular singer and so set his mind at ease by laughing and joking with him. John never forgot Tommy's help that night and because of it always held Tommy in the highest esteem.

So that first evening was recreated to some degree that night at the Beck Theatre with Clem backing John (this time with his own band the Tornados) and Tommy Bruce was also on the bill. I became, what I like to think of as, the final piece in the jigsaw, Realising how nervous John was I spoke to him about why he was feeling this way. He explained to me that it was nearly thirty years since he had performed on a live rock and roll show and said how worried he was as to whether to audience would actually want to see and hear him again after all these years. On top of that he was concerned as to how vocally sound his act would be.

I was amazed at how little confidence John had in his ability to please an audience. My reply was the only honest one I could give, I told him, "John you are a great actor and way back then when you played the part of Johnny St Cyr in *Harper's West One* you gave a performance of such quality that you went on to have a number one hit record with *Johnny Remember Me*. People will want to hear you sing that plus you have Clem Cattini and his Tornados behind you to look after you musically. You look great so don't worry just go out and be Johnny St Cyr and you will be fine."

That is just what he did and the audience loved him as I knew they would. I can speak from experience as a fan who bought the records in the fifties and sixties so I know what the fans want. I am just so lucky that thanks to Tommy Bruce so many of the stars that I had admired in the past showed that they are first and foremost people ... and I am so lucky that those people became my friends.

That night a link was forged between Tommy Bruce, John Leyton. Clem Cattini and myself. Whilst I would never claim that I helped John as much as Tommy had all those years before I do think that in me he had found another person who he could rely on not to let him down if. I think we all need to know that we have people around us who care enough to give us their support when we need it.

This seems a good time to make the point that I feel that friendship freely given is an honour, and a privilege to posses and certainly not a right. I will always endeavour to be worthy of the gift of friendship.

John Leyton came from a theatrical background so in some ways it is not surprising that his artistic talent would take him in that direction. His mother, Babs Waters, was a well-known actress on the London stage. and his father owned several theatres and cinemas.

John made the decision to attend drama school and in order to pay his way took a variety of jobs including that of a film extra. He appeared in various films, *The Square Peg* and *Doctor at Sea* being two of them. This experience would stand him in good stead later in his career when he would be appearing in Hollywood.

From my point of view, like many others, I first became aware of John Leyton at the end of the fifties when he got his first starring role on television. It was in the 1959 BBC adaptation of Captain W E Johns Biggles books. The story centred round the hero of the skies James Bigglesworth and his crew. The part of Biggles was played by Neville Whiting, who as John says was a fine actor, but I cannot find any record of his having done any future television work.

John played the part of Biggles's faithful sidekick Ginger Hebblethwaite. Because of his acts of daring-do he became the boyhood hero of every lad under the age of fifteen. Boys want to be brave and loyal friends and have the romantic idea that heroes are to be looked up to. Perhaps a bit more of that in the world today would be a good thing!

What I didn't know then, and would only realise when I met him for the first time some twenty-five years after that TV programme, is that John really is a true and faithful friend, who like Ginger Hebblethwaite will never let you down.

Incidentally, it might be of interest for some of you to know that some of the scriptwriting for the Biggles adaptation was done by Tony Warren. He would go on to write for a serial called 'Florizel Street'. This would become better known to us all as Coronation Street, the longest running soap in television history. Coincidentally, prior to John's rise to fame as a television star, he had been learning the skills of his profession at the Theatre Royal in York where he worked with someone who would go on to be luminary of television acting, Jean Alexander, who of course went on to play the wonderful Hilda Ogden in the aforementioned Coronation Street.

Following his time in rep John made the decision to go to London in search of an agent. After what turned out to be a rather lengthy search he found one in the shape of the young Australian Robert Stigwood. At that time Robert Stigwood was just starting to make his way in show business management. He had set up an office in Covent Garden. Stigwood's business acumen would help him to go on to become one of the most powerful men in show business. By allying himself with Stigwood John ensured that his talent would have the backing to ensure them both real success.

Robert Stigwood realised something almost immediately - that audiences are clearly attracted to John's charismatic live performances. So to capitalise on this Stigwood realised the time was right for good looking young men to enter the music business. John Leyton fitted the bill and Robert Stigwood had the contacts that would open doors for him.

One of those contacts was the now Legendary Joe Meek, who was at that time probably the most innovative young independent record producer around. Stigwood made the introduction and John soon found himself in Joe Meek's homemade recording studio at Holloway road.

John's success as a recording artiste was not immediate and the release of *Tell Laura I Love Her* on the Triumph label, did not bring the hoped for chart entry. This was due in no small part to Top Rank, who released the single, being taken over by EMI's Colombia label (Ironically John had auditioned at EMI Colombia whilst still at drama school. That audition proved to be his worst experiences in show business. Unfortunately John had had no say in the choice of song. Athough backed on piano by the late Russ Conway, the song *A Man On Fire,* did not suit his voice and so John had sung it badly making the whole thing an awful experience and made him glad to get out of the studio.)

This change of record company was unfortunate for John because Colombia already had an artiste under contract who had recorded the song and promotion of his version was already under way. The artiste was Ricky Valance so no more needs to be said. For some reason I do not understand why John's follow up disc *'The Girl On The Second Floor'* was not destined to be a hit.

However these reversals did not prove much of a set back to John's recording career because Robert Stigwood, who always had his eye on the main chance, had a plan. The plan was to put John up for the lead role in the new television series *Harper's West One*; John would play aspiring pop singer Johnny St Cyr in the show. Robert Stigwood then approached the show's producers with the idea that John should sing his new release *'Johnny Remember Me'* during the weekly show.

This idea proved to be a masterstroke and the recording soared to the top of the charts. This song with the soaring backing vocals of Lissa Grey has become one the most iconic songs from the sixties. That added to follow up hits with songs of the calibre of *'Hey There Wild Wind'* and my own personal favourite *'Son This Is She'* have ensured that John's place in the history of popular music is secure. It's still a mystery to me how *'Lone Rider'* didn't make the top ten. Various excuses about strikes, distribution and the like don't cut it for me, they could have re-released the record as it had hit written all over it.

Naturally John still considered himself, rightly in my opinion to be an actor first and foremost and was determined not to lose sight of his ambition to succeed in his chosen profession.

So, after he had appeared in many music tours and having worked with all the top artistes of the day, including the up and coming band The Rolling Stones, Robert Stigwood and John made the joint decision that for the time being at least John's serious acting career would take precedence.

With serious acting in mind and with the help of Stigwood's influence John landed the role of 'Willie The Tunnel King' in the now legendary Hollywood blockbuster *'The Great Escape'*. John Leyton's performance was of such a high standard that in spite of sharing the screen with already established acting luminaries such as, Richard Attenborough Steve Mc Queen Charles Bronson and Donald Pleasance, he was catapulted to international fame.

Because of the success of this film he was signed by Twentieth Century Fox and was in great demand. Playing leading roles in many unforgettable films including *'Von Ryan's Express'* in which he starred alongside Frank Sinatra and *'Guns at Batasi'* with Mia Farrow and Richard Attenborough. It came as no surprise when he was nominated for best actor in recognition of his incredible performance in this film.

Other starring roles came John's way for Cinerama in *'The Idol'* and *'Krakatoa East Of Java'*. John's success as an actor continued when MGM/CBS gave him the starring role in his own television series *'Jericho'* in which he appeared with Robert Lansing. During this period in his career John Leyton proved himself to be on of our best acting exports to Hollywood. This success was not just a credit to John's acting ability, because this is undisputed, it was also a credit to his appetite for hard work which his career is always reflected.

Charles Bronson and John Leyton in 'The Great Escape'
Courtesy of John Leyton and United Artists 2008

This has been clearly shown since his return to the UK as short sighted producers and casting directors have made him work extremely hard re-establish himself in the country of his birth. When in point of fact if the general public had any say at all in what finds its way on to our screens John would be on television every week.

Of course any artiste needs the right people working hard on his behalf and in Steve Etherington John has one of the best. I have great admiration for Steve who does all he can to keep to keep John in the limelight. Any of us who have tried to represent an artiste would wish to achieve the standards that Steve sets. He is a good hearted man and any time I have spent in Steve's company has been a pleasure and I wish him well in all his endeavours.

Q&A session at Welshpool town hall
John Leyton, Craig Douglas, Jess Conrad, Dave, Billie Davis, Clem Cattinni, Graham Fenton

John Leyton
Courtesy of John Leyton

I know that John has suffered health problems recently, but I am sure that the health and fitness he has built up over the years will help him to recover and come back stronger than before.

Margaret and I are very proud of our friendship with John Leyton, he deserves any and all success that comes his way. We hope that John and his lovely wife Dini, continue to have healthy and happy lives for many years to come.

Forty-Two

Tony Crane

Preface by Tony Crane.

Dave Lodge is one of the most genuine and honest people that I have ever known. In a business where there more sharks than you will ever find swimming in the oceans. We go back many years and I have always found him eager to help and promote all acts. Dave is liked and appreciated by everyone and I am proud to call him my true friend.
Tony Crane, The Merseybeats.

Tony Crane and Dave
Courtesy of Lou Rosenthal

If there were to be a template made to create natures gentlemen, there is no doubt that Tony Crane would be the model for it. Tony is a smashing bloke who over and above his prodigious talent has a sense of right and wrong that we would all do well to aspire to. Added to that anyone who has ever heard Tony sing knows that his throat must have been kissed by an angel at birth. His voice just flows into the atmosphere like liquid gold, it doesn't hit the ears it kisses them, there just isn't another like it.

Like me Tony has only ever loved one woman in his lifetime and I have always felt that is one of the things that makes me feel so close to him. One of the greatest regrets in my life is that Tony's wife Carole is no longer with us. Carole was a lovely lady and sadly I did not have the pleasure of knowing her very well or for very long but whenever I spoke to her either in person or on the phone she came across as a very warm hearted lady. I do know she was the love of Tony's life and that he will always miss her.

Tony Crane
Courtesy of Tony Crane

There would not be enough room in a book to tell you how much I admire Tony, so this chapter is just a very brief attempt to express that feeling.

Tony Crane as many of you will know is the lead singer with the band the Merseybeats and once again there is a show business link between us, two actually. One being that Tommy Bruce's lead guitarist from the Bruisers Peter Lee Sterling, who I also count as a friend, wrote '*I Think of You*' which of course, was a massive hit for the Merseybeats. The other is another mutual friend songwriter Barry Mason who of course discovered Tommy Bruce.

But there is another link between Tony and I that goes back over fifty years, that link is my father, Ted Lodge. Way back in the early sixties it was my habit, if I didn't have to work, to go into Stockport which is in Cheshire on a Saturday morning with my father. However on this particular Saturday I did have to work and so he went in on his own.

As he drove into the main street, Princes Street, after coming down Didsbury Road, as you could in those days before the town planners made a complete hash of the town, he saw that a crowd was to some degree blocking up the street. As he slowly continued his approach he realised that people had gathered outside a shop called The Toggery. This shop apart from giving its name to one of the local bands, *The Toggery Five*, also supplied most of the North West groups of the day. The problem was that it was on the second floor of the building and you gained access by along a narrow staircase

On this particular occasion the shop was being visited by one of the most popular groups of the day The Merseybeats. The word had gone out and it spread like wildfire to the young shoppers that The Merseybeats were in town, causing a large crown mostly made up of teenage girls to gather on the street at the foot of the stairs that led up to the shop. The lads came down and out onto the street to be greeted by this excited and screaming throng who were all eager to touch and speak to the stars who had just gone to the top of the charts with a song entitled '*I Think Of You*'.

Things were getting more and more out of hand as the fans tried pull the hair out the group members heads. They were scratching the lads and fighting to kiss them really, a very frightening experience.

At this point my dad who had stopped the van jumped out and struggled through the crowd to open the back doors, saying to the lads, "Get in and I will get you out of this." They all grateful struggled their way into the van and not without some difficulty my dad drove them away from the scene.

When they got out of the van as they were thanking him and shaking his hand my dad asked the question, who are you and why were they treating you like that? "My name is Tony Crane and we are the Merseybeats" came the reply.

My dad arrived home later and told the family about the incident, I was very put out and made the quite unreasonable comment, "the least you could have done was bring them home for a cup of tea". Just showing once again how unreasonable I was in my teens.

When I met Tony for the first time some twenty years later, the first thing that struck me was how right my father had been in his assessment him. My dad had commented that Tony was a really likeable young lad. By the time I met him Tony was a mature man but the qualities that made my father think as he did were clearly evident.

Tony Crane is without doubt a really likeable man with a generosity of spirit that is rare in these days of self obsessed people. Also Tony recalled the situation when I mentioned it to him and said that he had been very frightened, it should be remembered that he was only seventeen or eighteen at the time and such demonstrations of adulation by the fans had not yet become the norm.

Musically it all began for this likeable and talented Liverpool lad when he learned to play trumpet with his local church band at the age of eleven. Of course it was some time later when he met and formed a duo with another talented young lad, Billy Kinsley, that Tony's vocal gifts would get a public airing. Not to long after that the lads realised that the way

The Merseybeats with Manfred Kulman

forward for them in the exciting new music scene would be to form a group. So in 1961 Tony and Billy recruited Dave Elias, Frank Sloan and Billy Butler and called themselves *The Mavericks*.

Local success was soon achieved under that name, but after a while they decided to change the name to *The Pacifics*. This name only lasted for a short time, as they were not entirely happy with it. So the name was changed at Tony's instigation to The Mersey Beats. However the now legendary Bob Wooler decided it would be better if it were just one word to take the gap out and make merseybeats one word, hence THE MERSEYBEATS.

Bob Wooler was at that time the master of ceremonies at the Cavern Club and Tony and the other boys thought it wise to listen to him.

I do not intend that this narrative be a history of The Merseybeats career, rather recognition of Tony Crane's considerate nature and exceptional musical talent. It also has to be said that he has a level of business acumen that is rare in most walks of life, let alone in the music industry.

One thing I have never told Tony is that I bought all his records right through to and including the time when he and Billy appeared as The Mersey's in 1968. Proof of this is that my wife Margaret has had to put up with not just listening to the songs Tony has recorded, no hardship there, throughout the fifty one years we have been together but my attempts to sing them. We have enjoyed everything, *Mr Moonlight, I Think of You, I Love You Yes I Do, Wishin' and Hopin', It's Love That Really Counts*, to name just a few. Of course I would not forget my own personal favourite *Don't Turn Around*. Incidentally when Tony was on the Reelin' and a Rockin' tour with many other sixties luminaries, they had a vote as to which was the best song on the show, *Don't Turn Around* won hands down.

About ten years ago I was delighted when Tony gave me a recording he had made with Billy playing bass, of the old Troy Shondelle song *This Time*. On this recording Tony plays all the instruments and he harmonises with himself and I have to say that when I heard it for the first time the quality of his voice is so good that the hairs stood up on the back of my neck and I really felt the emotion of the song.

Tony's career has continued through more than five decades and I feel one of reasons for this is because of his love of melody. The beautiful ballads that he and the group have recorded all stand the test of time. The reason Tony continues to thrill audiences around the world is that he always has high quality musicians in the band, for example Bob Packham who started out with The Swinging Blue Jeans but joined the army at the start of the sixties on the basis that nothing was happening in Liverpool, Lou Rosenthal, Dave Goldberg who first came to my attention when he was in the band Perfumed Garden, were in the line up when we shared a trip to Germany. The band is augmented at times by Tony's son Adrian. Add to this to the wonderful harmonies Tony sings with Billy Kinsley who in his own right is undoubtedly one of the most talented men in the music business and you find yourself listening to the best of the best when it comes to vocal harmony.

The Merseybeats today
Courtesy of Tony Crane

Margaret and I who are life long fans of the group can only say that we are very proud to have the privilege of knowing that Tony Crane is our true friend.

Forty-Three

Graham Fenton

Those of us who know Graham Fenton all know that his musical success has not brought Graham everything he deserves. That said Graham has achieved great things, both as a recording artiste and performer. He is also a kind and thoughtful man who always puts the needs of his family first. His friendship once given to you can be relied through all adversities that come your way because, quite simply Graham Fenton is the much maligned good Christian who spends his life trying to help others. That he does this is very often to his own detriment.

Graham Fenton and Tommy Bruce

   Graham grew up in a music loving family, indeed there was always a good variety of music being listened to by Graham and his brother Ken who is an excellent reading musician, who plays double bass and Bass guitar for a variety of Jazz and Rock and Roll bands. Their sister Linda also loves the music and married a musician. Graham's mum was a real fan of Frank Sinatra and Elvis Presley, but it was a record that his dad bought that really fired Graham's love of Rock and Roll. The record was called *'Rock Around The Clock'* performed by Bill Haley and his Comets and Graham's dad became a real fan of the artiste and the genre. Hearing the exciting beat made Graham hungry for more of the same, his own record collection would feature the likes of Carl Perkins and Bo Diddley who he would later, in 1978 have the pleasure of touring with. However one man's records stood out for Graham and that man was Gene Vincent backed at that time by The Blue Caps, and it is not hard to recognise Gene's influence on Graham as a performer. To his great delight Graham has had the pleasure of working, recording and becoming friendly with, Dickie Harrell, Bubba, Johnny, Paul, Bobby and Jack Neal, collectively The Blue Caps on more than one occasion. Due to this relationship

Graham was also able to meet the producer of their 1950's recordings Ken Nelson at the same time he met Ken, Graham also took the time to visit Gene Vincent's grave at the Eternal Valley Cemetery and pay his respects. During this period Graham also took the time during the shows with The Blue Caps to pay tribute to Paul Peek, Jerry Merritt, and Cliff Gallup.

Graham's recording career has been a great success and he has received Gold, Silver and Platinum Discs in the UK, many other European countries and Australia, He has toured extensively throughout Europe, Australia, Japan the USA and of course the UK both with bands and as a solo artiste.

Although his greatest recording success came with Matchbox, who he still works with in the original line-up, the list of people that Graham has worked with reads like a who's who of rock and country music. I list just a few here but it is clear to see that Graham Fenton is an artiste of some prestige and highly respected by his peers. He has shared the stage with American artistes of the calibre of Bill Haley and The Comets, Gene Vincent, Carl Perkins, Jerry Lee Lewis, Johnny Cash, Linda Gail Lewis, Wanda Jackson, Brenda Lee, George Hamilton IV, The Crickets, Narvel Felts, Charlie Gracie, Don Everley, Janis Martin, Freddie Cannon and Sleepy La Beef. The list of UK artistes is just as impressive, Lonnie Donegan, Tommy Bruce, Heinz, Screamin' Lord Sutch, John Leyton, The Shadows, Marty Wide, Mike Berry, The Rapiers, Chris Black and The Black Cats, The Jets, Wee Willie Harris, Class of '58 and Jet Harris.

Graham looking every inch the rocker he was born to be

In spite of this body of work and his obvious talent promoters do not give Graham the work he deserves. This means that his legion of fans do not see as much of him on the road as they and he would wish. Graham Fenton is a kind and caring family man and a good friend to many including me. Graham takes pleasure in all things from the fifties era including American cars and British motor bikes of which he has owned many. Of course in many ways the music and the artistes from that era have been his life long passion. Indeed the only things I have found him to be more passionate about are his lovely wife Caroline and their two children Chrystal and Vincent. The world is a far better place with Graham Fenton in it, and we his friends are all the better for knowing him and having the privilege of sharing our lives with him. As Tommy Bruce would have said keep on rockin' Graham we are all with you.

FORTY-FOUR

TOM O'CONNOR

Tom O'Connor was born in Bootle on Merseyside and the only was to start any description of him is to say that he is quite simply a brilliant man. Tom has gift for taking real life scenarios and showing his audience the humour that is around us every day. He and his lovely wife Pat seem perfectly matched, they support each other in all aspects of life and support each other in charitable works, Most notably for handicapped children.

Tom O'Connor, Dave and Robin Gibb

Indeed it was through Tom's charity work that I first came to know him. He supports The Heritage Foundation, of which I was a director indeed he is a past President who continues to help the work and is an example to all of us who strive to do our best for others.

Tom O'Connor, as many of you will know, taught mathematics and was the deputy headmaster at St Joan of Arc's School in Bootle. At that time any aspirations Tom had to be a performer in the world of show business would have led to him being a singer ... he is still prone to picking up his guitar and giving his audience a song when the mood takes him. However it soon became clear that Tom had a natural gift for humour, and as he put it himself – "comedians get paid more". So in 1974 Tom took the decision to go full time in show business. Because by nature Tom is a sensible and cautious man he waited until he was twelve months ahead with advanced bookings for his comedy act before making the leap. He never looked back – in a very short time people realised he was an incredible talent who was not just a funny man but some one who could

235

harness his wit and natural humour and in so doing become a natural game show host.

Before long it was impossible to turn on your television set without seeing Tom O'Connor every night of the week. Shows like, '*The Tom O' Connor show*', '*Wednesday at Eight*', '*Night out at the London Casino*' and '*London Night Out*' gave every one the chance to see just how talented Tom O'Connor really is. Add this to no less than eight game shows, including '*Name That Tune*', *Gambit*', '*Zodiac*', '*Password*' and of course the unforgeable '*Cross Wits*'. all being ably hosted by Tom, we get some idea of the incredible ability he has to be different in each separate presentation of his art.

Of course Tom has not just been performing on television during the last thirty eight years, he has performed in major theatres including The London Palladium and cabaret venues throughout the UK and the rest of Europe. Tom has worked in America, most notably at Carnegie Hall in Manhattan, proving that unlike many of today's comedians his humour is such that it travels well and is relevant to who ever he is talking to. He still works incredible hard – only recently he entertained on five different cruise ships spending a week at a time on all of them. By his side is his wife Pat helping to keep him in tip-top condition and going through this gruelling schedule with him. Proving as I know from having my own wife, Margaret supporting me, that marrying the right girl is a big step towards succeeding in any aspect of life

Being in Tom O'Connor's company is a pleasure that is reminiscent of warm contented evening by the fire, with your favourite tipple, he has a happy knack of making you feel at ease and at peace with the world. It really is a pleasure to be in Tom's company and feel the warmth of his friendship.

Forty-Five

Philip Madoc

When you consider that Philip Madoc, with his rich deep mellifluous and resonant voice, was one of this country's finest actors it is perhaps surprising that there is so little known about him on a personal level. I put this down to the fact that Philip, although a talented intelligent and articulate man, was first and foremost a private man. A man who did not pursue 'celebrity' he relied instead on his high level of acting ability and this spoke volumes for him. That is not to say that he was reclusive or stand-offish, quite the reverse. In fact, I found him to be a good companion at social events, with great conversational skills and a wonderful sense of humour.

Philip Madoc

Philip Madoc was born in Wales and after university, having a gift for languages he became an interpreter. These talents gave Philip the opportunity to work in Russian, French, German, Italian, English and of course his native Welsh language. His career in the theatre extended to productions at the Bristol Old Vic, The Royal Shakespeare Company and The Royal Exchange. He made numerous appearances in the West End and has toured many productions nationally.

Philip Madoc's television career was both extensive and impressive. Indeed he first came to my attention with his portrayal of the relentless SS Officer Lutzig in the World War two serial *'Manhunt'* in 1969. Then in 1971 came his powerful performance of Magua in the BBC's adaptation of Jame Fenimore Coopers epic novel *'The Last of the Mohicans'*. Indeed since we first met in 1990 Philip told on a couple of occasions that Magua was the kind of role that he would have paid to have played, because he could feel the power of it from his first reading of the character.

The casting of this program was brilliant in that it brought two other fine actors, John Abineri as Chingachoog and Kenneth Ives in the part of Hawkeye to the screen. However more me Philip's performance stood out above all others and fixed him forever in my mind as a must watch actor. His list of credits is endless including his wonderful interpretation of the character of David Lloyd George in The BBC's *The Life and Times of David Lloyd George*. Another outstanding performance as DCI Noel Bain in 'A Mind to Kill' led to a feature film of the production with of course Philip reprising his role to great effect.

Philip's film career once again reflects not just quantity but quality. Performances in films of the calibre of '*Operation Crossbow*', '*The Spy who Came in from the Cold*', '*The Quiller Memorandum*', '*Shadow Falls*' and '*Best*' leave us in no doubt that Philip Madoc was indeed the consummate master of his art.

Philip had a fine sense of humour and an example is how he could turn a conversation that is perhaps becoming a little serious for a light social occasion back to a less sombre tone. I remember an occasion when he demonstrated this at lunch one day, a few of us had gathered together and in the course of conversation talk came round to the war and whether or not we, the British people were right to fight it. The general consensus was that we were and we all put our point of view with reasons why

Ann, Philip Madoc and Margaret

we thought Winston Churchill had been right to follow a certain course of action. Philip entered the conversation with the words, "My grandfather was treated appallingly by the Germans." All eyes turned to him, our ears eagerly awaiting his next words, our imaginations running wild thinking, "my god his grandfather must have been a prisoner of war, or if it were possible something worse." As the consummate professional he is Philip knew he had his audience in the palm of his hand and with perfect timing he held what can only be described as a 'delicious pause', then the deep sonorous voice loved by all his many fans he continued, "Yes the swine overlooked him for promotion on at least three occasions when he was far better qualified than those chosen". There was a stunned silence followed by uproarious laughter. Once again Philip Madoc knew just the right thing to say and to make sure we continued to enjoy the lunch. That is just one of the many reasons why I was proud and privileged to call him my friend as sadly Philip is no longer with us and Margaret and I really miss his companionship and humour.

Forty-Six

Vicki Michelle

Preface by Vicki Michelle.

When Dave Lodge first told me he intended to include me in his next book, I was very flattered. When he asked me to write an introduction to the piece, I was delighted to pay my own tribute to one of life's true gentlemen. Loyalty, commitment, honesty, reliability, generosity and integrity are all admirable qualities. Every now and then you'll meet someone with one or two of these virtues but in Dave, you will find them all and more.

Dave and Vicky Michelle

I first met Dave several years ago but have come to know him better mainly because of our mutual connection with the Heritage Foundation where Dave is currently a Director. When we first met he was also still manager of the late great Tommy Bruce and I shall always remember in particular the Tribute Luncheon he staged on behalf on behalf of the Foundation in memory of Tommy following his untimely passing. I know what a difficult time it was

for Dave but as ever the day was organised with his trademark dedication and professionalism and despite the underlying sadness of the occasion, it left me uplifted in the knowledge that there are people out there who really care about their fellow man.

I also have reason to be grateful to Dave for the lovely tribute he paid me at a recent Heritage Luncheon given in my honour. His kind words set the tone for what has become a very special day among my memories.

I could go on to mention that he never forgets any of my opening nights in the theatre. There will always be flowers, a good luck message or even a cuddly teddy bear from Dave and his lovely wife Margaret. I could also go on to mention how when recently I had a late night filming session for Emmerdale, Dave offered to make a 400 mile round trip to drive me home so I wouldn't have to wait for trains on a freezing station platform at night in the depths of winter because that's the kind of person he is but instead I will simply say, if there were more people in the world like Dave, it would be a much better place. I am proud to have him as my friend. Thank you Dave. Lots of love. Vicki Michelle.

I have no words to describe just how special Vicki Michelle is. So what follows can only be my very poor attempt to let you see something of the wonderful lady Vicki truly is. Stunningly beautiful, that much is clear, because heads always turn when Vicki enters a room. But there is so much more, Her beauty I think must come straight from her soul – so powerful is the radiance that exudes from her eyes and her smile invites you to be her friend, there is a wow factor that blows you away, right off the Richter scale. To husband Graham she is a wife who faces life and its challenges head-on and to her daughter Louise, she is I am sure just 'mum' with all the love that word inspires. For those of us who have the gift of her friendship, we have the most loyal, helpful and caring supportive friend that we could wish for.

Vicki Michelle was born in London and learned her craft in the early days at the Aida Foster Theatre School. Having appeared in several films and on television Vicki was as she says fortunate to be offered the role of waitress Yvette in a new BBC comedy series *'Allo Allo'*. This series which gave a light hearted look at the French resistance movement during the second world war. To put it mildly Vicki was an outstanding success in her role, in fact it made her a household name in the UK and the show ran for an incredible nine series.

Vicki Michelle as Ivette

Indeed the show which also featured Gordon Kaye, Carmen Silveria Kim Hatman and Rose hill to name but a few went on to tour the UK, Australia and New Zealand, smashing box office records everywhere. There were also two seasons in the West End.

But there is much more to Vicki Michelle's talent than her ability to play the part of a sexy French maid. Vicki has proven herself to be one of our most hard-working actresses. Her talents cover the full range of entertainment. If you want to cast someone for a serious or comedy role, if you want some one sing or dance look no further than Vicki Michelle … she will never disappoint you.

Vicki talent has shone in many performances. For me she was the definitive 'Miss Hannigan', in *Annie*. Her portrayal of a total amoral woman has to be seen to be believed. The critics gave her rave reviews and of course Vicki is no stranger to standing ovations and rapturous applause from her audience. Another musical in which Vicki gave a performance of remarkable skill was in fact her first. The show was the British musical version of *Beauty and the Beast*. In the part of the evil 'Bathsheba' and as she sang and danced her way through the show it was clear to all that a new star of the musical theatre had arrived on the scene.

In spite of the impressive body of work Vicki Michelle has to her credit I do not think the greater percentage of the British public realise what a wonderful talent she really is. One cannot look at the films she has appeared in, *The Sentinel*, *The Colour of Funny* and the *Greek Tycoon* without realising how varied the roles she plays really are. Vicki has featured in most of the top TV series over the last thirty years or so, such as '*Whatever happened To The Likely Lads*', *Come back Mrs Noah*, '*Are you being Served*' and the more serious roles in '*Softly Softly*', '*Minder*' and '*Play for Today*'. Then we look at her appearances on the game shows, such as '*Call my Bluff*', '*Blankety Blank*', *The 'Generation Game*' and '*What's my Line*' to see how her incredible personality lights up the screen. Of course any pantomime she appears in is greatly enhanced by her presence. If I were to list everything that Vicki Michele has appeared in I would need at least two books never mind the chapter I have afforded her here. For that reason I now intend to move on to her other roles in life.

Vicki Michelle cares more deeply for other people, than just about anyone else I have ever known. She is a tireless fund-raiser for good causes who supports several charities including The Heritage Foundation. An example of how Vicki supports her friends is that when Mac Poole and I put on an event to raise money for Tommy Bruce during his long and sadly fatal illness Vicki said she would attend. Vicki's idea of attending was to buy forty two tickets for the event, hire a coach and bring those people to see the show. When I asked her why she had done such a wonderful thing she said that Tommy and I were her friends so she it was just something she had to do. We have always liked and admired Vicki but that night our admiration turned to love. Margaret and I love Vicki as we would love a sister and there is nothing I wouldn't do for her. As I say she is a really special lady who brings joy and love to everyone she meets.

Vicki Michelle is a loving wife, mother sister and daughter before all else. Beyond that she finds time be a beautiful, talented and charismatic actress who still cares for and helps countless people. Really I have to say that Vicki Michelle appears to live at least three lives at once and in all of them she gives one hundred percent. For our lifetime she will have the love and friendship and respect of Margaret and I, Vicki will also be able to call on our support, anywhere anytime.

I would just like to mention Vicki's PA Nicki Edwards at this time, Nicki is another of life's special people who always puts others first. She and her husband Jon have a lovely family and we are glad that through Vicki we now have Jon and Nicki in our group of friends. We thank Vicki for bringing these two lovely people and their sons into our lives.

Margaret and Dave with Vicki Michelle

Forty-Seven

Alan Crowe

Preface by Alan Crowe.

I first came into contact with Dave Lodge many years ago. At the time I was looking to book Tommy Bruce to appear in some sixties shows that I was promoting at that time.

I also wanted Tommy to play in some charity golf tournaments I was arranging on behalf of clients. Since those early days Dave and I have remained in contact and those initial business associations have led to us becoming firm friends. During our friendship Dave has always been there when I needed advice, because like myself Dave has been there, done that and got the T-shirt in the entertainment

Alan Crowe

business. He knows what it is like to suffer financial reversals and has never allowed failed shows to come between us.

Dave is the consummate professional; he takes care to ensure that all parties involved in a production are happy with arrangements. He has the interest of the acts, promoters and venue at heart, as he says we want to do this right and come back again. Dave is a man who always makes time for his friends and to help others through his work with various charitable organisations. He is an extremely busy man who some how manages to find time to fit everything in.

Behind every great man there is an even better women, in Dave's case that woman is his wife Margaret. Margaret supports Dave through good times and bad and is probably the sweetest lady you could ever wish to meet.

Dave I hope the lord gives you the health and strength to carry on and that you and Margaret reap the rewards in life that you both so richly deserve, long may our friendship continue and prosper.

Alan Crowe Show promoter and sixties aficionado.

There are many people who will be surprised to find Alan Crowe in these pages as Alan has been unfortunate enough to suffer more reversals of fortune than anyone else that I know.

Due to those reversals several people have fallen out with Alan, usually over money. Personally even though I have suffered some heavy financial losses in show business, some of them involving Alan, I have always taken the view that life is to short to fall out over money. It has to be said that Alan always tries to do the best he can for all concerned. The one thing I do know about Alan Crowe is that he works very hard often for no reward, What he has tried to do over a number of years is keep the sixties music flame alive, this effort has frequently been to his own detriment. In spite of this Alan always bounces back with yet another idea for a great show.

So let's have a brief look at Alan Crowe's, stage name Ala Cra, achievements in the business. He has appeared as a DJ, Compère, Children's entertainer, Costumed character, Actor, Agent and Show promoter. Added to these accomplishments Alan has become published author, critic, publicist, not forgetting Community Champion. This an unbelievable list of credits achieved by an equally unbelievable character.

Indeed Alan's love of entertainment goes right back to his school-days in Welshpool. At the age of nine he was involved in a local production of 'Robin Hood' and apart from having a role in the play he was also co-opted into helping with the making of scenery and costumes. He also sang in Christ Church choir for several years. The school Alan attended was mostly attended by boys, therefore Alan was often called upon to take female roles in drama productions. His teachers recognised that he had organisational skills and so involved him in the backstage production of all their plays.

Alan picked some lighting skills during his school days so adding this to his hobby of collecting records he decided that here was a way to make a living, with this in mind he became a Mobile DJ. This developed his presentation skills and he moved into other aspects of entertainment including developing his own cabaret act. By 1980 Alan was working as a full time professional entertainer, working not just clubs but also major holiday centres. In spite of this Alan was not advancing in his career as much as he hoped, so heed to turn to promoting his own shows. In the course of this he worked with many of the famous groups from the fifties, sixties and seventies from both sides of the Atlantic. This gave Alan an enviable list of phone numbers, so he decided to start his own entertainment agency. He has gone on to stage various sporting events, (Golf, Cricket and Football) and in doing so has raised well in excess of £120,000 for charity.

Alan Crowe, Dave, Mick Bates Welsh Assembly member and Shobna Gullati

Alan has written for various magazines and also written sleeve notes for CD covers. This led him to go on to write his own Joke Books, (in the style of rag mags), Quiz Books, Country Music Cymru promoting the country music and line dance scene in Wales. He has also produced his own sixties magazine called *'Beats Working'*.

Although Beats Working is no longer produced but has become quite collectable on the nostalgia scene. Add all this to Alan's television appearances in various productions and not forgetting his role as a councillor on Welshpool Town Council .

Alan has used these experiences to take his literary skills to another level by writing books beginning with his autobiography, titled *'If it Wasn't for Bad Luck'*. He has followed this successful publication up by writing books about local history. The content of which includes interesting information about amateur dramatics and pantomimes in the area. His latest offering is titled *'Entertaining Mid Wales and Beyond'* In this he chronicles the careers of the many and varied and varied entertainers to emerge from or work out of the region.

Dave, Margaret and Alan Crowe

At the present time Alan is working on a number of other book projects, he also spends time reviewing various theatre shows for a number of online publications. As if these activities were not enough hard working Alan is out and about on a weekly basis, giving diverse and interesting talks on his entertainment career or local history to Women's Institute Groups, Golf Clubs indeed, anyone who books his talks. Also Alan shows his caring nature by working tirelessly for local and national charities, if you need a volunteer Alan is your man.

If like Margaret and I you count Alan as friend you will not be surprised to know, that he is a loyal and kind man who has often gone out of his way to help others.

FORTY-EIGHT

SCREAMIN' LORD SUTCH

Screamin' Lord Sutch, Lord David Sutch, or just Dave to his friends (Tommy Bruce always called him Screamin') was the epitome of how diverse the human species can be. The only way I can describe him is to say that he was an enigma.

Screamin' Lord Sutch

Dave Sutch was born in 1940 and brought up in London doing most of his growing up in Kilburn. I have to say I never met a man who loved his Mother more. In return for this devotion Annie Emily Sutch, in spite of spending many years of her life struggling to make ends meet after being widowed during the war, put her heart and soul into giving her wonderful son the best start she could in life. Annie came down to London from a little village called Woodhouse, just outside Sheffield at the age of eighteen. Before long she met and married the man who would be Dave's father. His name was George Sutch and he lived in Cricklewood. Dave would often tell us that his father knew Lloyd George ... the thing was with Dave there was no reason to disbelieve him. Sadly when Dave was only nine months old his father, a war reserve policeman was killed in a motorcycle accident as he was going on duty one night.

If his mothers first intention to return to Woodhouse had come into effect we can but wonder at the direction Dave's life might have taken if he had been brought up in Yorkshire. Luckily for his friends and fans Annie stayed in London and unwittingly gave her son the chance to become one of the most famous entertainers, and politicians in the country. Dave was quite simply along with Jess Conrad the best self publicist I have ever met.

I don't think anyone else could have named a party The Official Monster Raving Looney Party, taken the Loch Ness Monster as their mascot and made it into the most well known opposition party in the country ... Dave, Screamin' Lord Sutch did just that, in fact he turned that Monster Raving Looney Party into a national institution. Indeed the party is still represented in elections several years after his death.

On top of creating a political party Screamin' Lord Sutch was an incredibly exciting live Rock 'n' Roll performer. After being carried on stage in a coffin he would erupt with a blood curdling scream and go into his signature song *Jack the Ripper*. With his cape swirling and his top hat at a rakish angle he would go into a performance that was complete mayhem swinging a brazier full of hot coals. Health and safety would never allow it these days, the band playing fit to burst with hot coals flying everywhere! Dave's on-stage antics would often set fire to carpets and curtains in the Working Men's Clubs he performed in causing complete panic ... while he continue to sing as the band played on.

He would then fling the brazier to some poor fool who was in attendance and the excitement really started. Dave would go to the corner of the stage and produce a huge sword, a stick and a policeman's helmet. He'd throw the stick and the helmet to me and furious sword fight would ensue with me chasing him round the club, playing the part of the hapless constable who never caught Jack. I have scars on my knuckles to this day caused by that sword striking my hands when Dave missed the stick. Happy memories of a lovely man who brought a great deal of fun into our lives.

Incidentally another friend of ours Larry 'Teapot' Richards a very fine

Chris Black, Dave Sutch
Peter Stringfellow and Cynthia Payne

comedian and compère was also on the receiving end of that famous sword on various shows in the nineties, it's a good job the sword was heavy and blunt otherwise there would be a few of us missing fingers after sharing a stage with Dave Sutch!

I have to say that getting to know Dave Sutch was not what I expected. He was brash, loud and an extrovert on stage or public event but then would be the complete opposite when he was at home or travelling with you. Dave was never happier than when he was sitting with a mug of tea in his hand while wearing his carpet slippers ... not the sex, drugs and rock and roll that the press like to write about!

It was heart-breaking when Mac Poole phoned on the day of Dave's death to tell me he was gone. I had only spoken to Dave a day or two before on the phone and he had told me that for the first time in twenty years he was free of his debt to the tax man. We had a lovely conversation and he thought the future looked bright.

Once Dave Sutch became your friend he would make sure that your life was never dull. He never asked if you wanted to go somewhere with him, he would always phone and say we are doing this or going there – he never for a moment doubted that you would want to go on these jaunts with him ... and as he used to say only a death certificate would be accepted as a valid excuse for absence. Thanks for all the wonderful memories Dave, We are sure heaven is a better place for your being there. Margaret and I just wish you could have spent longer with us.

Screamin' Lord Sutch & Golly Goulding

FORTY-NINE

LEAPY LEE

Lee Graham

Lee Graham, who has become known to us all as Leapy Lee and was especially known to Tommy Bruce as 'little Lee off the Barking Road'. He was born in Eastbourne in 1939 and grew to be a real live-wire, a bundle of fun and energy who is the life and soul of any party.

Lee's life seems to have been full of twists and turns as through no fault of his own he's suffered more than his share of misfortune. In spite of that his enthusiasm for life is undiminished and the times Margaret and I have spent in his company have always been a real blast.

I personally think Lee was born to be an entertainer, it was I am sure to some degree reflected in his choice of jobs, he has variously been, a Bingo Caller, Club Manager and a barrow Boy on Portobello Road. His first band was somewhat aptly called I think, The Urchin Skiffle band. After all even at this stage in Lee's life, with his cheeky grin and sparkling eyes you could easily imagine him being cast as the Artful Dodge in Oliver Twist.

Leapy Lee has covered many aspects of entertainment in his colourful career including acting with many appearances in well known films as and extra. Lee also has worked in theatre in various productions, Including *Sparrers Can't Sing* and *Johnny the Priest*. He made his first recording *'It's all Happening'* for the Pye Records in 1962 and of course we all remember his first hit *'Little Arrows'* which was No.1 in eighteen countries in 1968. His appearance on *Top of the Pops* wearing a prisoner's suit covered in arrows was a little to prophetic as in 1972 Lee went to prison for a crime he didn't commit. I say this because having been told the true story of the events leading up to his arrest and conviction some years later

I have no doubt that he was framed, stitched up, what ever you want to call it. I won't tell the story here because Lee has published his own biography and the story of deceit and betrayal by people he thought were his friends is far better told by him. Suffice to say it cost him two years of his freedom and took away his chance to be one of the UK's greatest resident entertainers. Having said that, in countries around Europe and the rest of the world, Lee is still packing in huge audiences including ex-pats and holiday makers from the UK.

After spending 1976 til 1983 in Saudia Arabia following his release from prison in Lee moved to Mallorca and opened a bar with the late Andrew Ray – son of comedian Ted Ray. However it was not a successful business venture and so, in 1985, Lee started out as the cabaret entertainer that he is today.

I hope that I will be able to assist Lee in his desire to perform in the UK on a regular basis again in the near future as I am sure that people here will enjoy seeing and hear him perform over here again. Of course from the point of view of Margaret and I there are selfish motives involved in as much as we will be able to spend more time in his company than has been possible in recent times.

The other thing is that we will be able to hear him sing our favourite song among the many that he has recorded – his arrangement of Charlie Landsborough's great song, *'What Colour is the Wind'* to our mind is by far the best rendition we have heard.

Fifty

Tony Christie

Tony Christie
Courtesy of Tony Christie management 2008

Although the times I have spent in Tony Christie's company have been separated by a number of years. It is fair to say that I've known him for more than forty-five years. This time has include gaps of 10 or more years between our meetings so in one respect I would not expect Tony to consider me his friend. That said, I have great respect for him both as a man and as a performer and when he made his recent comeback I was more than pleased to write articles and review his shows for magazines like *The Beat*, in an effort to help to make sure it had the maximum impact.

We did enjoy a very pleasant meeting at this time and recalled people and places from the days we spent in each others company. He and his son Sean also made it possible for me to bring my good friend Peter Leonard, a big fan, to see Tony in a show at Doncaster. This was a really enjoyable occasion for Peter and I as we both share an appreciation of Tony's voice.

Tony spent many years working abroad, in 2002, for example he did a twelve city tour of Germany, which brought fans out in their thousands. Apart from a successful collaboration with British band *All Seeing Eye*, on the song Jarvis Cocker wrote for him, *'Walk Like A Panther'* in 1999 we had seen far too little of Tony in the UK in recent times. So I personally was delighted that Peter Kaye was instrumental in getting *'Is this the way to Amarillo'* released for Comic Relief in 2005. This gave us all the opportunity to see Tony Christie performing in the UK once again.

Born in Conisbrough South Yorkshire in 1943, Anthony Fitzgerald, aka Tony Christie, brought his own brand of hard work and talent to the Working Men's Clubs of the north in the Sixties. I first became aware of Tony when he was singing with a band called the *Trackers*. Since then I have been sure, like many thousands of his fans, that in him we had a very special entertainer. Long before he had a hit record people in clubs up and down the north of England were just waiting for him to get the break his talent, hard work and dedication deserved. Although Tony himself sometimes despaired of making the breakthrough.

We came close to losing his rare talent when a friend who, being aware of his growing disillusion with show business and a young family to support, offered to help him set up in business on his own. Thankfully though for Tony and fans his long overdue first hit *'Las Vegas'* went into the charts in 1970. This song would prove to be the catalyst that his career had been waiting for. Due to his collaboration with great songwriters of the calibre of Neil Sedaka, Mitch Murray and of course Barry Mason to name but a few Tony Christie would soon become the internationally renowned performer he is today.

Incidentally once again it shows just how small the show business world can be when I think that my friend Barry Mason, who discovered Tommy Bruce wrote *'Drive Safely Darlin'* For Tony. We all started out each not knowing the other but their talent is drawn together on these pages by each one being fated to know me to a greater or lesser degree.

Tony Christie has at various times been referred to as Britain's answer to one American or another, or even in his early days by ignorant people as a poor man's Tom Jones. To anyone who takes the trouble to listen to him sing it is clear that Tony's talent is unique. It is not just the power of his voice but the phrasing in his songs that sets him apart from singers he has been compared to. Anyone seeing and hearing him for the first time is in for an unbelievable experience; he is a charismatic performer with an almost unbelievable stage presence. When Tommy Bruce and I met him again down at Shepherds Bush studios on Mark Lamarr's *Never Mind the Buzzcocks* show and realised that his career was entering another successful phase we could not have been more pleased. His work ethic is second to none – even now when some performers might have been content to rest on their laurels and bask in the glory of previous success. Piccadilly Radio famously got it wrong in the early 90's when they suggested that he might have died ... not only was he very much alive he is back on the scene giving performances that will blow your socks off.

Dave Lodge and Tony Christie

In contrast to his on-stage performance off-stage I have found him to be quiet, courteous, almost shy man with a wry sense of humour. He has lived in Almeria, Spain with his wife Sue for many years and I am sure he will continue to divide his time between there and here. After all he is a fine golfer and the weather and courses are excellent over there. Having had the pleasure of meeting Sue I am sure that her love and support, is responsible in no small way for the continuing success in Tony's life. Because those of us lucky enough to marry the right girl are all aware of the contribution they make to our lives and well being. This very welcome return to the limelight was brought about in part by the now well-documented effect Tony's voice and his songs had on Peter Kay's mum.

It was also the effect, albeit indirectly, on Peter himself who listened to these songs as a child that lead *'Is This The Way To Amarillo'* being chosen as The Comic Relief song in 2005 and being re-recorded with Peter Kay.

It proved to be a phenomenal success and spent 7 weeks at No.1 with his 'Definitive' album at top spot too with a sell-out tour following suit ... Tony Christie was back on the road! So not only would charities benefit from Tony's endeavours through Comic Relief but also the scene was set for Tony Christie once again to show his existing fans, and a whole new generation of fans, just why I said he is unique. I hope our paths will cross again in the future and that I will have many more opportunities to hear and see the talent of Tony Christie.

Because of my own ill health and a few setbacks this book has taken six years to reach completion so there have been some changes for all of us.

I am pleased to say that in Tony's case there have been more successes along the way. Not the least of which has been a collaboration with a contemporary Irish folk group, *Rangari*, their line-up is Jean Kelly, Eliza Marshall and Tad Marshall. They have recorded an album called *The Great Irish Song Book*, giving Tony the chance to return to his family's musical roots, showing the versatility of his vocal talent.

I wish Tony continued good fortune and I look forward to many more years of listening pleasure from his music.

Fifty-One

Paul Melba

Once again I have to describe a friend as a gentleman because that is just what Paul Melba is. Modest and unassuming – he has a most incredible talent to mimic the voice and facial movements of many of the world's best known entertainers and celebrities of the last sixty years. Like all great artistes Paul has also put a great deal of hard work into achieving the status that he has in the entertainment world. His ability to sound exactly like the person he is imitating is all the more amazing. I often close my eyes when he is giving

Paul Melba

a performance because be it Johnny Mathis or Prince Charles, Paul's phrasing and diction convince you that the person you are listening to is really there.

In 1943 the show business world had its first glimpse of this very talented Liverpool lad. At the age of seven young Paul graced the Stage of the Argyle theatre and began a career that had him following in the footsteps of his father and grandfather. Paul's mother was a classical pianist so it is fair to say that he came from a show.business dynasty. It is no surprise that Paul Melba is at home with impressions of singers, actors and other celebrities when you look at the training he has had. He is a classically trained singer who was taught by Mr Francis's school in Liverpool, he taught Paul using the elbo canto style of Caruso; Paul followed this up with further training in London. He also learnt acting skills at RADA and attended The London Central School in Soho, He has said that from his point of view as an impressionist some of the lessons contradicted each other for example Elocution would teach him to say his A's in one way but vocal coaching for singing would have him produce opposite emphasis on the letters. Paul did very well for a number of years combining his acting and variety skills.

I suppose Paul Melba's full time show business career really began in 1956 when he was demobbed from the Marines. He built up a popular following whilst working in the many clubs and No2 and No3 theatres that were around at the time. As someone who paid to go and see Paul during this period I cannot believe that it took almost fourteen years for him to hit the big time. That said he was making a reasonable living and he was very popular with other entertainers. This is shown by the friendship he enjoyed with Matt Monro. Paul was kind enough on one occasion to tell me how he came to meet Matt and also to recount what led up to their last meeting. Paul was living in Crouch End at the time and he used to visit a milk bar in the area. There was a young girl working there, a nice girl and she and Paul would engage in conversation. He told her he was in show business, and she said she thought he looked the part. She then went on to say that her cousin was a singer by the name of Matt Monro, adding you won't have heard of him yet because he is still driving a bus, but he will be famous. Paul politely replied "oh really" and didn't think much more about it.

Some time later Paul found a new place to live in Clapham North, so he decided before moving to pop in and say cheerio to the girl in the milk bar. She was sorry he wouldn't be coming in any more but said it was good he'd gone in that day because her cousin, the singer, was sitting over in the corner. She introduced them and Paul and Matt got on like a house on fire chatting for some time whilst having a drink and smoking cigarettes. Their friendship lasted for many years.

When Paul became famous and appeared on TV, Matt noticed that he had a nervous tick on the side of his face. He contacted Paul and put him in touch with a Dr Fricke, in Baker Street London, who could help get rid of it. An appointment was subsequently made and he arrived on a very foggy day in London at the consultants to find an impressive array of photos of the celebrity patients of Dr Fricke – including one of Prince Charles. The technique Dr Fricke's employed involved the laying on of hands and Paul remembers the Doctors hands being quite hot, the treatment would seem to have been successful.

Just before they left the phone rang, it was Matt Monro phoning to see if Paul had arrived ok with the foggy conditions. He invited Paul and his then wife Didi to visit him and his wife Mickie. Paul said that would be great but he wasn't entirely sure of the area Matt lived and didn't think he could find their house as the fog was a real pea-souper. Matt Insisted and both he and his wife gave instructions on how to find the house. It took three and a half hours for Paul and Didi to find the house and when they arrived to find Matt, Mickie and their daughter Michelle waiting for them their faces were black from the fog through looking out of the open side windows of their car, this caused great hilarity.

Paul was immediately struck by how emaciated Matt looked as he had lost an awful lot of weight and his complexion was very sallow. When asked if Matt was ill, Matt said "Oh I got food poisoning while I was in Hong Kong, I am only just back." Matt showed Paul round the house including the garage which was done out with pigeon holes to accommodate all his musical arrangements. They had something to eat and Paul and Didi were asked to stay the night, Mickie saying Matt needs to take his medication and get some sleep because his illness is making him tired. In the morning Matt said they must meet up again soon – Paul said he was leaving to do an eight week working cruise on the QE2 and they could get together after that. OK said Matt I know a wonderful Italian fish restaurant in Charlotte Street, called I believe Pasquatories, we will have dinner there when you return. Sadly a few weeks into the cruise Paul received a phone call from Didi on the ship to shore telling him that Matt had died, Paul was devastated, of course as we all know now Matt had succumbed to the dreadful effects of cancer.

In 1969 Television producers finally picked up on the brilliance of Paul Melba's act. As he has put himself he was really good and his take off of James Mason had to be heard to believed. Modest as always Paul thinks he was good, I never met anyone who thought he was less than brilliant. Between1972 and 1976 Paul was appearing on London Weekend Television's hit show *'Who do You Do'* along side some superb impressionists. These impressionists included Peter Goodright, Margo Henderson, Janet Brown, Freddie Star, Aiden J Harvey and Roger Kitter. The list goes on as there is no doubt that the seventies were the golden age of British impressionists, also appearing on the show were, Faith Brown, Dustin Gee, Les Dennis, Little and Large, Lance Percival, Pat Dailey, Bill Wayne and Russ Abbot with and without the Black Abbots. It has to be said that none of these talented acts could eclipse the performance of Paul Melba.

In fact if talent counted for anything these days, Paul Melba who at one time had his own television show and was in demand for absolutely everything should still be a major star in this country. Unfortunately he had a serious accident which cost him the sight of one eye and kept him off stage for twelve weeks. Then as he says himself he took what turned out to be a bad career decision to spend too much time working on the lucrative cruise ships, which were it has to be said very lucrative and most successful for him. When he then tried to return to television and theatre work he found that producers and promoters have short memories for entertainers and work was hard to come by. Even though he is now living in Spain with Angie Hood a lovely lady, they have been together for seventeen years, probably eighteen by the time this book comes out, the British public have not forgotten him and it would be a wise decision if any promoter added Paul Melba to their show line up. The last time I had the pleasure of working with Paul was about ten years ago at the Lambeth Police club, I compèred and the other acts were Danny Williams and Tommy Bruce all the acts were backed by Paul Robert's band Flying High. Paul Melba as usual was the consummate professional in that respect nothing changes. I was recently interviewed on Vince Tracy's show on Spanish radio and Paul was in the studio at the same time as always we had great fun. We speak quite often on the phone and in one of those phone calls he told me that sadly his brother has recently passed away. In spite of this sad news Margaret and I wish both Paul and Angie many more happy and healthy years and we hope it is not to long before we meet up again.

Fifty-Two

Ruby Murray

Ruby Murray

Born in 1939, Ruby Murray had a lovely voice that seems to have been created by a childhood illness. She had swollen glands which required surgery and when she recovered she was left with her distinctive husky voice. Ruby's father was manager of the Ulster Hall in Belfast and Ruby liked to watch the performers who appeared there (Indeed, as mentioned earlier in the book another fine Irish vocalist Ronnie Carroll also made his debut there). Ruby Murray toured as a child singer and made her first appearance on television at the age of twelve. In 1954 at age nineteen she recorded her first single, *Heartbeat*, which got to No.5 in the charts. Twelve months later she hit the No.1 spot with *Softly Softly*. In fact that was the year Ruby achieved the remarkable feat of having five singles in the Top Twenty at the same time!

I was privileged to meet and work with Ruby Murray quite late in her wonderful career, but it was no less of an honour to meet her, share a stage with her and receive the gift of her friendship.

Ruby Murray had one of the purest voices you could ever wish to hear and it remained a perfect sound right to the end of her long career.

In the early days the hits came so fast and so frequently it seemed they would never stop and you couldn't switch the wireless on in the late fifties without hearing her lilting voice coming across the airwaves. Indeed as previously mentioned she had five hits in the top twenty at the same time, something no female artiste had achieved before. In fact it was another thirty years or so before a lady named Madonna equalled this feat in the 1980's although unlike Ruby, Madonna did not have her five hits in the

Top Twenty during the same week. No one except Ruby has ever achieved that. (See Guinness book world records). Indeed Ruby's record sales were quite simply phenomenal, she was never out of the charts with one record or another for an incredible 52 weeks, testimony to how loved by the public this lovely Irish lass was.

After touring Ulster as a child singer Ruby's performance was seen by producer Richard Afton. Under his influence she made her television debut at the age of just twelve. However stringent Irish laws in place for the protection of child performers halted her career and she had to return to school until she was fourteen.

Making up for lost time Ruby travelled to London with comedian Tommy Morgan and his travelling review. Once again Richard Afton would have a hand in her career – seeing her perform at the Metropolitan Theatre in London's Edgeware Road he quickly realised his original assessment that Ruby was developing into something special had been correct. Knowing that Joan Regan was leaving her position, as the resident singer on BBC television's "Quite Contrary Show" he offered the residency to Ruby, which she happily took. The things that happened in this year, 1954, were the catalyst to Ruby Murray's career because she was also signed to a recording contract with Columbia, by her recording manager and musical director Ray Martin. In addition to the hits named previously Ruby stormed the charts with wonderful recordings of songs like 'Let me Go Lover', 'If Anyone Finds This I Love You', (this with Ann Warren) 'Happy Days and Lonely Nights', 'I'll Come When You Call' to name just a few. A beautiful song 'You Are My First Love' was sung over the opening titles of the film musical 'It's Great To Be Young', ensuring yet another hit. Ruby Murray made film appearances in her own tight the most memorable for me being, 'A Touch Of The Sun', in which she appeared with Frankie Howard and Dennis Price.

Ruby Murray simply didn't stop working during the mid fifties. She had her own television show and Starred with Norman Wisdom in *'Painting The Town'*. In-between and during these shows Ruby also appeared in a Royal Command Performance and toured extensively in North Africa, Malta and the USA.

Ruby Murray with husband & Tommy Bruce (right)

Married twice – the first time in 1957 to Bernie Burgess who sang with popular vocal group the Jones Boys. Bernie became her manager and in the early sixties they actually toured as a double act. There was also some recording success for ruby with a song called *'Change Your Mind'* during this period. Married for the second time to impresario Ray Lamar, Ruby continued to perform with distinction in theatres and cabaret almost up to her sad and untimely death in 1996.

I came know Ruby and her second husband Ray in the eighties when I compèred some of the shows that Ruby appeared on and we became friends. Subsequently I booked her to appear in other shows that I was putting on for Tommy Bruce.

I found Ruby to be a lovely, warm and cheerful lady – very young for her years, she had a wonderful sense of humour and one thing that always made me laugh was her china tea service. With Ruby, image was everything, and being fond of a little tipple after the show she would have a drink brought to her in a china teapot … she would then pour it to her china tea cup. Ruby was always of the misguided opinion that nobody knew she had an alcoholic drink in her cup … but over the years it became common knowledge. While drinking it she would smile sweetly at me and say, "We have to have our little secrets don't we Dave?" It was my privilege to have this lovely lady as my friend and share happy times with her; I really miss her now she's gone.

Fifty-Three
Anita Harris

Anita Harris is vivacious, glamorous and talented, these things are a sure-fire recipe for success. The reality is that as with all things in life, lasting success is elusive and achieving it requires an incredible amount of hard work and determination, Anita Harris has these qualities in spades. Born in 1942 and having won a talent contest at the age of three it was clear by the time she became at teenager in the fifties that her beauty, charm and personality would lead her into the world of entertainment.

Anita Harris
Courtesy of Anita Harris 2007

Surprisingly she was first discovered as an ice dancer having skated and trained at Bournemouth Ice Rink from age three to fifteen. Anita was already championship standard when, just before her sixteenth birthday and having already partnered World Pairs Ice Dance champion Courtney Jones, she achieved recognition for her dance skills. Although she was not really looking to be in show business she was spotted by a talent scout at London's Queens Ice Rink shortly before her sixteenth birthday and invited to audition for a dance troupe *The Blue Belle Girls*. Before she could accept this chance Anita's parents had to go to Bow Street Magistrates Court to sign papers for a chaperone to take care of her on her travels. She then performed in Europe and Las Vegas. where she met and kept company with stars like Frank Sinatra and Tony Bennett.

After her six month stint in Las Vegas, doing three shows a night (the last one finishing at five in the morning) Anita came back to England. After spending a year at the Hampshire school of Drama she left and embarked on a singing career. The Cliff Adams singers recognising her talent and potential had no hesitation in bring her into the fold. These choral singers enjoyed great success on the wireless with the BBC's *Sing Something Simple* show. Of course Anita's success was always going to come as a soloist. Her first single was made while she was still in her teens. It was a Lionel Bart song recorded with The John Barry Seven, I believe, entitled *'I Haven't Got You'*. Unfortunately the songs release coincided with an equity strike which prevented its promotion and I have no doubt deprived her of a hit.

Anita counted the late Dusty Springfield among her friends and because of this had the opportunity to record a song written by Dusty's brother Tom. Released on the CBS label in 1967 (and bought by me as an expression of love for my wife Margaret) it was called *'Just Loving You'* and reached No.6 in the UK charts. Incidentally, it reached No.1 in South Africa and charted well in the USA, making her a truly international star.

The rest as they say is history. Anita Harris was now established as one of the best loved vocal entertainers in the country and around the world. The proof of this is her total of eight chart singles and many chart albums.

All the great songwriters, including Burt Bacharach, John Barry, Jerry Goldsmith and Leonard Bernstein have made it their business to work with her, and we – the record buying public, are the beneficiaries of their musical collaboration. Her Musical Arranger is the inimitable Kenny Clayton, who also has artistes of the calibre of Shirley Bassey and Petula Clark lining up for his services; Together they have been creating wonderful music for some years now. It is not surprising that Anita Harris has also achieved success in the acting world given her elegance and poise and talent. Unsurprisingly appearances in two of the *Carry On* films established her, not just as a sex symbol, but let cinema goers see that she is a fine actress as well. Stage productions have given her acting skills the real opportunity to shine and Anita has taken those opportunities with both hands. Those fortunate enough to have seen her performance as the crippled cat Grizabella in the stage musical *CATS*, will have marvelled at her ability to bring beauty and pathos to the role. An outstandingly enigmatic performance as Rachel in *'My Cousin Rachel'* is yet another example of Anita's acting skill. I would also like to mention that she received great critical acclaim when appearing in *'Stranger on a Train'* with Colin Baker.

Anita's list of television credits seem endless ... she co-hosted the *David Nixon Magic Show* appeared on *The Morecambe and Wise Show* and worked alongside Spike Milligan, Peter Sellers and Frankie Howard. Added to this were her own shows which included, *The Anita Harris Show* for the BBC, *Anita in Jumbleland* on ITV and most memorably *Anita Harris The Vocal Touch*. These programs resulted in many awards including Most Popular Female Television Entertainer and an award from the Montreux Festival for the BBC's Big Band Show.

Anita Harris is one of show business's great survivors, but blessed with the support of her husband, to whom she has been married for nearly forty years, Mike Margolis. Anita has overcome many setbacks in recent years – she was cruelly deprived of much of her money in the City Bank collapse ... but with hard work and diligence she has risen above her financial difficulties. On top of that her health was threatened when she suffered a cancer scare which once again with the love and support of her husband Mike she has fortunately recovered from. In spite of these setbacks and others besides Anita has bounced back stronger than ever, in her Millennium run of Peter Pan Anita broke all box office records at the 2,000 seat Manchester Palace Theatre. Added to this she has had a No.1 best selling fitness video and book entitled *'Fizzical'* and she continues to work tirelessly for charity.

Indeed she was the first woman President of The Heritage Foundation for the arts and entertainment, and indeed served two very successful terms

Anita Harris presents Tommy Bruce

of office. Having worked with the Heritage Foundation myself I have been able to appreciate first hand the benefits of her contribution to the work for the charity.

During my time with The Heritage Foundation I came to know and like both Anita and Mike, in fact she honoured Margaret and I by saying we were part of her little team.

I have to say, from my point of view, Anita Harris is a warm and giving human being always thinking of others first. She is elegant and beautiful, charming and charismatic. Anita is always immaculately dressed and looks the complete picture of perfection. When I asked her once what her secret was for looking so young and beautiful she replied, "If I am beautiful, it is because I eat lots of porridge oats and I have the love of a good husband in Mike, what more could I need?" One thing is for sure with an attitude to life like that Anita Harris will continue to be a beautiful woman and an outstanding human being. The people who have her friendship and that of her husband Mike are blessed indeed. Margaret and I look forward to our next meeting with them both.

Fifty-Four
Bob Monkhouse

Bob Monkhouse
courtesy of Bob Monkhouse 2000

It was with great sadness that I learned of Bob's passing; although I only met him a few times over the years there were two occasions prior to his death when I thought I would have the opportunity to spend more time in his company. One of the occasions was a charity function when Bob, Tommy Bruce and myself were to accept a cheque on behalf of the fund, helping others was some thing that Bob did through out his career, and the other was a lunch that was to have been put on by The Heritage Foundation, to celebrate Bob's many years in show business, sadly on both occasions his health prevented his being there. I shall miss him for his charm, his talent but most of all for the genuine warmth I felt in his company on the occasion we were together, he made me feel as though we had been friends for years and I looked forward to being in his company again. Like many other people some of whom knew him better than I and some who only knew of him as a performer I will miss him.

Bob Monkhouse died on the 29th December 2003 at the age of 75 depriving us all of the brilliant speed of thought and humour that was his trademark for 50 years. It would be easy to think that Bob had every thing in life so he naturally would be humorous, nothing could be further from the truth. Born on the 1st of June 1928 the parental affection most of us are blessed with eluded him and his much loved grandfather died when he was only 10 years old, the shock deprived him of the power of speech. He recovered only to be left with a stammer that he struggled with for the rest of his life. He once said that the emotional deprivations he suffered were the origin of much of his humour.

After he left school, having discovered his talent for drawing cartoons Bob worked for a short time as an animator for the Walt Disney studios in London, before joining the RAF to do his National Service. At the end of his service he returned to civvy street and in company with Dennis Goodwin began writing what turned out to be some of the most hilarious shows in the history of wireless. This in turn led to Bob writing material for Bob Hope, Jerry Lewis and other show business luminaries the day.

Bob Monkhouse's great success would be as a comedian in his own right, successful on stage screen and television he was rightly hailed as the boy wonder of British comedy. He was brilliant at fooling the public on Candid Camera with Jonathon Routh, then in 1967 came the Golden Shot his ready wit and natural charm made him nationally famous and lead him to a brilliant career as a game show host. Of course his career as a stand up comedian went from strength to strength in venues up and down the country though his material was more risqué in his live shows than on television he was never offensive and this endeared him to the British public.

The accolades to his many successes could fill this book suffice it to say, he earned every bit of his success for the dedication and effort he put into every aspect of his life, He wrote a very honest autobiography 'Crying With Laughter' in 1993 the same year he received his OBE. He also received a lifetime achievement award from The Television and Radio Industries Club in London. Those who knew him felt that family was the most important thing in his life; he married his second wife Jackie in 1973 but along with the happiness there has also been great sadness in death of his two sons, having suffered the loss of my own son I can understand the courage it took to continue his life in comedy, I am sure that like me it was only the support of a loving wife and remaining family that enabled him to go on.

He greeted the news of his prostate cancer in 2001 with great stoicism and bravery in spite of chemotherapy treatment being unable to contain the spread of the cancer to his bones, "I call it the Taliban because it is the enemy within" he said as he fought the disease and right to the end was still planning new projects. Once when asked how he would like to be remembered he replied, "I don't want to be remembered at all except by my granddaughters, my son in law and my wife. Fame is not an end in itself. It's as no worth except as a way of attaining something else. As soon as I am dead, there is no longer any point to it. My tombstone should read "Guess who I was – now push off"".

Bob Monkhouse
courtesy of Bob Monkhouse 2000

I am sorry Bob those of us who met you and those of us who saw you perform, know who you were to us and you will be remembered with much affection as long as the human race has a sense of humour.

Fifty-Five

Maggie Stredder

Maggie Stredder

Unbelievably Maggie Stredder, 'The Girl with the Glasses' has been making mens' hearts race since she joined the Vernon Girls in 1957. Although I am quite sure she had been doing that for a couple of years before she came into the limelight.

Maggie is a very beautiful lady who makes a mockery of the old adage *'men seldom make passes at girls who wear glasses'* because this lovely girl from Birkenhead has had all of my generation and a few from later ones gasping in admiration. Although she has been happily married to husband Jim for some years now Maggie is still a vision of loveliness in pink. She simply loves the colour. Some ladies might wear pink clothes or pink lipstick but Maggie can do all that and then on top of that she arrives in a pink car. It doesn't end there, because her home carries on the pink theme, even in the kitchen from the freezer to the kettle all is pink. I think that is why Maggie stays so young because she doesn't conform to the silly notion that as you mature there is a new colour code in your life.

Musically Maggie Stredder has had an incredible career, because quite apart from being one of the main focal points in the Vernon girls, with her vocal harmonies, Maggie is intelligent and looks so stunning, because of those two things success in her life was almost guaranteed, although she has never taken anything for granted and always worked hard.

Maggie left the Vernon Girls after several years of success on tours and television programmes, like Oh Boy! Where she worked with artistes of the calibre of Cliff Richard, Marty Wilde, Dickie Pride and Adam Faith to name just a few. Maggie took her vocal skills to another level when forming duo, 'The Two Tones and embarked on a tour of the US Air force bases in Germany. On her return to the UK and while working on Max Bygraves summer Special and then the Val Doonican TV Special Maggie decided to recruit a third voice in order to create a fuller sound and in doing so created the world famous 'Ladybirds.

The Ladybirds went on to appear in all most all the light entertainment shows on television, indeed it might have been them all as I remember them being on television all the time. They appeared with Les Dawson Show, The Two Ronnies, Morecambe and Wise, Tommy Cooper. Glen Campbell, Shirley Bassey, Little and Large and Paul Daniels to name just a few.

Personally I think that Maggie Stredder quite apart from her musicality and femininity which have both helped her career immensely has been able to add real business acumen and steely determination to the mix. Because of that Maggie's career has been able to absorb the vagaries and changes in the music industry and still flourish. There is no doubt that Maggie is a formidable lady.

The Vernon Girls, Shelia, Penny & Maggie, Tommy Bruce & Graham Fenton

When Hal Carter put the Solid Gold Sixties tours together he had no hesitate in including Maggie and two other ladies as a trio called The Vernon Girls, having seen them perform on Cliff Richards 30th Anniversary concert at Wembley. This is a wonderful memory of the former sixteen strong vocal dance group who used come dancing out of the back of the theatre and wend there way to the stage to the strains of the Mardi Gras waltz at the start of all the shows on Larry Parnes Rock and Trad tour. The two other ladies were the petite and lovely Penny Lister a former Ladybird and the glamorous and forceful Shelia Bruce, later after her second marriage Shelia Parker who has always been a vocal force to be reckoned with. These three ladies drove the name and the reputation of the Vernon Girls through to the 21st century.

These days Maggie has added after dinner speaking to her repertoire she is highly regarded on this circuit, I know this as I speak to many of the same organisations and they tell me about her visits also she has been voted best raconteur of the past ten years, by the Rotary Club, The Women's Institute and The Women's Club.

Maggie Stredder in every aspect of her career has always been quite sensational and long may she continue to wow her audiences.

Fifty-Six

Joe Dolan

Joe Dolan
Courtesy of Joe Dolan and Pye Records

Once again while I was writing this book we lost an artiste I greatly admired, Joseph Francis Robert Dolan, aka Joe Dolan. Joe and I used to meet at the Irish Clubs he played in Manchester during the sixties, The Astoria on Plymouth Grove and The Ardri in Coupland Street. Always friendly and likeable I found Joe Dolan good company and of course he had a wonderful voice. These venues gave young people in Manchester a real chance to enjoy first class live entertainment and in those days the entertainers were very approachable. Apart from Joe I met the incomparable Brendon Bowyer when he came with The Royal Showband one of his big hits was 'The Hucklebuck' an exciting dance tune which was recorded again in later years amid some controversy by Coast to Coast it seems they used Brendon's recording to great effect during their act. I don't know if that was true but I believe there was a court case about it. Bendon Bowyer and The Royal Show-band were massive stars in the UK and in the USA, they won a Karl Allen award in the UK for bringing more people into dance-halls here than any other band, In America they regularly packed out The Carenegie Hall. Their career really came to an end, I believe when Brendon fought Colonel Tom Parker in the courts for the right to be recognised as the writer of the *'Wonder of You'*. He didn't win but I for one believed him because I heard him sing it with his band some considerable time before Elvis recorded it and he introduced it as a song he had written.

Others I saw and met at the same time inclued Dickie Rock, Big Tom and his band The Mainliners, I have to say that Big Tom sang the best version of *Ashes of Love* I have ever heard and Larry Cunningham and the Mighty Avons, there is no doubt that Ireland at the time produced some of the finest singers in the world. There is no doubt that Joe Dolan ranks up there with the best of them and his great hit *Make Me an Island*. Is in my mind a timeless classic.

I met Joe again in the eighties during a time when I ran no less than seven Dublin Marathons and we enjoyed a few pints of Guinness on those trips ... after the race of course.

Of course Joe had several hits world wide not bad for a lad from Westmeath, who when asked what he did,used to say I sing a bit. He certainly did right from the very start when he started in sing in The Drifters Show-band with his brother Dan. He recorded his first single on the Pye Label, this was a cover of the Del Shannon B-side *The Answer to Everything* in 1964 and stormed in to the Top ten of the National charts. The hits continued in Ireland as he gained chart topping hits with *Pretty Brown Eyes* in 1966 an *The House with the White-Washed Gables* in 1967. His popularity was growing and the dates came thick and fast in England. He was also making a big name for himself throughout Ireland and on New Years Eve 1966 he performed at Belfast's vast Ulster Hall opening with his then signature tune *A Westmeath Bachelor*.

The Drifters were starting to drift at this time but Joe himself hit back with a great cover of French singer Francios Hardy's hit *Tar and Cement*. That was the fore runner of three other massive UK hits. *Make Me an Island, Theresa* and *You're Such a Good Looking Woman* made sure that Joe's career advanced not just in the UK, but Australia, New Zealand, South Africa and America as well.

In a very short space of time Joe Dolan conquered the whole of Europe with the help of the talented Italian producer and composer Roberto Danova, being instrumental in the million selling hit *Lady in Blue*. Joe's last UK chart hit as I remember was *I Need You* but that didn't stop people wanting to see and hear the talented Westmeath man on a regular basis.

Joe Dolan was a most courageous and innovative performer for whom distance and language held no fear. Joe performed to rave reviews in

Russia in 1978 a country most western artistes leave out of their tour itinerary. He followed this success by flying to Las Vegas to embark on a long season at the highly prestigious venue, The Silverrbird Hotel. Joe started his own studio in Mullingar and recorded songs like *Come Back Home and Wait til the Clouds Roll By*, he had his own label Gable by the 1990's and was able to release two innovative albums Joe's 90's the title so he told me a skit on the 60's TV show and 21st Century Joe on which he included songs previously recorded by the likes of Pulp, REM and David Bowie. With his last album, *Let There Be Love* Joe went back to the wonderful ballads that he sang so well.

Always willing to work and raise money for charities, in particular anything to help research into autism and never a man who worried about his so called image, Joe rerecorded *You're Such A Good Looking Woman* as a duet with television Puppet Dustin The Turkey, all the proceeds from the record were given to autism research.

It is cruel that we lost this great entertainer to a brain haemorrhage and even more cruel that his family lost him on Boxing Day 2007. Joe was only sixty eight not a great age to those of us just behind him in our sixties, but in that life span he used his talent to thrill audiences world wide, we will never forget Joe Dolan and his wonderful voice. I wish I had seen him again before he died because whenever I saw him we just enjoyed being together, I never told him how wonderful I thought his voice was. He knew though, that I bought his records so I hope he knew I thought he was one of the great singers on the world stage. We will always remember the 'Westmeath Bachelor' who with his voice, charisma and natural charm went out and conquered the world of popular music.

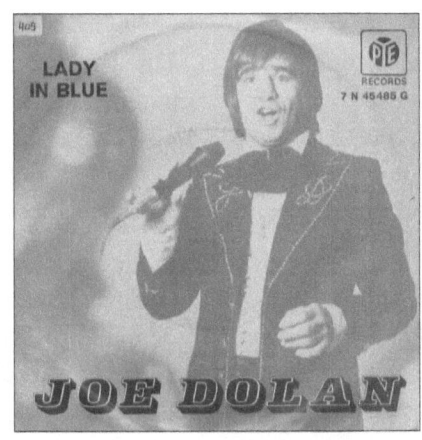

Joe Dolan
Courtesy of Joe Dolan and Pye Records

Fifty-Seven
Mike Pender

I have to say that the Liverpool sound for me was not epitomised by The Beatles. When they first became successful they left me cold. They seemed to be destroying, as another man I have had the pleasure of getting to know – David Jacobs would say, "My kind of music."Although their early recordings actually sound very good to me now, I never have got round to appreciating what I might term the 'psychedelic' music of the type they produced on the Sergeant Pepper Album.

Mike Pender
Courtesy of Mike Pender 2007

For me personally the music of Liverpool came from the Remo Four, The Fourmost , The Swinging Blue Jeans, Gerry and the Pacemakers, The Undertakers, Beryl Marsden, Karl Terry, Faron's Flamingos, Lee Curtis and most especially The Merseybeats and The Searchers. Although The Searchers featured other lead singers, from my point of view, with all due deference and respect for the other guys contribution, the sight and sound of The Searchers was and is epitomised by Mike Pender. So how lucky I feel that although I have met Frank Allan, Tony Jackson, John Mc Nally and Chris Curtis along the way Mike Pender is the one I feel I have come to know the best. Ask any fan who is among the most approachable of stars and the answer frequently comes back Mike Pender. Like Brian Poole, Tommy Bruce, Dave Dee and others in a select band Mike has remained the same person he was when he first started out.

When Michael John Predergast (Mike Pender) was born on March 3rd 1942 and it is most unlikely that anyone could have foreseen that he would grow into an incredibly talented musician who would help to change the nature of British popular music.

On leaving school Mike Pender started work in a guitar shop. He was already hoping to be a performer and so would look to play on gigs in a band with his friend John Mcnally I think at that time, 1959 the band was a guitar duo. He told me that he came up with the name for the band, co-founded with John, after going to see a John Wayne western The Searchers. Mike suggested and John agreed that would be a great name for the band. Shortly after that other people were added to line up in the shape of Tony Jackson (nicknamed Black Jake) and drummer Norman McGarry he was replaced in 1961 by Chris Curtis. Having first been fronted by Johnny Sandon for a brief period in 1960. The Searchers originally had Tony Jackson singing lead but having built and learned to play a customised bass guitar, Tony relinquished his position in the group to go off and form his own group The Vipers. This gave the opportunity for Frank Allen who had spent three years with Cliff Bennett's Rebel Rousers to make a very successful and long lasting entry into the group.

Courtesy of Mike Pender 2007

The group, by this time managed by Tony Hatch signed a recording contract with the Pye label, went on to have many top ten hits including several No.1's 'Sweets For My Sweet' being the first in 1963. Incidentally The Searchers second single which reached No.2 in the charts '*Sugar and Spice*' was written by Tony Hatch very successfully writing under the name of Fred Nightingale. As I have told Mike on several occasions over the years, as much as I have enjoyed all The Searchers recording, the one that I personally like the best is *'What Have They Done To The Rain'*. This plaintiff and haunting refrain has proved more and more prophetic over the years with the advent of global warming and acid rain and I feel could be a hit again if re-released.

I first met Mike Pender many years ago when he and Tommy Bruce appeared on the same bill, something that did not happen as often as I would have liked. I was immediately struck by his musical talent and vocal ability which I was already aware of but is greatly enhanced when you are fortunate enough to witness it close up. Since then we have usually just met like ships passing in the night on various shows – this is quite common in show business.

This seems like an appropriate time to mention Tony Sherwood who looks after business for Mike and many of the other sixties artistes, including The Merseybeats. Tony is a hard worker who takes the time to get things right on behalf of his artistes. It is no surprise them that he numbers among his friends not just Mike but people like Brian Poole and Tony Crane, who all speak very highly of him. My meeting with Mike of late have been on Derek Franks, productions like 'Reelin' and a Rockin' and the most recent 'OH BOY!!' but he always knows who I am and takes the time to link up with me. Indeed I have to say that Mike is a most likeable and gregarious man who is always the last to leave any theatre he appears in. This because he has time for everyone single one of the fans who come to him, he really listens to what they have to say and makes them feel special and he is always happy to have his photo taken or sign an autograph no matter how long his journey home may be. As I look to the future one of my greatest ambitions is to come to know Mike Pender and his delightful wife May better. Time spent in Mike's company is always time extremely well spent.

Fifty-Eight

Emile Ford

Emile Ford
Courtesy of Emile Ford

Emile Ford who started his career back in the late fifties and shot to fame with innovative reworking of standards like *What Do You Want to Make Those Eyes At Me For* and *Slow Boat To China* has to be one of the most likeable men in show business. That I came to know him well enough to share some of the experiences in his life is really amazing from my point of view because once again I never expected to do any more than just buy his records.

Emile Ford, or more correctly Emile Sweetman was born in Santa Lucia west Indies in 1937 the son of a government official. He could claim one of the finest musical pedigrees because his mother was an opera singer and she always took great interest in his musical aspirations. That said Emile was always more interested in the technical side of things, indeed his first ambitions were to be a sound engineer. His incredible understanding of the complexities of sound laid a foundation for the success of his own recordings and subsequently he created a sound system that he described to me as being simplistic and yet the quality of it is closer to perfection than many major recording companies seemed able to achieve with more sophisticated equipment and money. Indeed he would later tell me of a contract being taken out on his life to stop him from using the sound system for the benefit of other artistes. I do not know any more about this except to say that he disappeared for a period of about ten years during the nineties, when he resurfaced he told me he had been living in America under a different name during that time. Also his eyesight was deteriorating rapidly and has continued to do so to the point that he can hardly see at all.

However going back to the beginning of his musical career Emile having changed his name to Ford put a band together, calling themselves Emile Ford and The Checkmates. The line up as I recall included his two half brothers, George and David Sweetman, Ken Street, Alan Hawkshaw and John Cuffley. Emile honed his vocal skills working in a variety of venues that included I belive, The Buttery in Kensington, his first public performance, The Roebuck near Warren Street tube, The Breadbasket, The Macabre, in Soho and a place called Chiquitas. Emile told me that his first appearance with the band was he thinks at The Athenaeum Ballroom in Muswell Hill be that as it may Londoners were in the fortunate position of being in on the start of Emile Ford's career.

Emile Ford and the Checkmates *Courtesy of Emile Ford*

Winning a talent contest, at the Soho Fair in 1959 brought Emile to the attention of the now legendary Joe Meek, who was as impressed with Emile's skills as he was with his voice, Pye records would give him a contract as a result of his success. Although it has to be said that from 1958 onwards the rest of England had been getting the benefit of Emile's natural charm and vocal talent. This came about through the medium of television on programmes like *The Pearl Carr and Teddy Johnson Show*, OH Boy Six Five Special. Oh Boy!, Sunday Serenade and The Music Shop. Emile Ford's first single was produced by Joe Meek and put out on the Pye Label. The tracks recorded were '*Don't tell me your Troubles*' and '*What do you want to make those eyes at me For*'. Joe Meek favoured the first one for the A side but fortunately as it turned out Pye preferred '*What do you want to make those eyes at me For*' and Emile Ford and The Checkmates went to the top of the charts. Surprisingly there were those in the music business who didn't think Emile had a very good voice, he confounded these critics by following up with more hit singles and has been able to sustain a solo career up to the present day with his relaxed easy going style on stage. All this while running an audio service for other artistes.

I am glad to know Emile and I wish his eyesight problems could be cured because a man who has brought such exciting colours to his music deserves better. Although in his phone calls to he says he can still see them his mind. To quote another of his hits I think that Emile Ford would be a great companion on '*A slow boat to China*' because the knowledge and wit this man could share with us would make him a very interesting travel companion.

I thank this brave and talented man for his friendship and hope we continue in friendship for many years to come. .

FIFTY-NINE

JOHN ALLISON (THE ALLISONS)

John Allison
Courtesy of John Alford

In 1961 two young lads were catapulted to fame by appearing on what was then a serious attempt to find top performers and song writers, The Eurovision song contest. Singing a song, titled 'Are You Sure' written by John Alford (John Allison) The Allisons, Brian Henry John Alford (John Allison) and Bernard Colin Day (Bob Allison) took the song to second place in the contest and No.1 in the New Musical Express pop chart. This should have been the beginning of a long and successful career for the boys but in fact turned out to be a saga of mis-management, poor representation and real acrimony all round.

I have never met Bob Allison (Bernard Colin Day) but it seems that his commitment to show business success was never as strong as that of John Allison (Brian Henry John Alford). Bob was at the time an engineer and probably foresaw a good and well paying career in that trade. However I have known John for between twenty and thirty years since being introduced to him by Dave Sampson.

During that time I have come to know that John is as fervently committed to his music and his song writing as he has ever been. He is also passionate about the environment and determine to leave a better heritage and climate for future generations.

The Allisons story is like that of many other young artistes who came to the fore during the late fifties. Having had the little bit of luck that talented people usually need to make the step towards stardom their career foundered on the rocks of naïvety and poor representation. Their agent Tito Burns was revelling in the success of his number one artiste Cliff

Richard and did little to promote the duo. Their manager, Gerald Marks seems to have been clueless as to their potential falling on the success of 'Are You Sure', indeed he seemed more interested in his editorship of Disc Magazine. Indeed the original recording contract signed with Fontana Records was only for the release of one single, after the duo's success in the Eurovision Song Contest Fontana management called them back in to sign a revised contract.

The Allisons
Courtesy of John Alford

At this point you might have thought that Gerald Marks would have seized the opportunity to get a better deal with the company, or even looked to get a deal with a more well known recording company like EMI. EMI had turned down the chance to sign The Allisons earlier in their brief career and might have seen them as a better prospect with a guaranteed hit under their belts. Gerald Marks did none of these things merely allowing the boys to sign for the same meagre two and a half percent of the eighty five percent agreed in the original contract.

When you add to these poor management decisions to the two boys understandable ignorance of how the business ran and it is hardly surprising that in 1963 two years after their massive success with 'Are You Sure' and with two follow up singles, 'Words' 1961 and 'Lessons in Love' just scraping into the top thirty the duo disbanded.

Of course this was not the end for John Allison, with Bob returning to a career in engineering, many people would have let their show business dream go, not John he just shrugged his shoulders at the disappointment he felt and embarked on a solo career, singing and song-writing which continues to this day. Indeed when Tommy Bruce was ill towards the end of his life, John kindly stood in for him at my request on a show at New Brighton's Floral Pavilion Theatre, the year was 2004 I believe. When the Sixties revival shows started up John always tried to involve Bob in efforts in putting an Allisons comeback together but in the time I have known him John did not have much success in this direction, Bob always preferring to stick to what he perceived as the reliability of the day job.

There were a couple of other guys that John introduced to the Allisons at different times, their names being Mike and Tony, but they seemed to be more trouble than they were worth as far as John was concerned, bringing problems rather than solutions to the task of putting The Allisons, back on the road to success. Never the less John continues to work hard with the music that was, indeed is his dream and he never gives up hope that one day he and Bob will take the stage together again.

Courtesy of John Alford

In recent years John has been supported by a special lady by the name of Carol Shannahan. Carol has worked hard to help John sustain the belief that quality songs well sung will always have place in venues up and down the country. Sadly Carol's health has been very poor for the last twelve months or so and it is doubtful that she will be able to go out on the road with John in future.

In fact their regular trips on holiday down to the South of France have also been curtailed. Margaret and I having met and got to know Carol wish her health could be improved so that she could enjoy a better quality of life.

SIXTY

DAVE BERRY

Dave Berry
Courtesy of Dave Berry 2008

When David Holgate Grundy was born in Woodhouse, near Sheffield South Yorkshire on the 6th of February 1941 it is highly unlikely that anyone could have predicted that he would grow to be one of the most unique performers the UK has ever seen. To see the man who became Dave Berry perform is still a rare treat as he weaves a cloak of mystery around himself and the stage. Indeed were it not for the rare quality of his voice hanging hauntingly in the air you could almost believe he had become invisible. Dave uses a glove and the collar of his shirt to convince us that he actually appears from nowhere and such is his talent, we believe him. These rare gifts allied to his vocal talent will ensure that Dave Berry will always be a welcome performer wherever he chooses to appear.

Like all of the performers in this book it was as a fan I first came to know Dave Berry. I bought his record's starting with *'Memphis Tennessee'* in 1963 although this cover of Chuck Berry's song only just got Dave into the top twenty, eighteen or nineteen I believe, it served to let us know that someone special had arrived on the scene. More importantly for Dave to let Decca know they had an artiste who could sell records. The follow up *'My Baby Left Me'* did not quite make it into the top twenty for some inexplicable reason. Although I have to say that Dave's performance of the B-side *'Hoochie Coochie Man'* remains one of my favourites to this day.

However real chart success was not far away and *'The Crying Game'*, *'Little Things'* and *'Mama'* all featured in the top five. Once again we had the inexplicable failure of *'This Strange Effect'* not making it into the top twenty. This when in my mind and that of many other of his fans this song and performance of it had No.1 written all over it. Although I have to say that he hit the No.1 spot in Belgium and Holland where Dave still has a massive following he received an award for that song. Indeed he was so popular over in Holland that he once had to do a show inside a Lion's cage to protect him from being mobbed by the fans (although I'm pleased to say there were no Lions in it at the time). I was told about this by a Dutch fan, a young lady called Dorli, I later asked Dave about this – he remembered, saying there was still a strong smell of the animals in the cage. Television appearances on the top music shows of the day like *'Thank Your Lucky Stars' 'Ready Steady Go'* and of course *'Top of the Pops'* ensured that a legion of female fans spent what has known been as lifetime swooning for this likeable northern lad.

Dave Berry
Courtesy of Dave Berry 2008

I began meeting up with Dave in the mid-eighties while touring with Tommy Bruce and found him to be a quiet and likeable man. The first real conversation Margaret and I had with him, was at a venue called the Napoleon, later the Jive Inn in Openshawe Manchester, we sat talking and I got to know him much better than I had previously.

Dave went on to do Flying Musics 'Solid Silver Sixties Tours' appearing with Dave Dee, Gerry Marsden and may other of his contemporaries. I reviewed some of the shows he appeared in, including Derek Franks 'Reelin' and Rockin' shows' for various sixties magazines and he has always been most welcoming when he sees me.

I am pleased to say I was also able to help him get a cancellation fee from one promoter for a show that never took place. My friendship with Dave due to his career continuing to be a success is long distance, but I am always glad to have the opportunity to spend time with him and see him perform. As has been the case recently while he has being appearing with Mike Pender and Tony Crane. On these shows they have been backed by the Dakota's a band who although his health now prevents him from playing, had another friend of my teenage years, Mike Maxfield as a founder member. Mike was a wonderful lead guitarist, who in later time produced an Album for Tommy Bruce at his Court Yard Studios in Stockport.

Right from the very start with his own band The Cruisers, Dave Berry has always made sure that he has the best of musicians behind him. In the beginning it was guys like John Fleet, a fine bass and piano player, Roy Barber Rhythm Guitar, Frank Miles. Lead Guitar and Kenny Slade on Drums. Time went by and Frank White, Johnny Riley, Aloan Taylor and Roy Ledger all became part of the band for a time. Session Guitarists that Dave have worked with have all been the best around, in the shape of Big Jim Sullivan, Jimmy Page and John Paul Jones. As Dave has told me himself, in career terms it pays to have the best, in my opinion he is the best at what he does so he is right to want the best behind him.

Dave Berry
Courtesy of Dave Berry 2008

It came as no surprise his fans when in 1992, almost thirty years after it's original success *'The Crying Game'* became a hit all over again when it was used as the theme for the successful film of the same name.

It is clear that successive generations combine to ensure that Dave Berry remains a star.

Sixty-One

PJ Proby

PJ Proby
Courtesy of PJ Proby

It may seem strange that I include an American artiste in a book that has been about British entertainers but PJ Proby has been so much a part of the British entertainment scene for so long he just seems to belong here. Also his success for the most part has been in the UK and Europe, unlike some of the other American artistes, like Gene Vincent, Troy Shondelle, Freddie Cannon, Bobby Vee, Johnny Preston and Brenda Lee who I have been privileged to meet and get to know. PJ Proby has not had quite the same a success in the country of his birth, even though in my opinion he deserved it. He has had a life that has been filled with more than his fair share of ups and downs, but he has faced everything that life has thrown at him with remarkable fortitude.

Born James Marcus Smith (although I have always known him as Jim), on November 6th 1938. Jim began his search for stardom as soon as he graduated from Military School. In 1957 he move to Hollywood and set about the task of becoming a singer/songwriter and decided on the name of Jett Powers to help his career. Although he made a few records at that time, it was his song-writing rather than his actual singing, that brought him success, writing songs for artistes like Jack Scott, Ricky Nelson and Johnny Burnette who recorded *Clown Shoes*.

1961 brought Jim the name of PJ Proby, Jim took this name at the suggestion of his friend Sharon Sheely who was becoming well known as a songwriter. He also began recording for Liberty records, under this name but did not have any real success with the songs he recorded. Although he did have some success with a self penned number *Wicked Woman* which strangely he recorded under the name of Orville Woods. At this time Jim was also doing some security work for several named artistes or their management. He told me that these were exiting times, which usually meant making sure people didn't get to places they shouldn't by any means at his disposal.

Then Jim had a really lucky break another friend Jackie De Shannon introduced him to a man who had among other things helped to create an image for Gene Vincent, namely Jack Good. Jack who was the creator of television music shows 'Six-Five Special' and 'Oh Boy!' decided that PJ Proby would look good in velvet knee britches, buckled shoes, a smock top and a ponytail. Jim listened to Jack and at Jack's insistence came over to the UK in 1964 to be part of Brian Einstein's television special 'Around the Beatles'. Jim's performance encouraged Decca to give him a contract and he had two massive hits with rearrangements of two old ballads, *Hold Me* and *Together*, Pj Proby was on his way. Of course nothing is ever simple for Jim and there would be no exception now. Liberty Records still had Jim under contract and they took action through the courts to establish him as their artiste, the were successful and subsequent releases were made on their label. His first UK release for them was a fabulous ballad from the Musical West Side Story called *Somewhere* stormed to No.6 in the charts, his third hit of 1964.

Things could only get better or so it seemed at the time, but then we are talking about PJ Proby here and it seemed that fate always had a setback in store for him. In 1966 while headlining a tour that also featured Cilla Black and Tommy Roe on the ABC Theatre circuit, Jim not for the first time split his trousers on stage. The difference was as he told me that on this occasion Mary Whitehouse and Lord Longford were members of the audience at what I believe was the Fairfield Hall in Croydon that night. The headlines next day screamed out the news that PJ Proby had deliberately split his trousers exposing part of his anatomy. According to Mary Whitehouse and Lord Longford this deliberate piece of exhibitionism clearly demonstrated everything that was wrong with society on the sixties. That would have been fine if it were true but Jim is adamant that his trousers split across just above and below the knee,he also says that he wished it would have been possible for them to see what they claimed to have seen that far down his leg, but sadly it wasn't.

I believe him, so it would in the interest of publicising their clean up campaign, two pillars of society exaggerated the situation and turned a fairly innocuous incident into a national scandal. I cannot believe that Mary Whitehouse and Lord Longford were aware of the effect their actions would have on PJ Proby's career, but it was catastrophic. Jim was banned from theatres around the country and from making any appearances on television.

The one thing PJ Proby could still do was make records and so he went back into the studio and recorded another old ballad *I Apologise* which reached No.11 in the UK charts. Jim followed this success up with another half dozen recording in a period of eighteen months which all made the British charts. The most successful of these being another song from West Side Story *Maria* which climbed to No.8. Life was difficult for Jim during this period, royalty disputes with Liberty did not help. Although he did have a top thirty hit, *Niki Hoeky* in the Billboard hot 100 charts in 1967. He then return to America for a time, while he was there he recorded an album with the poignant title *Three Week Hero* this was released in 1969... Incidentally the band who backed him on the album, were known at that time as The New Yardbirds, later they became Led Zepplin.

However PJ Proby is nothing if not durable and in 1971 after he had returned from America he showed just how versatile his talent really is when he took on the role of Casio, in the rock musical called *Catch My Soul*. This production based on Shakespeare's *Othello* had a very successful run in the West End. Following on this success Jim worked for a time in the clubs up and down the country. Then in 1977 Jack Good came into Jim's life and career again when he cast him as Elvis in the successful production of *Elvis-The Musical* gaining rave reviews.

Like many other artistes PJ Proby has received poor managerial advice at crucial stages of his career. This advice has resulted in health and financial reversals, but thorough it all his talent and vocal ability has shone through. By 1990 Jim was living in Bolton Lancashire and I met him when he came to see a show that I was promoting for Tommy Bruce. It was very clear that Jim wanted to get back on the road and show that PJ Proby was still a force to be reckoned with. He appeared in a Granada Television documentary and the BBC featured him on 'This Week' and it seemed the PJ Proby show was back on the road. However just as things were getting going again Jim had a heart attack while in Florida. For Jim of course nothing deflects him from his career for long and on his recovery he set out on a fantastic rehabilitation of his career.

During the nineties PJ Proby recorded a duet *Yesterday Has Gone* with Mark Almond who had worked in a song-writng and production capacity on Jim's album *Legend* this album also benefited from the input of Neal X of Sigue Sigue Sputnik fame.

During this period Jim toured extensively on package shows including 'Sixties Gold' and he has also been touring in Europe right up to the present day. He has also toured Australia in recent times. In 2006 PJ Proby was an important part of Flying Music's 'Solid Silver Sixties' tour. In 2008 a fabulous Derek Franks show is touring with PJ Proby, Brian Poole, Chris Farlowe, Mike Pender and Vanity Fair. It is a fabulous production and of course, PJ Proby is still giving incredible performances, putting great physicality in his performances of his hit song *Hold Me* and I defy anyone to top his performance of one of his other hits *Together* a song recorded by many artistes over the years.

In 2002 Van Morrison had a song entitled *Whatever Happened to PJ Proby* on his album *Down The Road*, it would have been better to title it *What's Happening to PJ Proby* because something always is. PJ Proby has had more than his fair share of problems, most recently his much published brush with the DSS, but as with all the other reversals in his life Jim has rubbished their claims and efforts to destroy him and gets on with doing what he does best, entertaining people. Thanks Jim your friendship has brightened my life, long may you continue to live yours to the full.

PJ Proby with Dave and Margaret

SIXTY-TWO

BILL MAYNARD

Walter Fredrick George Williams was born 18th October 1928 in Heath End Surrey. You would have thought he had a name for success however, when he chose to enter the world of show business he was told that the name Williams was too common for him to use as his stage name.

He thought about for a while and then after noticing an advertising sign for *Maynard's Wine Gums* he decided that would do for his surname. And from his own surname of Williams he'd use 'Bill'. Using the name Bill Maynard the imposing 6ft,1in figure would go on to be one of Britains finest actors.

Bill Maynard
Courtesy of Bill Maynard 2003

Bill was educated at Kibworth Beauchamp Grammar school. He had it would seem, a fairly uneventful childhood. Although he did lose the middle finger of his right hand in an accident with a clothes mangel - a common household implement at the time.

His entertainment career seems to have started very early as he appeared as a child performer in the midlands. However Bill told me that in 1949 Ian Carmichael auditioned him for his first professional job in the theatre. Strangely enough more than fifty years later Bill would work with Ian in the television series entitled 'The Royal'

Bill Maynard's career has been nothing if not diverse. He has been a big band singer and indeed in 1957 he came fourth in the British heat of the Eurovision song contest also heading his own variety act.

As a film actor he appeared in at least nineteen films between 1969 and 1977, including five of the '*Carry On*' series and four of the '*Confessions*

Of' series. His theatre credits include, playing the title role in *'Hobson's Choice'*, he also played Daddy Warbucks in *'Annie'* and the West End Comedy *'Strippers and Ominroyd* to name but a few. His television credits include the lead in *'Oh No It's Selwyn Froggitt'* and its spin off *'Selwyn'*. Bill also brought his talents to *'Minder'*, *'The Sweeney'*, *'The Gaffer'*, *'The Life of Riley'*, *'The Royal'* and of course his most recent success *'Heartbeat'*.

In Heartbeat, his role as Claude Jeremiah Greengrass won him an award at Yorkshire's 2003 awards ceremony. He became Yorkshire Arts and Entertainment Personality of the Year. Bill Maynard certainly is an honorary Yorkshireman!

I first met Bill when a few of us including Don Lang, Tommy Bruce Craig Douglas, Dave Sampson and the Vernon Girls were doing the Six-Five Special Tour many years ago. The show was appearing at Leicester's De Mountford Hall. Unfortunately it was at this point in the tour that Don Lang's cancer worsened and he went into hospital and sadly died. During the show's interval Bill Maynard came to the dressing rom with a bottle of bubbly, a gift for Craig Douglas from Bill and his wife Tonia (previously Tonia Campbell, widow of the late speed ace Donald Campbell). Craig very kindly introduced me to Bill and I found him to be a truly delightful gentleman and I thoroughly enjoyed my conversation with him.

Bill Maynard is a genuinely open and honest man and during that conversation he told me about the colonial soap stars who were being paid vast amounts of money to appear in our pantomimes. His complaint was that unlike many of the British artistes the colonial artistes, while being talented actors, don't understand how to deliver the comedy required in a pantomime. He went on to say that while this situation continued he would not be appearing in any pantomimes, to my knowledge he has been true to his word.

Bill Maynard's strong belief in things being done in the right way coupled with his desire to right past wrongs led him to stand for Parliament in the 1980's. One of the other reasons that led Bill to stand for Parliament was a determination to stop Tony Benn getting back into the House of Commons as he truly believed this man was not the right one to represent the community Bill lived in. Bill stood against Tony Benn in the Chesterfield election, unfortunately the voters did not agree with Bill, so in spite of his best efforts Tony Benn won the election with Bill coming fourth.

Bill Maynard
Courtesy of Bill Maynard 2003

If you would like to know more about Bill Maynard then I recommend reading his brilliant autobiography 'The Yo Yo Man'. For my part I wish this talented and likeable man complete recovery from the several strokes he has suffered since 2001 and hope to be lucky enough to spend more time in his company.

Sixty-three

Faron

Faron and Dave Lodge

In August 2008 I was privileged to be invited to a ceremony to induct William Ruffley, Bill to his friends, aka Faron Ruffley of Faron and the Flamingos fame into the Merseybeat Hall of fame. For that invitation I thank Doug and Sasha Darroch proud residents of Fort Perch Rock in New Brighton. Apart from hosting two fantastic museums Fort Perch Rock has become a mecca for sixties music fans in general and merseybeat fans in particular, thanks to Doug and Sacha's efforts to promoting Operation Big Beat.

Born in 1940 William Ruffley was really following in his father's footsteps when he came into the music business. William, or should I say Bill's father was a fine musician who used to take his son along with him when times were hard and he would busk with his piano accordion, allowing young Bill to hold the cup for people to throw the coins in.

In 1947 Smiths Crisps held a talent competition to show that they were back in business after the war and with an inspiring rendition of Al Jolson's song *'Mammy'* Little Billy Ruffley won the competition. Incidentally Bill loved Al Jolson and his records but his family hadn't got one of the wind up gramophones of the day. His dad gave him a box of needles, so Bill, armed with his Jolson records and his needles, would go and visit neighbours who had a gramophone and ask to play his records.

By 1961 Billy Ruffley had progressed through The Tempest Tornados into a group variously known as The Ravens and Robin and the Ravens whose original line-up had included Nicky Crouch a fine guitarist who went on to further success with the MoJo's, Billy Jones, Eric London, with Trevor Morias on drums, Trevor later found fame with The Pedlars. The line up changed a few times with Eric London, on bass and Billy Jones leaving the band in 1962 and Dave 'Mushy' Cooper formally with The Undertakers came into the into the band playing bass and he was soon joined by Paddy Chambers. It wasn't to long before Dave Cooper left and Billy Ruffley (Faron) already the lead vocalist took over on bass. The band was a great success locally and Bob Wooler DJ at The Cavern, well known for his input with other local bands came up with the name Faron's Flamingos, Billy Ruffley becoming Faron. Bob Wooler also nicknamed Faron the Panda-footed Prince of Prance because of his energetic performance on stage, added to Billy (Faron) having unusual footwear, white moccasins.

Faron's Flamingos - *Courtesy of Faron, 2008*

There is a funny story to do with Faron's first pair of white moccasins, he had coveted a pair since seeing Cliff Richard on television in a pair but didn't know where to get them. Then by chance Faron saw that a pal of his had got a pair, so he asked where he could get them. As soon as he knew where to go Faron dashed of to the shop and purchased a pair, the price was £5.10s I believe, this was a week's wage for many of us at that time. That night proudly wearing them for first time augmented with his trade mark pink socks Faron kicked his foot out as part of his normal dance routine. The moccasin flew from his foot out into the audience where it was claimed by one of his adoring female fans, he never saw it again.

Faron's energetic style came about through the time he had spent watching films starring his hero Al Jolson this made for exciting moments on stage. I personally think Al Jolson in his day moved more suggestively than Elvis Presley he simply couldn't keep still when he sang.

The Flamingos' stage performance which included outrageous gymnastic performances from Faron and Trevor Morais was so successful; that the band was able to perform in France. This success almost caused them to miss Liverpool's beat explosion which followed The Beatles success at that time. Faron's Flamingo's contributed three great songs, *'Talkin' About You'* *'So Fine'* and a song also recorded by Lee Curtis and The All-Stars *'Let's Stomp'* to the fabulous Multi Artiste Album *'This Is Merseybeat'*.

Having secured a contract with Oriole Records at that time England's biggest independent record label Faron and the Flamingos recorded two songs to be put out as a single in 1963. *'See If She Cares'* and *'Do You Love Me'*. This song had originally been recorded with chart success by the American Motown group the Contours. However Brian Poole and the Tremeloes also recorded this song and achieved chart successes it was also a successful recording for The Dave Clarke Five. The story has since been circulated that Brian Poole and The Tremeloes success deprived Faron and The Flamingos of a hit. This is nonsense for two reasons; one is that Brian Poole is a friend of mine and he simply is not that kind of person. The story, which is as follows. When Oriole Records released their disc through Leeds Music in order to get the maximum promotion and airplay. *'See If She Cares'* was a Leeds Music publication so they issued that song as the A-side. Faron and the Flamingos did not have a hit with that song. By the time Leeds Music realised that they should have had *'Do You Love Me'* as the A-side as I have previously said had already been a chart hit for Brian Poole and the Tremeloes and The Dave Clarke Five so changing the tracks round and re-releasing was a pointless exercise. Also, as Faron put it Brian Poole is a lovely fellow and Faron has never blamed him for anything, as he says the music business is full of if only's.

Faron and the Flamingos followed the recording of *'Do you Love Me'* with the release towards the end of 1963 of *'Shake Sherry'* this had *'Give Me Time'* on the B-Side on the Decca Label but it just failed to make the charts. Disillusioned by their lack of chart success the group packed it in and by November of 1963 Faron's Flamingos were no more. Nicky

Crouch joined The Mojos, Trevor Morais Joined The Pedlars and Paddy Chambers along with Faron joined The Big Three. Despite of the lack of chart success Faron was highly respected by his peers, so much so that at one time he toured with Gerry and the Pacemakers as second vocalist.

Faron did reform The Flamingos in 1965 and enjoyed some success in France until the late sixties. On his return to Liverpool Faron kept a version of the band going and at one time included Brian 'Saxophone' Jones in the line up. Although he has been dogged by ill health in recent years, Faron remains one of Liverpool's much loved and well remembered stars. In fact he has recently made a CD with the Merseybeats which I am sure will receive great acclaim.

ourtesy of Faron, 2008

So there it is, a brief account of the career of one of the great entertainers of Liverpool's glory years. Billy Ruffley is a lovely man who I never tire of listening to, I hope in the not to distant future his biography will be written and published. I know that like his stage performances it will hold you spellbound. In a life that took him from not even having a gramophone to play his Al Jolson records on, to becoming one of Liverpool's favourite sons.

A life which has seen him inaugurated in to the 'Merseybeat Hall Of Fame at the same time as he lost his home and everything in it, in spite of this on the day of the inauguration Billy Ruffley aka Faron still performed for the fans and smiled all day. He is a great performer but more than that a great man and I am privileged to call him my friend.

Sixty-Four

Karl Terry

Karl Terry
Courtesy Terry Connor 2014

Karl Terry who started out his life as Terry Connor, is and incredibly talented and athletic performer whose energy and enthusiasm belie his age. His talent should have brought him more success than it has to date but that can be said of so many from the merseybeat era.

Since I met Karl at the late and in my opinion great Les Braid's funeral he has proved himself to a good and loyal friend to me

Karl Terry began his show business career in 1957, his desire be a singer prompted by hearing Bill Haley sing *Green Tree Boogie*. His first band The Gamblers Skiffle Group were formed due to the inspiration of Lonnie Donnegan, but they soon evolved into Terry and The Teenaces due to the advent of rock and roll. What is now regarded as the legendary band Karl Terry And The Cruisers came to be because Karl was a great admirer of Gene Vincent and Gene had released an album entitled Cruisin'.

The original line up of Karl Terry and The Cruisers was Dave Hamilton and Gerry Clayton, in fact they got together in Liverpool quite recently to reminisce about those early days. Karl actually appeared on the same bill as Gene Vincent at Liverpool's Olympia some time later. Karl Terry and the Cruisers became so popular that they frequently appeared on bills with the likes of Brenda Lee, Emile Ford, Bobby Vee, Johnny Kidd, Tommy Bruce, Karl Denver, George Melly and Freddie Starr to name just a few.

In fact on one occasion Karl Terry and The Cruisers even appeared at the Cavern on the same bill as The Shadows, Karl and the boys performance gaining praise from not just the fans but from the members of The Shadows as well.

Karl Terry's recording career has not brought him the success that it should have done but The *'Haunted House'* Album recorded on green vinyl has gone down in musical history as a classic. Also the last vinyl Merseybeat Album to be recorded *'Rock 'n' Roll That's All'* featured Karl and was produced in Germany by another friend of ours Manfred Kulman. Added to this Karl has recorded no less than fourteen original self penned songs on CD, including two songs which I think are absolute classics, *'Blues' Make My Brown Eyes Red'* and the brilliant *'Cigarettes, Cold Beer And Sexy Ladies'*. These songs have ensured that Karl Terry will never be forgotten.

Karl's talent has not been confined to music he has also had a career as an actor appearing in television movies with many of the outstanding actors of the last fifty years. These include Rod Stieger, Anthony Perkins, and Bernard Hughes.

As the years have gone by Karl has also appeared in theatre shows sharing the billing with the likes of Ken Dodd, Tom O'Connor, Mick Miller, Dickie Henderson and George Roper. Karl Terry has proved to be an entertainer of talent and longevity he has been recognised by his peers as one of the best to come of the fifties and sixties. Early in the Merseybeat era a band was put together for a special concert including musicians from The Beatles and Gerry And The Pacemakers, it says much for the talent of Karl Terry that he was chosen the be the lead vocalist for this hybrid band.

Karl Terry is always working for the good of others and has even tried to bridge to gap between the football supporters of Manchester and Liverpool by writing to the respective Chief Constables about the feasibility of putting on concerts in each town with bands from both places on the bill. So far they have not taken his idea up but maybe one day someone will see the sense of it.

From a personal point of view I was deeply touched by Karl's loyalty and friendship when Tommy Bruce was ill and he put on a benefit concert for him which combined the talents of The Sounds Of The

Sixties Organisation and The Mersey Cats. Artistes like Lee Curtis, King Size Teddy Taylor, Teddy was the man who among other things has been credited with teaching the Beatles how to sing, Geoff Nugent from The Undertakers, sadly no longer with us, all joining Karl on stage to pay their tribute to Tommy.

Karl Terry doing the splits on stage

Albie Wycherly was also in attendance, making the night even more special because Tommy thought a lot of Albie who has proved to be a good friend to me, indeed we share the same birthday. For me the highlight of the night was Karl's own special tribute to Tommy when he sang his own outstanding arrangement of *'Ain't Misbehavin'*.

My thanks go to Karl and the boys for giving us all a great nights entrainment. My thanks also go to all the fans who turned out and bought tickets for the event. I should also mention that The Sounds of The Sixties and The Mersey Cats raise a terrific amount of money for charities in general and children's charities in particular. This shows once again that the musicians and people of Merseyside have a heart of gold.

Keep playing the music Karl you have a special gift. Your friendship is of great value to Margaret and I and we look forward to more time spent in your company.

At the present time Karl, who has always been popular in Germany is working there under the auspices of that great man of German Rock and Roll, our good friend Manfred Kulman.

Sixty-Five

Geoff Nugent - The Undertakers

Geoff Nugent
Courtesy Geoff Nugent 2014

Gordon Geoffrey Nugent was born on the 23rd February 1943, as I recall and his destiny led him to be part of on of the most exciting live performance bands I have ever seen. That band The Undertakers would not enjoy the chart success that they deserved due in my opinion to poor management decisions and their choice of record label. That said The Undertakers did achieve legendary status in Liverpool and Germany where a different line-up including Geoff Nugent still perform today.

The Undertakers evolved from a group called Bob Evans and the Five Shillings, who then became the Vegas Five. The original line-up would seem to have been, Bob Evans on drums, Geoff Nugent, guitar and vocals, there was also a lead guitarist I believe called Ike although his last name escapes me and anyone else I have asked including Geoff. However Ike was replaced by a guy called Pete Cook who had previously played with The Topspots, Les Maguire, who would later join Gerry And The Pace Makers was on tenor sax, the line up was completed by Mike Millward. Mike would later be a member of The Fourmost, a lovely guy who sadly died in 1966. This sad event was I believe, just before his twenty fourth birthday.

When the name was changed to The Vegas Five in 1959 the line up was became, Bobb Evans, Geoff Nugent, Chris Huston, two lads from the Topspots called Jimmy McManus, a strong vocalist and Dave 'Mushy' Cooper who would also go on to be one of Faron's Flamingos, Brian Jones, who at that time was known as 'Boots' probably because of his style of play being similar to that of the great Boots Randolph, came in on saxophone.

The Undertakers
Courtesy Geoff Nugent 2014

The name The Undertakers seems to have come about by accident. It seems The Vegas Five were advertised to appear at a dance, but somehow a typesetter with the local newspaper managed to transpose the word Undertakers for an advert advertising a funeral director, putting The Vegas Five in it's place and vice versa. This made for some confusion. However the promoter of the dance, having sold tickets on the Undertakers name, persuaded them to go on that night using that name. The Undertakers having decided to keep the name developed the act with the gimmick of playing the Death March at the opening of their shows even at one point bringing a coffin on stage. This unusual entrance did seem to enhance their live performances for a while. Around the same time in 1961 the group merged with another Merseyside band Dee And The Dynamites who were based in Wallasey. Soon after the merger Bob Evans left the band and was replaced by Warren 'Bugs' Pemberton on the drums.

The changes in line-up seem to have been frequent and when in 1962 Dave 'Mushy' Cooper left to join the afore mentioned Faron's Flamingos, he made way for the talents of Jackie Lomax. Lomax's arrival had a big impact on the group and when Jimmy McManus, who seems to have had a bit of a reputation as a scrapper, left Jackie Lomax became the lead singer. This line-up was very popular in the London clubs because of their exciting stage presence. It seems to me that the driving force in keeping The Undertakers together both and now has been Geoff Nugent, although he didn't go to America with them. He has always been a caring man and he needed to stay at home for family reasons. I believe Geoff's not going with them may well have been one of the contributing facts as to why The Undertakers disbanded while over there.

Returning to their time in the UK before going to the USA, it would seem that The Undertakers' live performances were enhanced by a combination of Jackie Lomax's vocals and the fact they had a Gibson Guitar Line, possibly the first band in the country to have this. Added to these two things, Brian Jones great sound on saxophone improved their performance and style immensely. These changes made The Undertakers a band in great demand, for their live performances. The amplification and customisation of their sound was I believe brought about by Chris Huston who seemed to have an instinct for sound.

For reasons best known to themselves The Undertakers rejected offers of management from Brian Epstein and chose instead to be represented by local agent Ralph Webster and he certainly kept the gigs coming in the local area. By 1962 the Undertakers had a summer residency at The Star Club in Hamburg and this proved to be a big stepping stone in the boys career. This was because they had the opportunity to view first hand the performances of great American stars like Little Richard and Ray Charles. This experience helped Geoff Nugent and the other band members to reach another level of performance. When Pye Records gave them a recording contract in the spring of 1963 it really seemed The Undertakers were on their way to the top

Their producer was Tony Hatch who had been successful for Petula Clark and The Searchers among others. Unfortunately it seemed that Tony Hatch did not understand the music that The Undertakers were trying to make and as they had choice of music written into their contract they seemed to choose record around him rather than with him. The results were for the most part not a commercial success.

However Geoff Nugent was still playing to the very end and when ever and where ever the current line up of The Undertakers played they always received rave reviews. Margaret and I admired Geoff Nugents musical talents very highly and we have great respect for him as a man and a friend.. Sadly Geoff passed away in 2014, he is a great loss to the world of music and for Margaret and I another true friend has gone.

Sixty-Six

Harry Prytherch - The Remo Four

Harry Pytherch
Courtesy Harry Pytherch

Because Harry Prytherch is a recent friend, only in the last eight or ten years I don't know as much about him as I hope to in the future. What I do know about Harry is that he is a really good bloke and he is part of the very fabric of Liverpool music, therefore for these reasons he has a rightful place in this book. Harry Prytherch is a mine of information about the Merseybeat scene and with his narrated live music show 'Merseybeat' Harry with the help of his charming wife Doris has done much to keep the memories of Liverpool's Sounds of the Sixties alive. Harry is also one of instigators behind the Merseybeat Hall of Fame an organisation dedicated to ensuring that some of the innovative performers from the early days of Merseybeat who did not achieve the national and international fame their talent deserved, are not forgotten.

Harry Prytherch, having been inspired to play the drums during visits to his Grandmothers small Dance Hall. Having decided this was what he wanted to do Harry had to find the money to buy one. Like most of us who grew up in the years following the war, Harry did not have a lot of money. In order to buy his first drum kit he as, many of us did had a paper round which paid him the princely sum of sixpence a week. Harry saved up until he was able to at the age of fourteen to buy his Grandfathers old drum kit for £1.10s.

Harry was a member of his local football team and some of the other lads there had started playing instruments. Before long Harry was the drummer with The Remo Four unquestionable one of the best groups in Liverpool. Incidentally Harry and the boys would nip out in their lunch, from the day job to play gigs in the Cavern, becoming very popular on the local scene. The Remo Four had Colin Manley on lead guitar whose playing was unbelievably good even in those early days. Colin Manley would go on to be the Lead Guitarist in The Swinging Blue Jeans, while he was with them his playing would achieve legendary status, not just with the fans but also with his fellow musicians.

Courtesy Harry Pytherch

Sadly Colin died a few years ago as did The Swinging Blue Jeans bass player Les Braid, two fine musicians and lovely men who I was privileged to meet and spend time with. After Colin's death my good friend and incredible guitarist who played so many times for Tommy Bruce, Alan Lovell joined the last surviving original member Ray Ennis in the Swinging Blue Jeans.

It was during his time with The Remo 4 that Harry would meet and go on to marry, his soul-mate Doris, who has been by his side supporting all his endeavours through the years.

Harry Prytherch and The Remo Four should really have had greater success nationally, indeed world wide, because their musicianship was second to none. Perhaps being dubbed Liverpool's answer to The Shadows by some people held them back, Who knows? I can only say having seen them perform in the sixties myself, that I think there was much more to them than just being a Shadows clone band, for one thing they sang great vocal harmonies. The instrumental side of the band was due to Colin Manley,s desire to play great tunes from the likes of The Ventures and of course The Shadows, At the time they considered that they were the equal of bands like The Shadows, never trying to emulate them. Of course The Shadows, went on to have great success, while the Remo 4 while continuing to be much in demand as a live band for while, just couldn't find that elusive hit record.

Harry Prytherch was also a member of the first Super Group 'Unit One,' in this endeavour he was joined by other luminaries of the Liverpool music scene musicians who have left a tremendous legacy for future generations of Merseyside performers.

Courtesy Harry Pytherch

Musically sound and with his wealth of historical knowledge, as I have said before Harry Prytherch is keeping the Merseybeat memories alive. Harry is a really good man who cares about his contemporaries from those early days on the beat scene, even writing and performing in a musical play about the early days of Merseybeat music.

Harry Prytherch is a man to be much admired and Margaret and I are proud to number Harry and his wife Doris among our friends.

I can't believe it, I am calling the book back from the publishers so that I can add this postscript, Harry Prytherch has just collapsed and died, I have waited to write this until Margaret and I have returned from his funeral, so that I can tell you that an incredible number of people attended it showing how much Harry was loved and respected. God bless you Harry there will never be another like you. We will always have you and Doris in our hearts.

Sixty-seven

John McCane
The Last of the Breed

Big John McCane a big man in every sense of the word sadly passed away on Monday 15th March 2012. He left behind his beloved wife Susan and two fine sons, Harry and Cian, my heart broke when I heard this news. I cried bitter tears on hearing this news and my wife Margaret and I lost a wonderful friend. A man who like the name of his band really was the last of the breed.

John McCane

John McCane was possibly the kindest most caring man that I have ever known, certainly he is right up there with Tommy Bruce, who was my brother in all but name. The difference being that, Tommy and I shared a friendship that lasted nearly forty years. Whereas John and I barely had a quarter of that.

When we encountered terrible problems in our own lives John and his wife Susan, a truly remarkable woman of great courage, stood four square behind Margaret and I and fought like a demons for us. That he will never read this and know the love and respect that I felt for him, fills me with despair. It maybe that Susan will understand our feelings and know that for the rest of her life she has two people who will always be there for her.

I can only try to convey that love and respect for this lovely man in this humble attempt to write about this great man and his achievements.

Born in to Irish parents in Salford, England in 1959 John McCane would show from an early age that he was very different. It was clear to those who knew him that he didn't just have musical talent, he also had the drive and determination to achieve great things.

This musical talent would see him enrolled at The Manchester School of Music. He would show that he had great natural ability for playing musical instruments, also his vocal ability was second to none. Indeed His fronting bands vocal ability was second to none. Indeed he was described by his tutors as a very talented boy.

It wasn't long before his ability on bass guitar and fine singing voice came to the attention of local bands, Irish Show bands in particular and he was soon performing on that circuit.

These performances led in turn to session work and very soon he was fronting bands like Nevada and 16th Avenue. At this point I first became aware, as did many others of John's song-writing abilities, songs like an *'Only A Fool'* and *'Know the Dance'* brought him recognition and bookings at Pontin's Music Festivals.

In 1984 John met lead guitarist Mike Foly. Together in a band called Country Comfort they would stay friends and when in 1992 The Last Of The Breed was formed Mike would be part of that,

It should also be remembered that John always took the time to care for and help others.

One person who John was helping at the time of his death was Brigid Corcoran; It was clear to John that Brigid had the talent to succeed and he helped her as much as he could.

Sixty-eight

Colin Paul

Colin Paul is one of the finest gentlemen you could ever wish to meet., That he has blessed Margaret and I with his friendship is I think one of the most fortunate things that have happened in my life.

That good fortune came my way as a result of me taking several booking for Tommy Bruce to work with Billy Fury's brother Albie Wycherly, aka Jason Eddie. Colin and his band were part of most of these shows and

Colin Paul
Courtesy Colin Paul

it may surprise him to know that like me Tommy Bruce thought that Colin Paul was an outstanding entertainer. So much so that we would both stand in the wings and watch Colin's set.

Something else that may come as surprise to some people is to find out that Colin Paul was born in Brisbane Australia, it certainly surprised me. This event took place on June 8th 1962 and his parents who had gone to live in Australia in search of a new life would soon be returning to England. Colin's mum was homesick and wanted to show her new son to her family so they came home. This was probably a very good decision for Colin's future. They soon settled back in to the English way of life.

While he was still very young Colin discovered that he had a talent for mimicking other people. The breadth of this talent was surprising in one so young, he was able to mimic young and old very accurately, sometimes people were not always pleased by his humorous sending up of their little foibles. Family, friends, school teachers and celebrities all suffered from Colin's impressions, there is no doubt his parents were impressed by their shy son finding a way to express himself.

Courtesy Colin Paul

In my humble opinion the moment that would define Colin Paul's future career was when he heard a recording of the voice of the man who would become his idol in the future Elvis Presley. This was in 1970 and although he was only eight years old he knew that he wanted to become a singer. He resolved to overcome his natural shyness and get on stage and perform.

This was not just a dream it was a real ambition. That ambition would be achieved twelve years later in 1982 when he entered a local talent show and he won! That would be the catalyst that would inspire him to really become a performer.

He would not allow his courage to fail him and set out to find bookings in the form of local gigs and auditions. He was successful in his endeavours and soon became a popular performer in pubs and clubs around Manchester.

Eager to progress in his chosen career Colin formed his own band in May 1988 and by November of that year 'Raw Deal' were on the road. After four months of performing to rave reviews Colin and his band came to the notice of Manchester Radio DJ Neil Highley who suggested that they change the bands name to 'The Stormbeats'. Colin listen to Neil's advice and he and the band made more rapid progression.

Colin and the band enjoyed seven successful years touring the north West Clubs. Enough for some you might say but not for the likeable and talented Colin Paul. He wanted more so He stepped things up a gear and on the 12th of August 1995 'Colin Paul and The Persuaders' performed their first gig. That impressive gig lead to

Colin Paul & The Persuaders
Courtesy Colin Paul

booking all over the UK and Europe the reviews from their performances were of such a high standard that the chance to work in the USA on regular basis occurred. Colin took the chance with both hands. So he has become an international artiste of the highest calibre.

Of course Colin deserves to have a very happy family life and that was brought to him by the quite stunningly beautiful Sarah Lee, a lady who has the personality to match her looks is always kind and considerate to the people she meets. They have two lovely children, Grace and Jack and Colin and Sarah lee are perfect parents, they always make time for each other and the children not always the case in show business marriages.

Margaret, Sarah Lee, Colin Paul and Dave

Mind you Sarah Lee must have the patience of a saint, as she had to wait years for Colin to have a free Saturday so that they could get married. They finally tied the knot on the 8th of August 2008. Colin has no doubt that day and all the days since have been the best of his life.

Colin Paul is simply the best man he could be. He is an amazing entertainer who crosses boundaries that no other artiste would attempt. He is accepted by the Billy fury fans as a wonderful tribute act and this is proven every year at Blackpool. Then he is just as well received down at Hemsby with his tribute to the 'King' Elvis Presley. The bottom line is if a song can be sung Colin Paul can sing it, if you haven't seen and heard him then I strongly recommend that you correct that as soon as you can, you won't be disappointed.

So there you have it, I am sure if Elvis were still alive he would have Colin perform on one of his many trips to Memphis and there is no doubt he would be very impressed with the shy boy who started his life in Brisbane Australia.

Sixty-nine

Big Jim White

I have been extremely lucky to know so many talented people and this book would not be complete without a few words about someone who has an unbelievable talent, the one the only Big Jim White. For quite a while Jim was taking part in talent contests emulating his musical hero Elvis Presley. In fact he wasn't just taking part he was winning.

In 1977 two things happened that would change Jim Aplin's life from that of an ordinary hard working lad, to being recognised as charismatic young man from the North of England with talent to become one of the biggest theatre stars. The first thing that happened was the devastating news for millions of fans world wide that Elvis Presley had died. The second thing was that with a change of name, to Big Jim White realised that he had the capability to do more with his life than just win talent competitions with his tributes to his hero.

Big Jim White

More than this people around him were starting to be aware that he was something special. Before long that realisation was spreading to people up and down the country.

'The Forever Elvis Show' was being promoted in all the countries theatres and in a very short space of time Big Jim White was receiving rave reviews for his quite stunning tribute to 'The King'. From Preston to Portsmouth, Leicester to Lowestoft and all points North, South, East and West. Jim's Whites natural talent added to his enthusiasm and drive to be the very best he could be, meant that he was taking everywhere by storm.

This mercurial rise to the top brought Jim White to the attention of the legendary entertainer PJ Proby. PJ was so impressed by the level of Jim's performance that he decided to share what he knew of Elvis and his style of performance with Jim. PJ Proby also shared his experience and stagecraft with him and he really appreciated all the help and advice PJ was giving him, although going so far as to tear his trousers on stage at the Kings theatre Southend did seem to me at the time to be taking PJ's advice a step to far.

Jim Whites performances were quite simply amazing and had the Local and National newspaper reporters writing about how stunned they and the public were by the power and quality of Jim's voice. Also they were amazed by the accuracy of his mannerisms and movement, saying that this was simply an incredible tribute.

During a phenomenal period of more than ten years the Forever Elvis Show became the worlds longest running and most successful Elvis musical. This prompted The Stage and Television Today newspaper to give Jim White the most fulsome praise for his starring role.

During this time at the request of The Elvis Presley Appreciation Society, Jim appeared on the Terry Wogan Show in front of millions of viewers to mark the tenth anniversary of Elvis's death.

But Big Jim White is not a performer who lives on past performances, his power and passion on stage have to be seen to be believed. Jim is not an Elvis impersonator, although many who are would love to achieve Jim White's high standards of performance. Jim's show is a tribute that keeps the memory of the King's performance and stage presence alive. When people come to a show to see Big Jim White's act for the first time they may come as Elvis fans but they go away stunned by Jim's mesmerising talent and when they come back, as they always do, they always come back because it's Big Jim White.

Jim has the support of his good friend Ged Ford who is always there when he is needed. Ged is one of the most optimistic men I have ever known and no matter how low I am feeling when we meet up, my spirits

may be when I see him I always come away feeling uplifted. Incidentally Ged provided management for Gene Vincent on his last tour of the UK. I am sure with Ged as his friend Jim White will have support in his life when ever he needs it.

Margaret and I have had the privilege of knowing Jim White for more than 40 years and we became friends during that time. Jim is a good and loyal friend in good times and bad. Like the rest of us Jim has known hard times. But no matter what life has thrown at him, his true nature and talent have always shone through, Jim White is a good and decent man, who Margaret and I are proud have as our friend.

Seventy
Chris Black

Preface by Chris Black

I have been best friends with Dave Lodge for over 40 years, and in all that time we have never had a cross word.

This must be some kind of a record in the music business. A business which many of you know, is cut throat and frustrating, there is a price for everything and you rarely find any who will help you without wanting something in return. Dave Lodge doesn't even take commission off an artiste, what he tells you is the fee is what you get.

I got a special buzz when I first met Dave, from that moment I knew we would be friends, what I didn't know was

Chris Black with Brenda the Fender

that we would become like brothers. The thing that made the difference with us was Dave becoming Tommy Bruce's personal manager. When Tommy told me that Dave didn't take commission from him and they didn't have a contract I was amazed, I had never heard of such a thing. I asked Dave about it and he explained, 'the prevalent attitude in this business is that the artiste works for the manager or agent, my view is that I work for Tommy and it is not for me to take his money away from him, we shook hands, that is enough, I trust Tommy and he trusts me'. I watched and as the years went by the relationship and the friendship became deeper and stronger. Dave is a hard worker and I could see Tommy getting better paid for his performances than he had for any time since I had known him, He was also getting outstanding money from previous gigs, were the cheque a was in the post, but previously never arrived!!

It was a pleasure watch Tommy and Dave working together, they made a great team. Each of them had their own strengths, Tommy with his talent as a great rock and roller and all round entertainer, Dave with his people skills and determination to get things right for Tommy. They were the best of pals always having a laugh and a joke, like two brothers really. When you saw them together you always felt better, their good humour was infectious.

Dave has the ability to converse and work with any one and his approach has gained him lasting respect, you know that is hard earned in this business. Even now that Tommy has passed away and Dave doesn't do much in the business he is still held in high esteem

I am very proud, like many others, to have Dave as my best friend, and we talk and email each other several times a week. He has so many great stories locked away and at last he has put some of them in a book.

The book is of historical content re the 50's & 60's and goes all way to July 2006 when Tommy sadly died.

Dave himself has had a busy varied life and was a top athlete in his day, taking part in Marathon's, Triathlons Rugby, Swimming, Cycling, and few other sports.

Dave has gained amazing respect in the music business (which has to be earned) and he has made many lasting friends, due to all the years, that he has worked at Tommy's side. He is a most amazing guy and so easy to get on with, and everybody was in awe when Tommy sadly got "Big C" and Dave continued to take care of business through thick and thin to the very end..

God Bless You Dave you are my hero !!!! ROCK & ROLL.

Dave's Book is a fabulous read ... If you are reading this you will have made a good decision and bought it.

I have just put (8) Tommy Bruce, Chris Fender Black & Blackcat's new (never seen before) video tracks from 1984 on You Tube. Have a look and listen, and see for yourself what a great act Tommy was !

I have dedicated "Bony Marony" to Dave Lodge, Tommy's fantastic manager to show in some small way my appreciation for what Dave did for Tommy over the years. I'm glad to say that Dave and I are getting it back together with loads of laughs and happy times are coming up again !!!

YouTube link to my videos :

I hope you enjoy them ... a little bit of history !

https://www.youtube.com/user/clocksprings

Teenage Chris

It would be impossible not to mention my dear and good friend Chris Black. Chris and his Fender guitar have been blasting their way round the Rock and Roll scene for the best part of 60 years. In various Chris Black and Blackkat or The Blackcats have been blowing audiences away up and down the country. Chris is, as Tommy Bruce would say is a hard worker and he has promoted shows written songs and backed many of the top artistes from the sixties including Brian Poole, Tommy Bruce and Ricky Valance. Chris is a big man with an even bigger stage presence, I am really glad he is in Margaret and my life. He is a loyal and true friend who will never let you down.

Chris Black is one our favourite people and his contribution to what I tried to achieve with Tommy Bruce is immeasurable. Thankfully we have CD recordings and DVDs to remember their performances together. He is often referred to as the wild man of rock and Roll, But There is much more Chris than that, he has a kind heart and much of what he does for the benefit of other people.

So how did it all begin for Chris Fender Black the man who can only be described as an enigma, in fact the Oxford English Dictionary should put as the definition for the word enigma, Chris Black. You only need to see him perform once to understand what I mean. However back to the beginning, it was a very unusual start for Chris who actually found his first guitar as a young lad, in the rubble of a house bombed during the war.

Chris in the early days
Courtesy of Chris Black

The house was next door to the one Chris Veness as he was then, lived in with his family, in Ilford Essex and as he rooted around he found his way to what had been the cupboard under the stairs. He started digging in the rubble and his surprise and delight he found a battered acoustic guitar. Of course being Chris he immediately put metal strings on it, only Chris could make it worse, he wound the strings so tight that the neck bent like a longbow and Chris couldn't hold the strings down past the fifth fret. Chris didn't mind that because as he said he could make it twang and just as important play skiffle tunes on it.

Chris very quickly found a few like minded lads and formed a skiffle group and always quick off the mark when it came to a name he called them Mike Stand and the Jack Plugs. Determined to succeed Chris soon arranged the first gig, like many things in those early days the venue was an unusual one, it was down in Kent known as Chislehurst Caves. Underground there was no electricity so, no sound system or lights, so it was an acoustic gig lit by candles. There were several bands performing but the audience loved Chris's flamboyant style and he really enjoyed starting to feel like an entertainer. He now started to feel what he was born to be, a guitar hero and he loved playing skiffle.

There was no way Chris or any of us could have what was coming next, but we were the luckiest generation everything was new and we were getting opportunities in life that our parents and grandparents never had. The catalyst for musical change was a film called the 'Blackboard Jungle' Chris felt he had been hit with base ball bat what a buzz and appearing in it was an unexpectedly exciting band, Bill Haley and the Comets, they sang *'Rock Around the Clock'* and was impossible not to get up and dance to it. Rock and Roll had arrived it generated an excitement that we had never felt before, our generation in our seventies still feel it today, nothing was ever going to be the same again. Suddenly we had Elvis Presley and our new music was coming fast.

Chris and Dave

Chris Black is a self taught guitarist, he has never had a lesson, but he had a good ear for the music being played by Scotty Moore and Bill Doggett and he new the British youth were impatient for groups of there own to bring this sound to venues that they could dance in. Chris was going to give it to them but he had a couple of problems, he didn't have an electric guitar and he didn't have an amplifier. What he did have was an idea of how to improvise, an ability that has stood Chris in good stead all his life. He knew a guy who worked in the medium of television so he fitted an electric pick to his old guitar and got the guy to make him an amp. It was a monster a metal base and visible glowing valves and loose wires trailing all over the place. Needless to say Chris was on the receiving end of several electric shocks, he was fighting a war with his equipment and winning the audience loved it. Audiences loved his exciting and sometimes raucous style. He really was Rocking and Rolling now his hair Teddy boy style, Quiff and DA life was good and he was taking the South of England by storm.

But as always with Chris Someone threw a spanner in the works. The Government, in 1957 called him up for National Service keeping him, like many another young man, for two years. So his quiff went during his first army hair cut and Chris did his basic training before shipping out to Cyprus. As soon as he got there Chris started canvassing his fellow squaddies, looking for musicians to form a Rock and Roll band. He was successful, and soon had group that he called for obvious reasons the NS Six. Before long he found a venue for them to play in a café on Ledra Street Nicosia. This area was known as The Murder Mile, and there were Machine gun guards on the doors to prevent terrorists throwing bombs

Courtesy of Bob Harrison

into the café, these boys really were on active service. Of course there wasn't a fee for these performances. just free steak, chips and beer.

Just when the group were really rocking the army transferred them to Iserion Barracks in Germany. Of course Chris soon had the group playing again and they became very popular. So much so that Chris had arranged for them to appear on German television. However the army chose to ship Chris back to the UK to await his demob.

So it was December 1959 and Chris was back in Civvy street, he re-formed the band, adding a saxophone player and calling it Unit 7. The lads were together from 1960 until 1964, playing venues like the 2i's and the Whiskey a Go Go.

In 1962 feeling the time was right, Chris bought a new Fender guitar on HP, it would take years to pay for but it was worth it. He named the guitar 'Brenda the Fender' (and actually married the guitar on *Pebble Mill at One* more than thirty years later.)

1964 would see the end of the line for Unit 7 even though they were playing on shows with the likes of Gene Pitney, Johnny Burnette and Wee Willie Harris. The reason the band split and went their different ways was continual cost. This cost was caused by the groups van and equipment being stolen on at least three occasions. The group had gone their separate ways and Chris had to find a day job to pay the bills. Of course he was still playing part time and planning for a full time return.

This comeback would come in 1978 when he put the Blackcat group together although it was short lived and that line-up split in 1980. But with the bit back between his teeth Chris soon had new personnel in the band and when Tommy and I met him for the first time in the early eighties he was really Rocking and Rolling. Chris was backing everybody appearing with all the acts at Butlins, including the Americans that were being brought over by Barry Collings and Mike Lee Taylor. Chris had an idea for a legends of the sixties show and he and Didi Melba decided to promote.

It should have done really well with performers that included, Jess Conrad, Don Lang, Tommy Bruce, Terry Dene, Heinz and Screamin' Lord Sutch in the line up. However the wheels came off the tour in Spain. Ronnie Night, Barbara Windsor's ex husband helped get everyone home as told in Tommy Bruce's biography, 'Have Gravel Will Travel'.

Dave Dix an exciting Saxophone player was part of the band that Chris had when backing Tommy and the other guys on The Legends tour as was the late Gerry Chapman who was one of the most brilliant piano players I have ever known. He was also Chris' oldest friend.

Undaunted by any reversals, Chris continued on and came up with his C'mon Everybody show. He has toured that up to the present day, enjoying great success. It is I think an opportune time to write Chris' philosophy on guitar playing into this chapter, it goes as follows, 'You can have lessons to teach technique on the guitar, but you can't teach 'Feel', that is God given. Without 'Feel' playing guitar just becomes a boring battle between musicians. I don't believe anyone has ever put it better, if any man has 'Feel' for playing the guitar, it is Chris Fender Black.

Chris shows expertise on the keyboard too... computer keyboard that is with an early design for the cover of this book

Sadly Chris Black passed away in January 2016... Rock and roll will never die not while Chris Black is playing Brenda the Fender.

Seventy-one

Bob Harrison

Bob Harrison

Although the man himself does not agree, one of the unluckiest men to have performed during the sixties was Robert (Bob) Harrison aka Bobby Sparkle he lived in Heaton Moor Stockport at the same time I did. I first got to know him when he was performing at Sale Locarno in the band Bobby and the Blue Diamonds, The line up was Bobby Alan, Kevin Mottershead on Lead Guitar, Chris Barry Rhythm, Ken Clark on Bass Guitar, with Joe? (neither Bob or I are able to remember this lads surname) on Drums.

Bob, Chris and Kevin then went to Germany with changes in the line-up Ronny Clary on Drums, There had previously been other changes that included Deke Rivers and Ronnie Berks who went on to be second violin with The Lynsey String Quartet, These various line-ups making for some very talented musicians in what for the most part was a local Stockport band.

Although we were not friends until the Sale Locarno days I knew Bob slightly before that as I said previously, because he lived in Heaton Moor, Stockport, just round the corner from me and then later in the sixties we were living in different houses on Cranbourne Road also in Heaton Moor.

Bob Harrison had, indeed still has the most tremendous voice, that added to the fact that he is a charismatic and handsome man should have ensured that he enjoyed great success in show business, but it seems it was just not meant to be.

With a slightly different line-up The Blue Diamonds went to Germany in 1964, at some point Bob recorded a song penned by Tony Crane of The Merseybeats fame, in Luxembourg, I believe. For a brief period the band was known as The Dolly Mixtures

In my opinion, because it featured three girl singers, one of whom was married to Karl Green from Hermans Hermits. Before going on to what was undoubtedly the band's most successful incarnation The Mixture. Of course Bob's ability to be in the wrong place at the wrong time, led him to leave the group after the recording of *'The Push Bike Song'* as we all know the song was a massive hit but Bob though his voice probably contributed to the records popularity was not part of that commercial success.

Once again because of the vagaries of popular music at the time and his own choices Bob Harrison was denied the opportunity to fully capitalize on his talent. In spite of this the fact was that he did come to the notice of the now legendary Joe Meek and indeed Bob went to the Holloway road studio to record a song that was picked up by Heinz, who was in the studio on that day. Because of these and other outside influences I believe Bob Harrison chance to have been one of the massive stars of the sixties was missed. Perhaps a good manager making decisions on Bob's behalf would have made the difference.

Bob Harrison very often recorded demos of songs which went on to be recorded by artistes of the calibre of Tom Jones and Englebert Humperdinck, I think his interpretation of these songs probably encouraged these artistes to choose them.

I met up with Bob again a few years ago and we have stayed in touch, his good looks and charisma have not left him and neither I believe has his voice. I have to say that in my opinion Bob's live performance of the song *'Yellow River'* is unsurpassed by any other vocalist, also his rendition of *'White Christmas'* would have impressed Bing Crosby himself.

Bob Harrison is a thoroughly decent man and I am sure we will remain in touch as the years go by. Margaret and I will always have a place in our hearts, for the heartthrob from Sale Locarno, the one and only 'Bobby Sparkle'.

Seventy Three

Other people who have been there along the road.

There are other people who I have been privileged to meet and become friendly with but for different reasons have not had their own chapter in the book. These people are still important to me, although I do not know enough about some of them to write about them at length.

The list is endless and when I mention some of them just by name they may mean nothing to you the reader, but they mean so very much to Margaret and I. There are those who may expect to have been mentioned, but are not and I can only say to them I am sorry, because their absence will only be due to my memory failing me while I am typing. It does not mean that their friendship is any less important to me.

I have written this book in the hope that some measure of the affection, respect and regard Margaret and I have for the people who have and are sharing my life and who are allowing me to share in their life as we travel along the road, will be reflected in these pages. The most incredible thing that has come from this book for me, it may be that I am repeating myself here, is the depth of affection and respect that has been shown me by the people I have written about.

It should be noted that among the people mentioned at the end of this book are a few people who while not being friends are respected acquaintances who always take the time to speak to me. It really is incredible that people who were just names on cast lists for the first thirty years of my life now in many cases share their time and their lives with me.

As I write this section it has sadly come to my attention that a lovely man who it has been a pleasure to know has passed away. Shane Fenton aka Alvin Stardust, was born and christened Bernard William Jury on the 27th September 1942 passed away on the 23rd of October 2014. He will be very much missed by family, friends and his legion of fans. My last meeting with him was in 2006 just before the death of Tommy Bruce. We shared a dressing room in the Pavilion Theatre New Brighton and we had a long happy conversation about friends we had met and known along the way.

Dave Harmon, is a man I greatly admire, although I have had the pleasure of meeting and speaking to him on several occasions I cannot truly claim to know him or claim him as a friend. Dave Harmon who really came to prominence with the band of the incredibly long name Dave Dee, Dozy, Beaky Mick and Tich is without doubt one of the most courageous and caring men I have ever met. David Harmon bought his first guitar at the age of twelve having saved the money from a summer job and then going on to play in a skiffle band with a friend John. The band was called Johnny Nichols And The Dimes I think. Dave told me the groups name was a play on the American expression working for Nickels and Dimes. However Dave's father who was also I believe a talented singer in his day, did not think music would be a full time occupation so he wanted his son to do something with a more reliable future. With this in mind at the age of seventeen Dave applied and was accepted into the police force. The only thing I know about Dave's time in the force is the much documented story about him being the first person on the scene at the car crash in which Eddie Cochrane died. I also know that he ensured the return of Cochrane's guitar to the family in America. Dave Dee, Dozy, Beaky Mick and Tich, Real names Dave Harmon, Trevor Ward-Davies, Ian Amey, John Dymond and Michael Wilson got together as a band in 1961 but it was three years of playing on the circuit including the Star and other clubs in Hamburg, before the lads finally got a record deal with Fontana. They had several hits including *'Bend It' 'Zabadak'* and *'The Legend of Xanadu'* before Dave finally split from the band in 1969, Dave then had a brief spell as an actor and solo singer before he became Head of A&R With Atlantic Records, he also had his own record label for time. In spite of ill health Dave Dee was still a regular performer of The Solid Silver Sixties Tours and his alter ego David Harmon JP has twice been a magistrate, in Brent, North London and Macclesfield Cheshire.

For myself I have always found Dave Harmon to be both charming and courteous, a man who refuses to take anything but the best from life and who tries to share that best with the people he meets. It is with great sadness that I write that Dave lost his brave fight against ill health. My wife Margaret and I lost a dear friend with his passing.

Jimmy Cricket

Jimmy Cricket is another truly wonderful gentleman who takes a simplistic approach to comedy that belies the comic genius he possesses, that added to the fact he has as yet unpublished talent as a song writer, he also plays a mean saxophone. His lovely wife Mae is one of the finest singers I have ever heard indeed I hear traces of my dear friend Ruby Murray in Mae's voice. Long may Jimmy, his wife Mae and their family continue to thrive.

Nelson Keene is a smashing bloke, Nelson was Tommy Bruce's friend from the Larry Parnes days and a man who I still speak to from time to time at his home in Australia. Dave and Ann Robins who I have said in the past are in my opinion, under the name of The Chevron's, the best vocal duo working on the northern club circuit, they are also fine solo performers who have worked with many of the artistes mentioned on previous pages. Special mention has to go to Dave in this other persona as Dave Robins, once again for his help in putting the photographs into order for this book. Indeed without Dave's computer skills in restoring old pictures a lot of the photos you see on the pages of this book, would not have made it into the book at all.

Nelson Keene

Tony Harte and his wife Julie have proved themselves to be really good friends. Tony and I worked together on the Rock and Roll Thunder tour and he has gone on to do invaluable work, in creating both Tommy Bruce's Memorial Website and my own Website, now defunct. In more

Tony Harte

recent times Tony has been making his name as the lead singer of the current Martin Murray line up of The Honeycombs, although as I write this I hear that Martin is once again no longer part of this Honeycombs line up. Tony's wife Julie is a fitness instructor and a very capable and attractive lady. Terry and Chris Jones from The Spinning Disc record shop who quite simply gave 100% of themselves to helping the rest of us. Terry sadly died a few years ago but his wife Chris still gives her friendship and support to each and everyone of us. John and Doreen Eckert two wonderful people whose friendship Margaret and I value greatly. The lads in that great band Vanity Fair who are still giving performances of the highest standard, all I can say to Mark Dean Ellen, Steve Oakman, Eddie Wheeler and Bernie Brilliant is keep on going lads you will continue be popular for years to come. Tony O'Keefe and his great band the Shakers, who play Merseybeat music like it used to be played way back in the sixties.

Johnny More who in my mind is the only man who ranks alongside Paul Melba as an impressionist has with his irrepressible good humour bounced around my life for many years. Indeed it is only his keenness for work and golf that keep him on the road travelling so much that has

Dave, Sue Upton & Johnny More. Enjoying a Champagne breakfast at the home of Sir John Mills

precluded my being able to get to know him better. I have to say that Johnny More's impersonations of Billy Eckstien and Frank Sinatra will never be bettered by anyone.

Neil and Maureen Crossland who together are two of the best people we know, it seems to me that their first thought every morning is for the benefit of someone else it is a privilege to have the honour of their friendship.

Mike Willetts and his wife Maria a man who has great stories to tell about the sixties.

John Cross

Paul Cross, the youngest drummer to ever play at the Cavern Club

John Cross his wife Carolyn and their two sons Paul and Jack are among our closest friends. John's Group Rave On is simply one of the best groups around and with son Paul on drums are well worth the admission fee.

Pat and Joan Whelan, they know why.

Other people like, Rod and Nora Doleman who are always kindness it's self to Margaret and I.

Brigid Corcoran

On the country scene Brigid Corcoran who many of us feel is the future of country music in this country, her incredible talent is aided by the hard work her husband Stephen Corcoran puts into helping her career.

Of course there is my great friend Manfred Kulman from Germany and his lovely wife Cherie. Then there is the very beautiful and talented Suzi Jari. Suzi has incredible vocal ability and a wonderful personality, I have known her since the early stages of what is sure to be a long and successful career. I am pleased to say that she regards me as her friend and she knows I that I will help her in any way that I can to achieve her goals.

Margaret and I have also been privileged to meet Malcolm Vaughn who thrilled us all in the fifties with recordings like '*Saint Theresa of the Roses*'.

Jimmy Melia

Malcolm is a really lovely person who is always immaculately dressed and is a perfect gentleman.

Glyn Dooley a man who has an incredible voice but more than that he and his wife Di are loyal friends. Ray Dexter for his enthusiasm.

Jimmy and Irene Melia who show their friendship in many ways. Indeed though he won't thank me for telling you Jimmy is one of my heroes, this in spite of the fact that my father who was himself highly decorated in world war two being awarded among other thing's the Military Medal, spent his life telling me to be my own hero by living the best life I could. Jimmy Melia has to be an exception to that rule, he served on HMS Coventry under a great captain David Hart-Dyke during the Falklands war and as many of you will remember HMS Coventry was sunk and Jimmy with his shipmates many of whom did not come home finished up in the burning sea. Jimmy as he puts in himself 'did his duty', knowing the man as I do this phrase will cover far more than we know, he is to modest to tell us more. But this is not the reason why this incredible man is one of my heroes, the reason quite simply is because of the way he lives his life. The only way to truly describe him is to say that he is a real man and I am proud to know him and have his friendship.

Jimmy & Irene Melia

I should also mention exceptional Guitarist Pete Bardsley who apart from his guitar playing skills took many of the photographs of me with the sixties performers.

Frankie Connor is a lovely guy and a perfect gentleman, for many years now he has been

Frankie Connor
Photo Courtesy of
Frankie Connor and BBC

heard on Radio Merseyside, playing the kind of music our generation (in my case 70 plus) like to hear. In the sixties apart from being in a band, 'The Hideaways' who played at the cavern on more than 250 occasions Both he and the band were very popular with the fans in those days, Frankie is also a gifted songwriter. Frankie was a very talented footballer, who played at Goodison Park the home of his favourite team, Everton. He played for the All Star merseybeat team, who included another man who I have great admiration for, entertainer and DJ, Vince Tracy. My wife Margaret and I in common with all who know him, love and respect Frankie very much, and hope to share his friendship for many more years.

If I am speaking of local performers from the Manchester area it would be impossible to forget Rockin' Ricky (Eric Nugent) and his wife Hilary because of their contribution to the music scene over the last forty years. Ricky had a hit in Europe with *'Someone'* and more recently sang the Michael Cox song *'Angela Jones'* on a Joe Meek, compilation disc. Incidentally Mike lives happily with his family in New Zealand these days. Returning to Ricky he made this recording in the company of an array of talented people like John Leyton, Jean Vincent and Clem Cattinni, this I think

Rockin' Ricky & Dave Lodge
In the Grapes in Matthew St, Liverpool

was a fitting recognition of Ricky's efforts over the years. The CD was made at Alan Wilson's Western Star Studios. Alan is responsible for a lot of good stuff being brought out in the nostalgia market. Great hearted man that he was Ricky sadly passed away in 2015 leaving a void that can never be filled, We are blessed to still count his wife Hilary as our friend and the memory of Rockin' Ricky and his Velvet Collars not forgetting his Rebounds will never fade.

Also a man I have to mention is John Beecher, John is a great guy whose Roller Coaster records label is famous all over the world. John was one of Mike Berry's Outlaws in the early days but he knew that his forte was in the recording studio creating sounds for other artistes. He has gone on to be incredible successful and by the time this book is published it is hoped that John and I will have brought out a CD of Tommy Bruce's live Saturday Club appearances.

Bill Farley, a wonderful man who was a good friend to us all in his lifetime. Bill was a record plugger in the sixties and then a record producer, in fact among his many credits he produced *'I See A Red Door and I Want To Paint It Black'* for The Rolling Stones. Bill kept trying right to the end of his life and if people want to succeed in that side of the business his was without doubt the best example to follow. The lads from the band Wall Street who I mentioned at some length in Tommy's biography.

Keith Loftus & Wall Street backing Dave Sampson

Led by Keith Loftus a lovely man who is more than worthy of a chapter in his own right and who unbelievably succumbed to a heart attack whilst I was writing this part of the book. I have to say Keith was a wonderfully gifted and talented rhythm guitar player who took over on lead when the previous lead guitarist, Pete Piggott left the band just as Wall Street started to become an integral part of the sixties revival shows that were being promoted in the late eighties, Keith took it all in his stride and through hard work and dedication became one of the best known lead guitarists in the North of England. I can see Keith now in my minds eye with his red Fender guitar in his hands a cigarette stuck in the top of the fret, tousled hair, cheeky grin on his face simply loving the rock and roll. I wish Keith had lived so that I could have let him know how much I appreciated the help he gave me in those early days when he and Wall Street took over from Chris Black's Black Cats and backed Tommy Bruce, Heinz, Wee Willie Harris, Screamin' Lord Sutch, Dave Sampson, Jess Conrad and not forgetting 'The Classy Lady' herself Miss Pat Francis who appeared as our opening act on all those ' The Way It Was' shows, Pat was quite simply a phenomenal vocal talent who put her family life with husband Kevin Fitton before her show business career, there is no doubt that Pat would have been a top star in the music business. Pat Francis quite simply had it all, good looks and a charismatic stage presence added to a wonderful and powerful voice.

That I was able to go on and elevate Tommy Bruce's career back into the major theatres throughout the UK was due in no small part to the lessons I learnt while on the road with Keith and Wall Street. Tommy knew this and there was never a time when we didn't enjoy our shared memories of Keith and the boys in the band.

There was much more to Keith than just his remarkable self taught musicianship, he was a fully qualified electrician, indeed he passed his City and Guild Certificates. Ever my true friend he rewired my house at no charge once again showing the depth of his friendship. Keith was kind and considerate but he was nobodies fool and always spoke his mind, In my eyes he was quite simply everything a man should be. Margaret and I will miss this man who I nicknamed Rockin' Ron Bacardi, later shortened to Rocky by friends and other band members. Our our love and support will always be with the lady in Keith's life his wife Debbie and their family, please remember what I told you Debbie, There is no doubt that Keith saved the best to last.

Bass player was of course the erasable and loveable Peter Colleton, this man is without doubt one of the most naturally talent entertainers I have been privileged to know and I am proud to call him my friend. Piano Player Danny Thurston a real gentleman in every sense of the word, Johnny Hart, another man sadly no longer with us who I admired and respected greatly on Drums and percussion, talented Saxophonist Bill Drain a thoroughly decent and Christian man, Paul Ashford affectionately know to Tommy as Stacy Keach who took over on Drums, how could anyone not like Paul, to this day he combines boyish good looks and charm to his percussion skills, yes like me he can be infuriating but I liked having him around and he certainly brought all the pretty girls along to the shows. The Reverend Ian Darby otherwise known as Rinswind on guitar, a clever and articulate man who shared his relaxation skills

Guitar George

with us all and I for one have reason to be grateful for that. Graham Marshall who performed backing vocals and also looked after the band on the road, a likeable and hardworking man, who again I am pleased to consider my friend, who along with wife Ann, Debbie's sister, did much to keep the show on the road. Although I am writing about the musicians of Wall Street at this time it is fitting that I should mention the man who is possibly the most naturally gifted musician I have ever met Keith's great friend, and also I believe a friend to me the incredibly gifted George Borowski. Forever known as Guitar George, he is an inspiration to others including Keith who had a failed audition for George's band many years ago.

This failure did not prevent the two of them becoming firm friends and sharing a mutual admiration for each other. Indeed while Keith and I were in what I consider to be our purple patch with 'The Way It Was' show George guested with Wall Street and played some unbelievable music. I remember one night in the Napoleon, later to be renamed the Jive Inn when George with typical modesty set up in the corner beside the stage and there in the shadows played some unbelievable rhythm fills while we all listened in awe.

The New Bruisers - Steve Bird, Mac Poole, Tommy Bruce, Roger McKue, Pete Windle

335

Legend has it that George is the Guitar George named by Mark Knopfler in his Dire Straits Hit '*The Sultans of Swing*' who knows the full truth of it? I do know that ever the shy and modest man George always shuns the question. It is true that George and his band worked on shows with Dire Straights and that Mark Knopfler admired George's playing and his guitar. We can all have our own beliefs but I suspect the only two people, they being Mark Knopfler and George himself, will ever know the answer and I doubt that George will ever tell.

I can not leave this section without mentioning someone who was for many years special to Keith Loftus, Sandra Mills, a lovely girl who Margaret and I liked very much, personal reasons took Sandra and Keith in different directions, but Margaret and I always have a place in our hearts for Sandra and will always wish her well.

Other great musicians who have lived their lives in the music business in a way that is worthy of their own book. This includes guys like Roger Mckue, Bobby Patrick, Pete Windle, Dave 'The Prof" Lane, Steve Bird and Dave St James.

The very lovely Lynn Cornell who apart from being one of the Vernons Girls was a regarding star in her own right, fans may remember her hit '*Never on a Sunday*' and of course the first one I bought I think was called '*Demon Lover*'.

Paula May

Paula May and her husband Roy Holt are two special friends of ours who are working together to make a successful career in the music industry for Paula who has an outstanding vocal talent. Their support for Margaret and I during the most difficult period of our lives is a testament to what true friendship is all about. Keith Wood who keeps the music and the memory of the 2i's coffee bar alive down at the 100 Club Oxford Street London,

Effie and Peter Smith my aunt and uncle sadly no longer with us who were like a second mother and father to me. Roger and Rita Day again my aunt and uncle who were inspirational in every sense, Roger has passed away now but left me and many others the inspiration of Kipling's *IF*. Rogers sister and my aunt Susan who inspired my love of literature and also was a good companion during my childhood we wish Susan and her husband Don long life and happiness.

Of course I can never forget another aunt and uncle Betty and Jim Topping who died some years ago but who supported me emotionally on many levels.

Pat and Joan Whelan two people who really understand the word friendship. Knowing them really enriches our lives.

Ged Ford a fine man who has the most optimistic outlook of anyone I have ever known. Dave and Ann Chevron who I mention twice under their real and stage names, they have worked hard to become the outstanding vocal duo working in the British club scene not only that they are both excellent artistes in their own right who once again are valued friends and they make a constant contribution to our every day lives.

Dave and Mark Wilsmore

Mark Wilsmore who keeps The Ace Café just way it has always been for Bikers and Rockers for the last fifty years.

Dean Memphis

Pete Bardsley a simply incredible guitarist who has enhanced every band he has ever played with, he is also a decent man whose friendship I value. Pete also took several of the photos used in this book.

Dean Memphis, known to Margaret and I by his given name of Rob Lewis who along with his wife Tracy and their lovely children are a simply wonderful family. As an entertainer Dean is one of the most dynamic and energetic

337

performers I have ever seen, more than that Rob and his wife Tracy have proved to be remarkable and supportive friends during the most difficult of times.

Kevin Anthony (Ken Oldham) is simply the best of the swing singers around today it really amazes me that this man who has performed and won awards around the worlds not given his full respect in this country.

The unbelievably talented Les Reed who and his wife June who give their support in so many ways, the world is certainly better with them in it. The equally talented Barry Mason who wrote so many wonderful songs with Les Reed and if it were not for Barry I might never have met Tommy Bruce because Barry started the whole thing off and for that I will be eternally grateful and I will always consider him my friend. Barry it has to be said has a great sense of humour and very often uses it against himself. For example he tells the story of being in the gents toilet at the BBC and the guy standing next to him was whistling *'Delilah'*, I wrote that said Barry, "Oh no you bloody didn't" came the reply, Les Reed did, quite right said Barry, "Les wrote the music but I wrote the words," the guy considered this for a moment before replying, "So what, I'm not whistling the bloody words!!" Nice one Barry I can never hear the song without remembering the story.

Bert Weedon and his lovely wife Maggie, Bert was more than just a remarkable guitarist he was a special man, sadly he is no longer with us.

Ronnie Hilton who proved his friendship in many ways.

Comedian and compère Larry 'The Teapot' Richards, Larry served in Northern Ireland with great distinction, something that everyone seems to have forgotten now, but I never will. He and his wife Pam are simply the best of people and I really feel that Larry was deserving of more success than came his way, incidentally Pam has been fighting illness for

Larry 'The Teapot' Richards

a long time now and we all hope that the future holds better health for her. Pam sadly lost that fight. Our hearts go out to Larry, we will always try to be there for you mate.

That great rock and roll piano player Freddie 'Fingers' Lee who regrettably has been really ill of late, we all wish him well.

The incredibly talented and very lovely Kay Garner who is sadly no longer with us, was simply one of the most caring and considerate people we have ever known. It has been one of the greatest pleasures in our lives to know Kay, she was a wonderful jazz singer who also excelled in all music genres sadly she was not to achieve the stardom her talent deserved but those of us who knew her, miss her enthusiasm and drive.

Sue Glover a friend of Kay's and another incredible vocal talent. Sue like Kay did not receive the individual acclaim that her voice deserved but along with her sister Sunny appeared in vocal groups and enjoyed success. Sue is a warm hearted and generous person whose friendship we all value.

Penny Lister formerly with the Ladybirds and The Vernon Girls, who has been very ill of late, I hope she will have won her battle with cancer by the time this book is published.

Sue Glover & Kay Garner

Gary Storey and his wife Julie with their band The Graduates, they are real fans of Tommy Bruce who also became friends as time went by. Shel McRae formally with The Fortunes is a very talented guy and I am glad to have got to know him because he is a really genuine man.

Mike and Maria Willetts, Mike played drums in a band that backed Tommy for a while in the sixties and became friendly with him. That friendship was renewed in the nineties and continued until Tommy died.

Manchester rock and roll legend Pete Whetton, better known to you all as Pete Maclaine. Pete has overcome all the setbacks that life has thrown his way, including Brian Epstein taking his band to be Billy J Kramer's benefit to continue playing his kind of music. More than fifty years down the line you can still hear Pete Maclaine and the Clan, playing rock and roll at the Bull's Head in the Market Place in Stockport.

Another Stockport lad whose parents had the off-licence in Heaton Moor when I lived there is Mike Maxfield, Lead Guitarist with Billy J Kramer and the Dakotas, Mike has suffered ill health and tragedy and I hope that only good things come his way in the future.

Del and Karen Richardson who keep the music alive on Radio Caroline's Good Rocking Tonight show and provide all those of us who love music with CD's through their record company Fury Records.

Another DJ Mike 'The Mighty' Quinn who knows the business and has become my friend only recently but I feel as though I have known him all my life.

Cissie Stone an absolutely fabulous rock and roll singer who blew audiences away when appearing with Tommy Bruce and Screamin' Lord Sutch on the Legends tour. Cissie is an amazing performer and a wonderful person.

Cissie Stone, backed by Wall Street

Fred Fielder also a DJ, a man whose larger than life persona belies his kind nature, Fred has always put a lot into keeping sixties music alive.

International wrestler Al Markett who in his other persona of Alf Margate was a work colleague in the early sixties and who I met again on the celebrity golf circuit when I was travelling with Norman Wisdom. Some other wrestlers I have known include, Billy Two Rivers, Cowboy Jack Cassidy, Jackie Pallo, Mick McManus, and Les Kellet who all crossed my path along the way, enriching my life with their presence.

From the world of Rugby League, the talented Widnes and Great Britain Player Reg Bowden who I have unfortunately lost touch with, Mick Martin and Walt Tabern both International players who took time out to be friendly to me indeed Mick Martin arranged a trial for me at Leigh, but I chose to continue to play Rugby Union.

From the sport of Rugby Union there are to many to mention here but a few that really stand out are Internationals Josh Lewsey, Mike Leadbetter, the Irish Lion Willie John McBride, Steve Smith, Bill Beaumont and of course, for me a man met first by my good friend Peter Leonard, Rob Andrew, in my mind without doubt the best fly half I personally ever saw play for England, a contentious opinion I know but Rob's ability both physical and mental to turn the course of a game that seemed to be lost had to be seen to be believed.

Good hearted men like Ian Freeman, David Graham and John Novelli who I became involved with through The Heritage Foundation have enriched my life on a sometimes daily basis.

Through that organisation I was able to meet such luminaries of the acting world as Sir John Mills CBE who was always the perfect gentleman, his lovely wife Mary Hayley Bell and both his talented daughters Juliette and Hayley. We even enjoyed a champagne breakfast at his home.

To have met and been in the company of probably our biggest Sixties super star Cliff Richard is an amazing memory as I bought all his singles in the sixties and while I can not claim to have been his biggest fan that title must go to my sister Christine. Among the people I know, there is no doubt that his strong work ethic and his much publicised Christian ethic have made him worthy of the success he continues to enjoy.

The gorgeous Stephanie Beacham who grows more lovely every time I see her, Paul Shane who lived his life in his own way is sadly another no longer with us. Herbert Lom was a marvellous man with a great sense of humour. Sylvia Sims, Shirley Ann Field, two lovely ladies, also John Inman who I knew all to briefly as he passed away while I was writing this

John Inman

book but who I liked immensely, Jeff Stewart a fine and likeable man and John Savident. Cliff Bennett who is a great blues singer and rock 'n' roller, a real gentleman and I'm very pleased to know him. Bip Wetherall one of the most talented men I know who does a lot for other people.

I must not forget Robert and Linda Raine my great friends. Robert is mentioned in the first chapter as my childhood friend, he and his wife Linda and also their talented and likeable son Edward are true friends. The late Frank Moses and his widow Nancy Moses, my friendship with Frank goes back fifty years and his wife Nancy can only be described as a caring and Christian lady. Sadly Frank was another who passed way while I was writing this book, we miss him.

This book would not be complete if I did not mention the redoubtable Paul Barrett. An agent who helped me by just being there with his friendship throughout my time in show business. Paul is a big man in every sense of the word fiercely loyal to his friends, totally reliable in all things and honest to a fault. This physical giant of a man would never let you down. My pride in having his friendship is immeasurable.

I must mention Lord Jeffrey Archer who was kind enough to talk with me about my literary aspirations before I finished Tommy Bruce's biography. Thanks to him I am here at the end of another book. This man who has no edge on him at all has been kindness itself and who on only our first meeting said please, no need to call me anything but Jeffrey. I have to say no matter what opinion others may have of you Jeffrey, you have my respect and admiration for a life that continues to have every single minute filled.

I must mention my sister Christine and her husband Dennis, they have had their own struggles in life but after more than forty years of marriage they still find time to help others.

While I was writing this book I was saddened to hear of the sad passing of two men who I considered to be giants of the show business world they would have made it on to these pages anyway, it saddens me that I cannot look forward to more time in their company. Calle Neillson a lovely person who I was only privileged to spend time with socially on one occasion but who strengthened his friendship with me in many phone calls. Calle died suddenly from a heart attack a terrible loss to his family in particular but also to his friends.

The other man was Derek Franks who also succumbed to a sudden heart attack. Derek was a gentleman who always ended his phone calls to me with the words, "Don't be a stranger, keep in touch". Unusually in this business Derek was a promoter who I never disagreed with because right or wrong he always displayed the natural courtesy of a gentleman. His family, particularly his wife Debra and friends will miss him. From a personal point of view I will never forget Calle and Derek two of the very best people I have ever met in any walk of life.

I value the continuing friendship of Tommy Bruce's son Thom and his wife Lisa also their sons Bailey and Bo. Thom is a really talented singer songwriter and I live in hope of helping him gain much deserved recognition for these talents. Tommy's daughter Lorraine is one of this countries finest stage actresses.

The very talented Mark Wynter, who moved over from being a top recording star with hits like 'Venus in Blue Jeans', to being a most accomplished actor in theatre productions and musicals. To date nearly all my contact with Mark has been on the phone, but I am hopeful I will see more of him in the future.

Not knowing as much about the following people has not stopped me from realising what fine gentleman and great musical talents they are. For example Bruce Welch rhythm guitar player and song writer from The Shadows is a kind, considerate and courteous man who sadly I meet up with at to many funerals. That said I enjoy his conversation and company and hope that I will get to know him better. Also Brian 'Liquorice' Locking a simply incredible musician who apart from being Jet Harris's replacement in The Shadows has been playing for a wide variety of people over the years including Marty Wilde, Adam Faith, Eddie Cochrane, Vince Taylor and Gene Vincent. He also played in a harmonica band with Vince Eager in the early days. Incidentally Brian's nickname comes from playing the clarinet, known in the business as a liquorice stick. Brian is a devout Christian who lives his life in a Christian way, he is a quiet and gentle man who is loyal to his friends. I am proud to be considered a friend by this lovely man

I place great store in the fact that both Danny Williams and also his son Tony afforded me the privilege of the writing the sleeve notes for the last of his albums issued by EMI. Indeed I like to think that Tony and I through are friendship have been able to elevate his own career to that of actor/singer with his wonderful voice and my promotional skill. Once again we find teamwork comes to the fore.

One lady who made it possible for Margaret and I to get through the last few years is Mrs Anne Jones, Anne has been tremendous and without her support many of the things that have been achieved including this book and the one before it, would not have been. So our heartfelt thanks to you Ann.

I have recently been fortunate enough to meet a man called Golly Goulding. I met him through his band The Paul Hayes Collection and we have gone on to become friends. This is a great band, with very talented Line up Paul Hayes, Lead Vocals, Golly Goulding Lead Guitar, Gary Pugh on Bass Guitar and Rod Cairns on Drums. Golly introduced me to Paul who I am pleased to say has also become our friend. Paul Hayes' rise to prominence, is due in part to the programme *Cash in the Attic*, however he has a love of sixties music which he performs with great enthusiasm and I find that the pleasure he gets from the performance transmits to the audience and this is helping to keep our generations music alive for a new generation.

Added to that the fact that if I had not shared an important part of Tommy Bruce's extraordinary life and able to write about the whole experience and our friendship, in his biography *'Have Gravel Will Travel'* and then to go

The Paul Hayes Collection

on in this book and write about the friendships that are Tommy Bruce's lasting gift to me.

These friendships have been a gift that is beyond price, but value of them and all that entail is immense. Thank you Tommy for making my life more wonderful than I ever dreamed it could be and bringing your lasting presence to it all. I live in hope of us getting together the next time around.

Big Jim Sullivan, Dave & Brian 'Liquorice' Locking

Colin Pryce-Jones & The Rapiers

This book would not be complete if I didn't mention Colin Pryce-Jones, lead guitarist with his band The Rapiers, who is not just a wonderful musician he is in fact a marvellous man. He is a true Christian who always puts others first. Colin and his wife Janet are lovely people and Margaret and I are blessed to have them both as our friends.

A good friend and fine entertainer, Dave Wickenden, is also in my thoughts.

Finally, and indeed I think fittingly, I refer to some great sportsmen who played the game of American Football people who I never met but who for me epitomised the ideal of friendship and team work. Firstly Chicago Bears running back Gayle Sayers, (I actually spoke to this great man on the phone once), 'The Kansas Comet' who in spite of only playing sixty eight games in the NFL was honoured by them in 1967, 1968 and 1970 with their award for Most Valuable Player and also inducted him in the NFL Hall of Fame recognising him as the greatest running back in the first fifty years of NFL history. My reason for including him is not because of those awards, or any of his fantastic achievements but because of his great friendship with team mate Brian Piccolo an incredibly talented and courageous fullback who had voted ACC Player of the Year but sadly died of cancer at the age of twenty six in 1970. The love, respect and support that ran through their friendship has been immortalised in a book and a film 'I Am Third' and I am not ashamed to say that their story moved me to tears. This was compounded by Gayle Sayers wonderful tribute to Brian when he was presented with the award as Pro-Footballs Bravest Player by the New York Football Writers. On receiving the award in recognition on of his determination in coming back from serious knee injuries that would have finished many players careers he said, "This Trophy should not have come to me it should have gone to Brian Piccolo, compare his courage with the courage I am supposed to posses." He later gave the trophy to Brian. This story of two remarkable men sums up for me what my life has been about, teamwork, love and friendship, nothing else has ever been important. In this context I would like to mention the Oakland / LA Raiders team and in particular their tight end Todd Christianson who very emotionally said, "There is only one sin, that of ingratitude." He was not guilty of that and that team epitomised teamwork in it's purest form. I hope that in this book I have shown that I live by that belief.

Just as I was finishing this book having already suffered a serious accident that ended my sporting career, only six weeks after competing in the Malta International Triathalon, Margaret and I found ourselves suffering one of the greatest betrayals of friendship imaginable, by a person not worthy of being named in these pages. It was almost enough of betrayal to make us give up on our belief in friendship, loyalty and teamwork. We were literally in complete despair. Amazingly just when we thought that all hope was gone we received the most wonderful support from the people close to us proving that every reason I had for starting this book was valid. At this point we do not know if we will get the results we deserve, but we do know that many of the people in this book are helping, supporting and praying for Margaret and I.

For example my god-daughter Karen Dare sent an email of love and support. Karen and her siblings, Mandy Palmer and Steven Leonard have been of tremendous support during what can only be described as an ordeal and a trial by fire.

That we still have the support of these special people, including my sister Christine and her husband Dennis Brown, their daughter, my niece Sandra Brown, Peter and Lynda Leonard, Ken and Christine Eyre, their son Toby and his wife Claire, Brian and Pam Poole, Tony Crane, Frankie Connor, John and Doreen Eckert, Pat and Joan Whelan, the late Dave Sampson and his wife Wendy and Roy and Paula Holt, Jon and Nicki Edwards, Dr Eileen Bradbury, Dave and Ann Robin's, the late John McCane and his wife Susan, the late Mac Poole and his wife Maria and many others all equally important, can only be described as a gift from God that I will try to be worthy of every day of my life.

In a life where I have done my share of wrong, I have always tried to do the right thing and also it could never be said that I am guilty of ingratitude, because both Margaret and I are truly grateful that the people on these pages gave us the chance to share their lives.

As I come to the end of this book about the wonderful people I have known and those I continue to know, hopefully this is not the end of the story. I look back and think of the things their influence has enabled me to achieve. The Palmeres I have been awarded in life and in sport are all appreciated. The ones I appreciate most are in the form of the gifts of friendship given to me by the people in the pages of this book. It has been our experience in life that when God closes one door in your life, in due time he always opens another, even though sometimes it is pure hell in the hallway.

Dave, at his happiest delivering a calf!

Dave and Margaret with Bruno their Dog

So our thanks go to you Karen for reminding us on that morning that although the choices we make in life are our own and enable us to pick our team, God always provides the squad we select from.

As I come to the end of 'The Long Road' and look towards the next adventure. I can pause and reflect on where me and Margaret are now.

We are now both in our seventies and have returned to our roots in the Northern countryside. We have two cats, Brandy and Oscar, and a large German Shepherd-Cross dog called Bruno – these pets are loving companions. I'm from a farming family on Grandfather's side, and grew up with cattle and sheep and as recently as a couple of years ago had some cattle and had the joy of assisting in the delivery of some calves.

Although I was injured in an accident a few years ago and move slowly with the aid of a walking stick we take great pleasure in walking (or in my case hobbling!) around the lanes near our converted barn.

I'm currently working on my next book, with a very different subject matter than my previous ones. Margaret is a member of a local singing group and we are both active in the local community. Our motto is - keeping busy keeps you young!

Dave Lodge.

Also by Dave Lodge

The Official Tommy Bruce Biography

The amazing story of how a young cockney lad went from 'barra boy' to a teen singing idol. A unique insight into the 1960's rock 'n' roll scene when Tommy Bruce and contemporaries such as Billy Fury, Johnny Kidd and Joe Brown were doing the rounds together. In this fickle world of show business many friendships don't stand the test of time. Not so that of Tommy Bruce and Dave Lodge, his manager, friend and author of this biography. We see how their partnership has endured since the 1960's unhampered by contracts, surviving on friendship through the highs and lows. The book is a testimony to Tommy's affable style both on and off stage making him a well-loved character in the industry for the past five decades.

Price: £6.99

Paperback: 280 pages / 100 B&W photographs
Publisher: Pixel Tweaks Publications (July 2015)
ISBN-13: 978-0992751487

www.ingramcontent.com/pod-product-compliance
Lightning Source LLC
Chambersburg PA
CBHW020607300426
44113CB00007B/543